THE
CODE
OF THE
HOLY
SPIRIT

PERRY STONE

**CHARISMA
HOUSE**

Most CHARISMA HOUSE BOOK GROUP products are available at special quantity discounts for bulk purchase for sales promotions, premiums, fund-raising, and educational needs. For details, write Charisma House Book Group, 600 Rinehart Road, Lake Mary, Florida 32746, or telephone (407) 333-0600.

THE CODE OF THE HOLY SPIRIT by Perry Stone
Published by Charisma Books
Charisma Media/Charisma House Book Group
600 Rinehart Road
Lake Mary, Florida 32746
www.charismahouse.com

Unless otherwise noted, all Scripture quotations are from the New King James Version of the Bible. Copyright © 1979, 1980, 1982 by Thomas Nelson, Inc., publishers. Used by permission.

Scripture quotations marked AMP are from the Amplified Bible. Old Testament copyright © 1965, 1987 by the Zondervan Corporation. The Amplified New Testament copyright © 1954, 1958, 1987 by the Lockman Foundation. Used by permission.

Scripture quotations marked KJV are from the King James Version of the Bible.

Scripture quotations marked NIV are from the Holy Bible, New International Version. Copyright © 1973, 1978, 1984, International Bible Society. Used by permission.

Cover design by Justin Evans
Design Director: Bill Johnson

Visit the author's website at www.voe.org.

Library of Congress Cataloging-in-Publication Data:
An application to register this book for cataloging has been
submitted to the Library of Congress.
International Standard Book Number: 978-1-62136-261-6
E-book ISBN: 978-1-62136-262-3

First edition

13 14 15 16 17 — 9 8 7 6 5 4 3 2 1
Printed in the United States of America

Two men directly impacted my life at the beginning of my ministry: My father, Fred Stone, and his uncle, Rufus Dunford. My father was a mighty prayer warrior and a strong believer that God's *charismata* (gifts) were all intact within the body of Christ and could be manifested through fasting, prayer, and obedience. His Uncle Rufus was miraculously healed of a deadly brain tumor through prayer in the early 1930s and also received the gift of divers tongues (1 Cor. 12:7–10) in which he could (only under divine inspiration) speak to foreigners in their native tongue and witness of Christ to them. The amazing aspect of this gift: Rufus only had a third-grade education and no training in foreign languages. It was a gift from God for the purpose of preaching the gospel to men from European nations who came to work in the mines.

I personally witnessed my own father operate in all nine gifts of the Spirit, and I received Uncle Rufus's prayer for an impartation of these gifts in my life when I was eighteen years of age. Both Dad and Rufus made lasting impressions upon my life and ministry. Today I dedicate this book on the Holy Spirit to their memory, as they lived this walk by example and not in word only. I suggest that the reader read with a prayerful and open mind to gain the most benefit from each chapter.

Contents

Foreword

M Y WIFE, CHERISE, and I have been friends with Pam and
Perry Stone for more than twenty-five years. Our friendship
goes back to the days of youth camp, where both Perry and I
received a calling to ministry and encountered the Holy Spirit in a life-
changing way. The insights and revelation that Perry has from God's
Word have always amazed me. His extensive studies and research of
the Bible makes him a reliable source of godly information and inspiration.

Over the years I've heard Perry preach and teach on many topics,
but the most powerful message that Perry preaches, in my opinion, is
when he speaks on the Holy Spirit. I've witnessed more people in my
church and family receive the baptism of the Holy Spirit as a result of
Perry's teaching than any other teacher or preacher I know. To put it
simply: nobody teaches about the Holy Spirit better than Perry Stone.

Perry also has carefully studied and researched the spiritual connection between God's Word and traditional Jewish beliefs and teachings. This book you are holding, *The Code of the Holy Spirit*, adds a
whole new level of understanding to any other teaching about the Holy
Spirit as it explores the Spirit's role and relationship in your life from
a Hebraic perspective that is based on traditional Jewish truths. From
the fascinating revelation of the tri-unity of God in Jewish writings
to prophetic promises of an end-time healing and reviving, Perry will
unveil important truths that will strengthen your faith and inspire
you to "give the more earnest heed to the things [you] have heard"
(Heb. 2:1).

I highly recommend *The Code of the Holy Spirit* by my friend Perry Stone and consider it one of his most powerful and impacting messages. Let it change your life as you discover afresh the supernatural infilling and gifts of our precious Holy Spirit. Allow your vision to be expanded, and begin to grow in the grace and knowledge of God through this insightful study of the Holy Spirit.

—JENTEZEN FRANKLIN
SENIOR PASTOR, FREE CHAPEL
NEW YORK TIMES BEST-SELLING AUTHOR OF *FASTING*

Chapter One

MIDNIGHT AT THE
WESTERN WALL

At midnight I will rise to give thanks to You,
Because of Your righteous judgments.
—Psalm 119:62

I<small>T WAS A</small> chilly November night in Israel as four others and myself were making our way toward the famed Western Wall in the Holy City of Jerusalem. As we approached the wall, the beams of white light from a huge Hanukkah lamp cast a somewhat mystical glow on the ancient limestone wall, making the large ashlars give off a yellowish iridescent aura. As we entered the sacred compound, we could hear a mumbling of the high-pitched and lower-sounding voices of mingled prayers, sounding to a casual listener like a distant thunder rumbling across mountains. Countless men were facing the stone wall, rocking back and forth in a rhythmic motion as these midnight worshippers sent words upward from one of Judaism's holiest sites. The wall was lined mostly with men in long black coats and black hats, identified as Orthodox Jews. Others were clothed in white Jewish prayer shawls, called *tallits,* and fur hats, and they lifted prayer books close to their eyes to pull from the pages every word needed to be spoken. This was Jerusalem's Western Wall at midnight!

However, our assignment was not to join in midnight prayers at the wall. We had received a personal invitation to join a leading rabbi for questions and discussions at his rabbinical offices, located to the left of the wall in an apartment-type stone building. The stones matched the style and shape of the wall but were much smaller limestone blocks. In nervous anticipation I would be meeting with a beloved rabbi, Yehuda Getz, a brilliant man with exceptional knowledge who loved Americans and had numerous Christian connections, including Jewish and non-Jewish friends who admired his love for God and the Bible.

Arriving in his modest office, I was impressed by a large shelf of artifacts—some discoveries from recent excavations in tunnels—and by the numerous sets of Hebrew commentaries lining the wooden bookcases. The rabbi welcomed us, with my close friend and tour guide, Gideon Shore, serving as the translator. We began with personal greetings and a few brief comments of appreciation for his time, and the rabbi opened the door, allowing us to ask whatever question we desired.

My first question concerned the actual location of the tree of life and the Garden of Eden. I shared my theory that the center of the garden was actually the Temple Mount. He smiled in agreement and quoted numerous Jewish schools of thought that also confirmed this often unheard theory.

The second discussion concerned the possible location of the long-lost ark of the covenant. The rabbi pulled out a yellow note pad and began a mini-lecture on the formation of the Temple Mount, the expansion under King Herod, and the many hiding places and secret chambers cut in the original limestone under various levels of the mount itself. He then related a story of seeing the ark in 1981 in a battered condition, surrounded by rock and debris, in a small crack that opened to a secret chamber. He viewed it by looking into a mirror and shining a light into the crack. Later I saw firsthand the area, which was sealed up by the Department of Antiquities. Because the area was in the direction of the Dome of the Rock, the sacred Islamic mosque on the Temple Mount, no one was permitted to continue digging in the area.

At this point the conversation shifted, and the rabbi began asking me questions. He asked what I personally believed as a man who accepted the Scriptures as inspired. I knew the rabbi was a *mystic* and believed in midnight and early morning prayers, and also accepted God's supernatural presence and power as a fact and not some emotional self-induced experience. I related how I believed in the covenants of God, including His redemptive covenant, and continued to express a belief that exorcism (expelling evil spirits) was possible, to which he interrupted and said, "Good! I have a man at the wall who dresses in white and says he's Elijah, and he has some type of deceptive demon. Help me cast it out of him, as he causes many problems!" After smiling, I decided to express to him a fact of my personal experience that I knew could be received with skepticism or controversy, but it was a part of who I was and an important aspect of my personal prayer life. I told him I believed in the Holy Spirit, His anointing, and the gift of speaking with other tongues as a prayer language the Lord gives a person who receives His Spirit. To my amazement, he replied with a smile, "Oh, you mean you have experienced the language of God!" It was said as a matter of fact, without any puzzled look or an eye of unbelief.

The Language of God

Being a fourth-generation minister who grew up in a full gospel church, I had heard the terms "speaking in tongues," "speaking in an unknown tongue," "the prayer language of the Spirit," and the theological term "glossolalia." Yet I had never heard the phrase "the language of God." Yet this phrase actually described the experience in a more complete manner than some of the terms we had used growing up. There was almost a poetic flow to the words… "the language of God."

When I asked for his explanation to the phrase, he replied by giving a Jewish tradition that I had never heard or read in the past. My only regret is not asking him for a personal explanation on his references. However, since he was a leading rabbi with tens of thousands of hours of study and stacks of books I have never or may never read, I simply meditated upon his answer.

The rabbi replied, "It is among the traditions that when the high priest would enter the holy of holies on the Day of Atonement, he could communicate to God in a language that only he and God understood. This ability to speak in and understand the language of God only occurred when the high priest was in the holy of holies, and after he exited the sacred chamber, he was no longer able to speak that heavenly tongue." I was amazed at his comment, and my mind went immediately to the words of Paul where he wrote: "Though I speak with the tongues of men and of angels..." (1 Cor. 13:1). I knew there were earthly and even heavenly dialects, and that no voice was without significance (1 Cor. 14:10). I also knew that there were numerous reasons in the New Testament for the vocal gifts of the Spirit (1 Cor. 12:7–10) and that God Himself was the originator and giver of all good gifts (James 1:17). The conversation went deeper into God's supernatural gifts and manifestations, and I left the rabbi's office about an hour later, walking past the yellowish glow of the wall and away from the rumbling voices of midnight seekers into the normally bustling but now quiet streets of Jerusalem. My interest was piqued, and my spirit rejoiced as my heart set out to discover the lesser known or understood details and insights concerning the Holy Spirit, or as I have called it, the *Hebraic roots of the Holy Spirit.*

Most denominations and Christian faiths have a theological thesis forming a doctrinal statement concerning the Holy Spirit, identifying Him as a part of the Godhead (Col. 2:9). However, others expand this statement into a more detailed commentary of systematic theology by making the mystical belief of the Holy Spirit a more practical application for a person's spiritual commitment, while limiting His supernatural manifestations to a previous generation. There is a third group that details the biblical references to the Spirit and maintains that the nine spiritual gifts (1 Cor. 12:7–10) have never ceased but were inactive during times of spiritual apostasy and restored in full operation until the return of Christ.

I was raised by a very doctrinally sound and spiritually strong father, who I saw operated at some point in his life in all nine spiritual gifts referred to in 1 Corinthians 12:7–10. I learned so much from Dad's teaching and more by the experience of watching him *flow* in the anointing of the Holy Spirit. However, even after sitting under Dad's ministry for years and spending thousands of hours in biblical study, I actually knew very little if anything about the marvelous insights that are discovered when I remove my Western glasses and pick up the Hebrew shades that allow me to see the Holy Spirit through Jewish and rabbinical eyes and to eat the fruit of the Hebrew tree of life.

That December night in Jerusalem my knowledge had been increased, and my desire to study from a Hebraic perspective was stirred and remains stirred to this day. Looking to the left, I passed the wall again on my way through security to the old gate. It was now one o'clock in the morning in Jerusalem, and the Jewish mystics were gathering for special prayers. They believe that as the earth becomes still, the voice of God can be more easily heard within the spirit of the seekers. The large numbers of men remaining in prayer caused me to think, "It must be true with so many men praying here. Apparently they understand something about night prayers that we in the West don't."

There are some who relegate the operation of Holy Spirit gifts to a previous time in church history, and others may be apprehensive to travel a lesser-known road to gain understanding that just may contradict their religious upbringing. However, I encourage you to read all of this book and then to pray in your own way for the spiritual illumination required to walk in the Spirit and be blessed by His presence.

Chapter Two

IS GOD THREE—
OR IS GOD ONE?

In the beginning was the Word, and the Word was with God, and the Word was God.

—John 1:1

THIS TITLE QUESTION was the first controversy I experienced when sharing my faith with Jews and even Muslims living in the Middle East. They both viewed Christians as believing in three different Gods, when in their faith tradition they believed in only one God. One of the most difficult theological mysteries to explain in simple human terms is the tri-unity of God, called by theologians in the West, *the trinity*. The Christian explanation of one God in three distinct persons is actually a major stumbling block to Jews, who believe there is only one God who manifests as one spirit. Even the Muslims teach that Allah (God) is not begotten, and neither does God begat, and they continually maintain that God has no son. Thus, when a person expresses the traditional Christian concept of God as *three in one*, or that *God's son is Jesus Christ*, opposition immediately arises from two of the three monotheistic (one God versus polytheistic, or many gods) religions—Judaism and Islam. How do we explain the plural nature of God and the terms "Father," "Son," and "Holy Spirit"?

One of the great New Testament writers, John, penned the Gospel of John; First, Second, and Third John; and the Book of Revelation. John begins his Gospel by saying, "In the beginning was the Word..." and uses the Greek word *logos* for "Word" in this reference, indicating a name for Christ Himself, who was the visible divine expression of God on earth, dwelling among men (John 1:1, 14). The Word was with God and was God.

We read in 1 John 5:7–8:

> For there are three that bear witness in heaven: the Father, the Word, and the Holy Spirit; and these three are one. And there are three that bear witness on earth: the Spirit, the water, and the blood; and these three agree as one.

Three names are identified here: Father, the Word, and the Holy Spirit. Later in John chapter 1, the apostle moves from calling Christ the "Word...made flesh" (v. 14, KJV) to calling Him the "only begotten Son" (v. 18); he also said that he bears record that Christ is the "Son of God" (v. 34). Thus we see the Father, His Son, Jesus Christ, and the Holy Spirit, or Holy Ghost (*Ghost* is the older English translation and *Spirit* is the newer translation: however in Greek both terms are the same—the Greek word *pneuma*, a word for "life," "breath," and "spirit"). John wrote, "These three agree as one" (1 John 5:8). Thus there is one God manifest not just as three names or titles, but three spiritual personalities. The number three is significant in Scripture as it alludes to a unity of three items. Notice the threes in the Scripture:

The Threes of Scripture

Sun, moon, and stars	The unity of the cosmos
Clouds, stars, and heaven	The unity of the heavens
Crust, mantle, and core	The unity of the earth
Abraham, Isaac, and Jacob	The unity of Israel
Faith, hope, and love	The unity of the Spirit
Body, soul, and spirit	The unity of man
Man, woman, and child	The unity of the family

The Threes of Scripture

Outer, inner, and holies	The unity of the temple
Israel, Jerusalem, the temple	The unity of Israel
Foundation, walls, roof	The unity of a building
Father, Son, and the Word	The unity of the Godhead

In Christianity and Judaism we both believe there is only one true God, the Creator of heaven and earth and the God of Abraham, Isaac, and Jacob. However, Judaism cannot accept the idea that Jesus Christ is deity or God, and certainly does not accept that God's *Son* is Jesus Christ. The emphasis of *one* God is seen in the prayer called the *Shema*, found in Deuteronomy 6:4, which reads: "Hear, O Israel: The LORD our God, the LORD is one!"

The central word here is the word *one*, which in Hebrew is the word *'echad*. The word *one* is found about 1,360 times in the King James Version of the Old Testament. However, *one* is translated as *'echad* 387 times in the Torah and translated as *one* a total of 687 times. The meaning of this single word can be "a union, a quantity or the ordinal number 1." In our Western concept, the word *one* means the single number one—like one tree in a garden, one specific car in a parking lot, and so forth, and certainly it can mean *one God*. However, in places where it is used in the Old Testament, there is another application.

One early example is the creation of Eve. In Genesis 2:24 we read: "Therefore shall a man leave his father and his mother, and shall cleave unto his wife: and they shall be one flesh" (KJV). Adam was a man, Eve was a woman, created from his rib, and therefore they were one in flesh—two people but one in emotions, will, and desires. This word *one* is also *'echad*. This is the same word used in Deuteronomy 6:4, "The LORD our God, the LORD is one." The word *'echad* is also used in Genesis 11:6, speaking of the multitude of people at the Tower of Babel as one people. Jeremiah 32:39 indicates that the people of Israel were "one heart" (unity). Ezra 2:64 identifies a large multitude of people ("whole congregation together," KJV) that assembled as one in Ezra's time. Thus the understanding and broad use of this Hebrew word is the first hurdle to overcome in understanding the unity of the

Godhead. One is not just one, but one can be more than one being united as one.

In the Beginning

Moses penned the Book of Genesis in the wilderness and received a divine revelation in Genesis 1:1 concerning the beginning of Creation, in what is termed *ages past*, or the countless ages prior to the formation of Adam. Notice the tri-unity of God revealed in the first three verses of the Bible:

- Genesis 1:1—"In the beginning *God* created the heavens and the earth..."

- Genesis 1:2—"The earth was without form, and void; and darkness was on the face of the deep. And the *Spirit of God* was hovering over the face of the waters."

- Genesis 1:3—"Then God said, 'Let there be *light*'; and there was light."

Genesis 1:1 reveals *God* as Creator; the Hebrew word God here is *'elohiym*, which is an early name for God used throughout the Book of Genesis. However, in the second verse we read that the *Spirit* of God is moving upon the waters. The word *Spirit* here is *ruwach* and can be translated as, "wind, breath, and spirit" in the Old Testament. In the flood of Noah we read where God sent a "wind" to pass over the earth and dry up the waters. Wind is the same word here, *ruach*, but notice it is a *natural wind* and not a wind of the Holy Spirit, such as came in the Upper Room on the Day of Pentecost (Acts 2:1–2). In Genesis 1:2 the Spirit of God Himself is brooding over the waters as God prepares to bring light out of the darkness.

The third verse is quite revealing, as God said, "'Let there be light'; and there was light." This light was not the cosmic light of the sun, moon, or stars, as these heavenly lights were formed on the fourth day of Creation (vv. 14–19). Here the Spirit and light are joining together on the first day of creation (vv. 2–3). When I asked Rabbi Getz what the light was on the first day of Creation, he stated that it was an unknown light that was connected to the glory and presence of the Almighty. Further researching the apostle John's comment in the introduction of his Gospel, the "Word" (Christ) is present at Creation, and John said: "The light shineth in darkness; and the darkness comprehended it not" (John 1:5, KJV). One translation reads, "And the Light shines on in the darkness, for the darkness has never overpowered it [put it out or absorbed it or appropriated it, and is unreceptive to it]" (AMP). What or who was this light?

With God appearing in verse 1, and the Spirit moving in verse 2, then the Word (Christ) is the light in verse 3; thus the Godhead appears in the first three passages in Genesis. Notice how John, in chapter 1, connects the Word of God to "light" (John 1:4–5, 7–9). Later John would record where Christ said that He was the "light of the world" (John 8:12; 9:5). In fact, Christ speaks that He is the light at numerous times in John's Gospel (John 3:19–21; 11:9–10; 12:35–36, 46). To prove that the first day of Creation was the supernatural light and glory from Christ, we read concerning the New Jerusalem in Revelation 21:23, "The city had no need of the sun or of the moon to shine in it, for the glory of God illuminated it. The Lamb is its light." And in Revelation 22:5, it is written, "There shall be no night there: They need no lamp nor light of the sun, for the Lord God gives them light. And they shall reign forever and ever." If the Lamb of God is the light of the New Jerusalem, then He was the early light of Creation on the first day!

When John wrote that there were three bearing witness in heaven—the Father, the Word, and the Spirit—Genesis 1:1–3 confirms this statement as fact. There is no doubt that John was referring back to the original Creation to indicate the three manifestations of God Himself, revealed in the earliest moments of the Creation of the world.

Who Is the "Us"?

It has been pointed out that the Genesis 1:1 name for God, *'Elohiym*, is a word with a *plural masculine* ending. To help understand this, in English we have boys' and girls' names. However, at times a name for a boy is also used for the name of a girl, such as Jackie. Thus when saying, "Jackie," you must know if Jackie is a boy's or girl's name. If

I say "she," you know Jackie is a female, and if I say "he," you know Jackie is a male. In Hebrew, the ending of the Hebrew words can indicate if they are a feminine or masculine word, or if the word is a singular or a plural word.

In Hebrew the word *'Elohiym* is a plural word, as has been noted by Christian scholars and Jewish rabbis who are divided over their opinion to the plurality. Traditional Christian scholars will note that this word is literally translated as "Gods," indicating not three Gods but the three divine natures of God manifested through three who are in unity and bearing record in heaven—God the Father, God the Son, and God the Holy Spirit. The Hebraic interpretation would be that the plurality is simply an indication of the numerous characteristics of God.

There are several passages in Genesis that also hold clues to the fact of the plurality. Notice when Adam was created, God spoke, saying, "Let Us make man in Our image, according to Our likeness" (Gen. 1:26). The *Us* in this passage is plural, and God is speaking to someone other than man himself. The common rabbinical interpretation would say the *Us* were heavenly angels that were present at the creation of Adam. Certainly angels were there at the formation of the first man, as we read where God informed Job of the beginning of Creation and questioned him saying:

> Where were you when I laid the foundations of the earth?
> Tell Me, if you have understanding.
> Who determined its measurements?
> Surely you know!
> Or who stretched the line upon it?
> To what were its foundations fastened?
> Or who laid its cornerstone,
> When the morning stars sang together,
> And all the sons of God shouted for joy?
>
> —JOB 38:4–7

The main challenge with the angels being the "Us," is the remaining part of the verse—to make man in "Our image, according to Our likeness." Again, the "Our" mentioned twice is plural. The word *likeness* in Hebrew is from a root meaning, "a resemblance or a form." When

Moses later spoke of Adam and Eve being created, he said that they were made "in the image of God [not angelic spirits]" (Gen. 1:27).

When speaking of man being in God's image, I recall debating a young theology student years ago who believed that God Himself was a spirit that had no form whatsoever, and when we arrive in heaven, we will see a light with no form. I told him he was confused by the *Wizard of Oz* movie he saw as a child. His point was that God dwells in light (1 Tim. 6:16) and manifests as a fire (Ezek. 1:27); thus He has no form. It is true that a spirit being can change its form or manifest in various forms, as the Lord appeared in a pillar of cloud by day and fire by night in the wilderness (Exod. 13:21–22), and the Holy Spirit manifested in the form of a dove at Christ's baptism (Matt. 3:16). Even angels who are normally invisible can manifest at times in a human form. (See Genesis 19; Hebrews 13:2).

In reality, the prophets of the Bible who saw God in dreams and visions gave certain key descriptions of Him that are very comparable to the actions of those humans created in His image. In Daniel 7:9 the prophet penned that the Ancient of Days was seated on His throne, and His hair was white like snow. In 1 Kings 22:19 Micaiah saw the Lord sitting on His throne and the host of angels on either side. When Ezekiel witnessed a vision of God, he described a sapphire throne and the likeness of a man above it, with fire from His loins up and fire from His loins down (Ezek. 1:25–27). The prophet Isaiah also saw the Lord sitting upon His throne with His outer garment (called "the train") filling the temple (Isa. 6:1). In Revelation 4:2 John saw One sitting upon the throne with the appearance of a jasper and a sardius stone, and in Revelation 5:7 He held a book in His right hand.

There are numerous verses throughout Scripture that identify God with the same characteristics found in the human family. We know God is a Spirit (John 4:24); however, the Bible also gives concepts of God as having a form, a shape, or a particular composition.

The *face* of God

> The LORD bless you and keep you;
> The LORD make His face shine upon you,
> And be gracious to you;
> The LORD lift up His countenance upon you,

And give you peace.

—NUMBERS 6:24–26

The *finger* of God

But if I cast our demons with the finger of God, surely the kingdom of God has come upon you.

—LUKE 11:20

The *hand* of the Lord

The word of the LORD came expressly to Ezekiel the priest, the son of Buzi, in the land of the Chaldeans by the River Chebar; and the hand of the LORD was upon him there.

—EZEKIEL 1:3

The *arm* of the Lord

Therefore say to the children of Israel: "I am the LORD; I will bring you out from under the burdens of the Egyptians, I will rescue you from their bondage, and I will redeem you with an outstretched arm and with great judgments."

—EXODUS 6:6

The *eyes* of the Lord

For who has despised the day of small things?
For these seven rejoice to see
The plumb line in the hand of Zerubbabel.
They are the eyes of the LORD,
Which scan to and fro throughout the whole earth.

—ZECHARIAH 4:10

The *ears* of the Lord

And Samuel heard all the words of the people, and he repeated them in the hearing of the LORD.

—1 SAMUEL 8:21

The *mouth* of the Lord

The glory of the LORD shall be revealed,
And all flesh shall see it together;
For the mouth of the LORD has spoken.

—ISAIAH 40:5

The *mind* of the Lord

> Then they put him in custody, that the mind of the LORD might
> be shown to them.
> —LEVITICUS 24:12

The *heart* of the Lord

> Thus saith the Lord GOD: "…Yet thou art a man, and not God,
> though thou set thine heart as the heart of God."
> —EZEKIEL 28:2, KJV

All men on the planet, who are created in the image of God, carry these same nine physical and internal characteristics that are identified with God Himself. I do not believe these characteristics are for the purpose of human men attempting to create a visible image for man on earth of the Almighty, but these are actual active parts of God Himself.

The pronoun "Us" continues to be used at various places where God is speaking. In Genesis 3:22, right before God drove Adam and Eve out of the Garden of Eden, we read, "Then the LORD God said, 'Behold, the man has become like one of Us, to know good and evil. And now, lest he put out his hand and take also of the tree of life, and eat, and live forever….'" God again addresses a person (or persons) who is present with Him at the time when Adam fell into sin. From a Christian perspective, the "Us" would refer back to the three present at Creation—the Father, the Word, and the Spirit. This is clear from deduction of the fact that only Adam, Eve, and a serpent are recorded in the narrative.

The "Us" at the Tower

The incident in Genesis 11 of the building and eventual destruction of the Tower of Babel holds another clue to the tri-unity of God. When God saw that these men were united to build a tower and believed there was nothing that could restrain them if they remained united, God spoke and said, "Come, let Us go down and there confuse their language, that they may not understand one another's speech" (v. 7). The "Us" is another plural reference that indicated others are present with God, and together they "go down" (from heaven) to examine the tower and confound the people's languages. From a Christian perspective the Holy Spirit would have been present at this event to confound the languages, as He was the sole source of the many languages imparted to the believers on the Day of Pentecost, when they began to "speak with other tongues, as the Spirit gave them utterance" (Acts 2:4).

Babel was the division of languages, and Pentecost was the coming together of the nations to experience the kingdom of God in action.

Christ said that, "Before Abraham was, I AM" (John 8:58). This verse indicated Christ existed long before Father Abraham, as the "Word of God" (John 1:1–2). He would have been present at Creation and would have known information about the past that others living on earth in His day were completely unaware of. In Luke 16 Christ tells of a rich man and a beggar who both died, and the beggar was carried to paradise in Abraham's bosom, and the rich man found his soul in hell. Christ mentioned Moses and the prophets in the story (v. 29). This narrative was not a parable as some suggest, but a literal story Christ would have known, as He preexisted with His Father and had observed at some point the actions of a rich man and a beggar. Christ spoke about little ones (children) who are assigned a guardian angel in heaven who always beholds the face of the heavenly Father (Matt. 18:10). Christ's preexistence enabled Him to know this connection for a fact, as He had been with the Father before His supernatural conception on earth. Christ also spoke of how in heaven men are not married or given in marriage but are as the angels (Matt. 22:30). These and other revelations of things in heaven revealed by Christ were not known or understood to the devout Jews of His day, but they were known by Christ, since from the beginning He was "the Word" and was with God (1 John 1:1; 5:7), prior to supernatural conception.

The Holy Spirit has also been on earth from the earliest stages of Creation when He was moving (brooding) and hovering over the surface of the water (Gen. 1:2). As believers we often view the coming of the Holy Spirit at Pentecost as His first official arrival to this planet. However, the Holy Spirit came upon the various judges in the Old Testament. We read where the Spirit of the Lord came upon Othniel, Gideon, Jephthah, and Samson in the Book of Judges (Judg. 3:10; 6:34; 11:29; 15:14). Under the first covenant He came *upon* men, but under the new covenant of promise He *abides* within men. This abiding within men is identified as being "baptized with the Holy Spirit" (Acts 1:5). The word *baptized* or *baptism* is often connected to the thought of being baptized in water (Matt. 3:6). However, the writer of Hebrews spoke of the "doctrine of baptisms" (Heb. 6:2). There is more than baptism in water, as in the New Testament there are three main "baptisms" assigned for the believer. The first is the baptism occurring when the Holy Spirit baptizes a believer into the body of Christ (1 Cor. 12:13), which is initiated when a sinner repents and his or her name is placed in the heavenly registry of the Lamb's Book of Life (Luke 10:20). A newly "born again" (John 3:3) believer is automatically baptized or brought into the universal body of Christ, which is the community of all believers who have a redemptive covenant.

The second baptism is the baptism in water after repentance. When a sinner repents, Scripture commands that person to be baptized in water, which is a picture of being buried with Christ and raised a new creation with Him (Acts 2:38). We read:

> Buried with Him in baptism, in which you also were raised with Him through faith in the working of God, who raised Him from the dead.
> —COLOSSIANS 2:12–13

> There is also an antitype which now saves us—baptism (not the removal of the filth of the flesh, but the answer of a good conscience toward God), through the resurrection of Jesus Christ.
> —1 PETER 3:21

The third type of baptism is the baptism of the Holy Spirit, which is given exclusively to the children of God who are redeemed and in covenant with God. Christ said in Acts 1:5, "John truly baptized with water, but you shall be baptized with the Holy Spirit not many days from now." A sinner must repent before receiving the Holy Spirit baptism in the same measure believers did. (See Acts 2:4; 10:46; 19:6.)

Each member of the Godhead has a specific assignment for those in covenant. God our Father is the Creator; the Son, Jesus Christ, is presently the High Priest or heavenly advocate making intercession continually for men who pray and seek forgiveness and cleansing of sins, and He answers our prayers. The precious Holy Spirit is the Comforter on earth who is working with us to strengthen our faith and our walk with God.

During the Old Testament we read of the activity and actions of God working in Israel among His covenant people. In the New Testament Christ is the central figure of the new covenant, establishing the church and the manifest kingdom of God on earth. Since Pentecost the Holy Spirit has been the power source of enabling the church to fulfill the Great Commission of spreading the gospel of Christ to the world.

How Can Anyone Describe the Trinity?

Any theologian who believes that he or she can totally explain in simple terms the Godhead has a great challenge. At times the only way of understanding spiritual matters we cannot see is to compare them to the natural world, which we see. For example, in John 3:3 Christ uses a term saying you must be *born again*, a phrase in Greek, *gennao*, meaning, "to procreate, and, figuratively, to regenerate." It is to conceive a new birthing or a new creation. However, when a child is being born, there is a threefold process of birth—descent, rotation, and crowning. The descent is when the infant drops into the birth canal, rotation is when the infant turns and prepares for birth, and the crowning is when the face of the child is seen and the process concludes with the cutting of the umbilical cord. When you're born again, you must descend, or humble yourself before God; you must then repent, which is to turn from your wicked ways; and the crowning process is when you are face-to-face with your new Father—the Almighty!

This example may seem weak, but an egg has three parts: the outer shell, the yoke, and the egg white. Take an egg and hold it, and it is one egg. Open the shell and lay it aside, separate the yoke and the white, and you have three distinct parts of the same single egg. There is one God, and His eternal breath is His Spirit, which is the breath of the holy place and manifests as the Spirit of God. God is both light and love, and in the beginning He separated the light and love into a manifestation called *the Word*. We discover both the light of the gospel and the love of God revealed in Christ—the living Word. It was necessary for God to manifest as flesh through Christ, just as it was necessary for Christ to defeat Satan in a human body, giving us the same authority that He Himself carried.

The Tri-Unity in Jewish Writings

In the West believers have the Bible and often use different biblical commentaries (such as Barnes, Matthew Henry, and so forth) to discover the more detailed meaning of words and verses. Among Jewish rabbis there are numerous rabbinical commentaries based upon the written Word of God and upon what is termed the Oral Tradition. These include the Babylonian and Jerusalem Talmuds, including the Mishnah and the Gemara (all parts of the oral laws and traditions); the Zohar; the Kabbalah; and other minor writings used in yeshivas (Hebrew schools), especially rabbinical studies. One of the main books among Jewish mystics who have achieved a *higher level* of spiritual enlightenment is the Zohar, a word meaning "radiance." The book was compiled by Rabbi Simon ben Jochai and his son, Rabbi Eliezer, years following the destruction of Jerusalem in AD 70. Christian scholars have pointed out that in the Targums (paraphrases of Scripture) and in the Zohar there are references that appear to allude to the triune nature of God.

The unusual references to the "tri-unity of God" in the Zohar were noted by a medieval Christian scholar named Pico della Mirandola. Several books were written by Christian writers such as Petrus Galatinus and other writers, writing as far back as 1677, that began to explain the various passages written by the Jewish mystics who were attempting to explain the plural meaning of God's Hebrew name *Elohiym*.

In the Zohar one noted rabbi was instructing his son, and the question is asked, "How can they (the Three) be One? Are they verily One because we call them One? How Three can be One can only be known through the revelation of the Holy Spirit."[1] In another section, Rabbi Simon ben Jochai explained the word *Elohiym* as three substantive beings or divine persons in unity as one.

The Ancient One is revealed with three heads, which are united as One, and that Heads is thrice exalted. The Ancient Holy One is described as being Three; it is because the other lights emanating from Him are included in the Three.[2]

Rabbi Bechai noted that in Genesis 1:1, the word *Elohiym* is a compound of two Hebrew words, which he translates the name as, "These are God." The plural form of the name is expressed by the Hebrew letter *yod*, found in the name *Elohiym*.

One of the often overlooked passages is when Moses was in the desert and came across the burning bush. We read in Exodus 3:2–4:

> And the Angel of the LORD appeared to him in a flame of fire from the midst of a bush. So he looked, and behold, the bush was burning with fire, but the bush was not consumed. Then Moses said, "I will now turn aside and see this great sight, why the bush does not burn." So when the LORD saw that he turned aside to look, God called to him from the midst of the bush and said, "Moses, Moses!"

Rabbis point out that an *angel* appeared in the flame of this bush, yet God's voice called to Moses from the midst of the bush. The rabbinical comment on this narrative notes that this angel is the "redeeming angel" that God informed Moses would go before Israel during their journey in the wilderness.[3] This angelic messenger would be the same guardian angel God promised to Israel that would follow the nation throughout their wilderness struggles, observing them through the pillar of cloud by day and fire by night (Exod. 13:21). The Almighty said that His name would be on this angel and that if Israel sinned, this angel would not forgive their transgression. (See Exodus 23:20–23; 32:35).

Let us see if there is a tri-unity of God found in the narrative of Israel in the wilderness. First, God throughout the journey is seen speaking to Moses from the door of the tabernacle in the form of a cloud, known among Jewish sages as the *Shekinah*, or manifest glory (Exod. 33:8–11). We read that God spoke to Moses "face to face, as a man speaks to his friend" (v. 11). Thus God Himself is manifest on location at the tabernacle in the wilderness. Far above the tent is a manifestation of the pillar of cloud by day and fire by night (Exod. 13:21). Hundreds of years later in the temple of Solomon the manifestation of the "glory cloud" was a visible manifestation of the Holy Spirit demonstrating God's glory among the Hebrew people at the dedication (1 Kings 8:10–11). On the Day of Pentecost there were "tongues of fire" that sat upon the believers, which was a visible manifestation of the Holy Spirit (Acts 2:1–4). Thus, the cloud and the fire are linked to the visual manifestations of the Holy Spirit's presence. The angel who followed the nation of Israel had God's name on him and was given authority over the power of forgiveness.

> Behold, I send an Angel before you to keep you in the way and to bring you into the place which I have prepared. Beware of Him and obey His voice; do not provoke Him, for He will not pardon your transgressions; for My name is in Him.
> —EXODUS 23:20–21

This angel was the *redeeming angel* given the assignment of ensuring Israel eventually made it through to the Promised Land. This is the same angel Joshua spoke to after crossing the Jordan River, identified as the "captain of the Lord's host [armies]" (Josh. 5:15, KJV), and he required Joshua to remove his shoe from his foot—the imagery of the angel in the burning bush and God instructing Moses to remove his shoes from his feet (Exod. 3:5).

These manifestations—God speaking at the tabernacle, the cloud and fire, and the angel in the cloud observing Israel—again reveals the Godhead as the Father, Christ the Son, and the Holy Spirit.

There are many mysteries concerning the Godhead and what we term the trinity that are challenging to explain with human intellect. However, the Scripture is clear in both Testaments that there is a manifestation of the Father, the Son, and the Holy Spirit. Our book will explore the third person in this divine tri-unity, the Holy Spirit.

Chapter Three

THE MYSTERY OF THE
RUACH HA-KODESH

And when He had said this, He breathed on them, and
said to them, "Receive the Holy Spirit."

—John 20:22

THE TERM *Holy Spirit* appears forty times in Acts, five times in
Matthew, four in Mark, thirteen in Luke, three in John, sixteen
in Paul's epistles, five in Hebrews, two in Peter's epistles, and
is not alluded to in John's three small epistles or in Revelation. Since
Luke wrote the books of Acts and Luke, the Holy Spirit is mentioned
in those two books fifty-three times, demonstrating that the writer,
Luke, believed the role of the Holy Spirit was very significant. Luke
was a physician and gave specific narratives in Luke that are not found
in the other three Gospels. Luke provided great details into the births
of John the Baptist and Christ. John's parents, Zacharias and Elizabeth,
were old, and she was barren. Mary was a young virgin. Both births
were a result of a miraculous conception, which to a medical doctor
would have been an interesting aspect of his narrative. (See Luke 1.)
The conception of Christ occurred when the Holy Spirit overshadowed

Mary and the seed of God's word was implanted within her. It is called the *Immaculate Conception* (Luke 1:35).

In the Old Testament Hebrew, the phrase *Ruach ha-Kodesh* is the term used for "the Holy Spirit." The word *ruach* is a word translated several ways in the English Bible, such as "spirit," "breath," and "wind." The word *ha* is used as the word *the* in Hebrew, and the word *kodesh* refers to "holy" and "holiness." In English we say *spirit*; in Greek the word is *pneuma,* and the Hebrew word is *kodesh.* E. W. Bullinger commented that: "The meaning of the word is to be deduced only from its usage. The one root idea running through all of the passages is invisible force....In whatever sense it is used, (it) always represents that which is invisible except by its manifestations."[1] The word *ruach* is used nine different ways in the Old Testament, and the Greek counterpart, *pneuma,* is used fourteen different ways in the New Testament. For example, Jesus said His words were "spirit, and...life" (John 6:63). The idea of words being spirit is that words cannot be seen with the eyes just as a spirit is invisible to the eyes, but words can be heard, and once God's words are received in the human spirit they produce life! In the Scripture there are three significant titles used for the *Ruach ha-Kodesh*: the *Holy Spirit,* the *Spirit of the Lord,* and the *Spirit of God.*

Philo, who lived from 20 BC–AD 50, in *De Specialibus Legibus* (4:123) identified the Divine Spirit with the "breath of life upon the first man," which is the rational soul. The famed rabbi Maimonides discussed eleven degrees of prophecy, of which the second from the lowest stage is prophecy through the *Ruach ha-Kodesh.* He ascribed this type of prophetic inspiration to the biblical prophet Balaam (Num. 22–24), the high priest when reading the Urim and Thummim (Exod. 28:30), and the seventy elders to whom the Spirit was imparted in the wilderness (Exod. 24). David and Solomon both penned their books—Psalms, Proverbs, Song of Solomon, and Ecclesiastes—under the inspiration of the *Ruach ha-Kodesh.*[2]

In the time of Christ, His Jewish audience was aware of the *Spirit* of God and the concept of the Spirit being identified with *ruach,* or *wind, breath,* and *spirit.* This is perhaps why in John 3:5–8 Christ compared the Holy Spirit to the wind.

> The wind blows where it wishes, and you hear the sound of it,
> but cannot tell where it comes from and where it goes. So is
> everyone who is born of the Spirit.
>
> —JOHN 3:8

Wind cannot be seen just as the Holy Spirit cannot be seen and is invisible to the eyes, yet wind can be felt just as the Spirit can also be felt when He is present among us. Likewise, wind is invisible, but you can see its effects when the strength of its force manifests. The same is true with the Holy Spirit. Some of the Hebrew terms used in connection with the Holy Spirit are:

The Spirit	*ha Ruach*
The Holy Spirit	*Ruach ha-Kodesh*
Spirit of the Lord	*Ruach Adonai, Adonai*
Spirit of God	*Ruach El*

By the time of the second temple, the era of Christ's birth and ministry, the rabbis believed that prophecy had ceased with the Hebrew prophets Haggai, Zechariah, and Malachi, giving rise to a widespread concept called *bat kol*, or "the daughter of the voice" (Yoma 9b).[3]

As an example of this, the rabbis speak of men who were righteous and had the *Ruach ha-Kodesh*, or the Holy Spirit, rest upon them. A story is related in the ancient times that when rabbis gathered in Jericho, a divine voice announced to them that there were two among them who were worthy of the *Ruach ha-Kodesh*.[4] The rabbinical idea of inspiration ceasing after the last Hebrew prophets penned their books and the future revelation manifesting from a heavenly voice is interesting for the following reasons. Malachi is considered the last prophet after the Babylonian captivity to prophesy to Israel, and scholars estimated there is a gap of about four hundred years from Malachi to the public ministry of John the Baptist, the "voice of one crying in the wilderness" (Matt. 3:3). Historically there were no major prophetic voices during this entire season, called *the inter-testament period*, identified with this gap that exists between Malachi and John the Baptizer. (See Matthew 3.)

When John appeared as the wilderness baptizer, preaching the

kingdom of God, Christ, about age thirty (Luke 3:23), came to the
Jordan River to be baptized by John. When Christ came up out of the
water, the heavenly voice echoed from heaven, placing divine approval
upon Christ by announcing, "This is My beloved Son, in whom I am
well pleased" (Matt. 3:17). This voice was a public announcement from
heaven for those standing at the Jordan observing this historic event.
This moment marked a special *inspiration* upon Christ and His ministry. The second narrative unfolds after the baptism and when Christ
concluded forty days of fasting. He departed from the Judean wilderness to His hometown synagogue in His hometown of Nazareth. There,
Christ read from Isaiah's prophecy:

> The Spirit of the LORD is upon Me,
> Because He has anointed Me
> To preach the gospel to the poor;
> He has sent Me to heal the brokenhearted,
> To proclaim liberty to the captives
> And recovery of sight to the blind,
> To set at liberty those who are oppressed;
> To proclaim the acceptable year of the LORD.
> —LUKE 4:18–19

Had Christ ceased reading at a certain section of Isaiah and closed
the book, the service would have transitioned as normal. However,
Christ closed the scroll and announced, "Today, this Scripture is fulfilled in your hearing" (v. 21). Since the belief at that time was that the
Holy Spirit's inspiration and prophetic voice had ceased, then Christ,
in the eyes of the hometown people, was bordering on being self-
delusional, as this Isaiah passage was considered a Messianic prediction, and Jesus was simply, in their eyes, a *hometown lad* (v. 22). Later
in His public ministry, the proof of divine inspiration was witnessed
in Christ's teaching, and the power of God was demonstrated through
His miracles.

The rabbinical theory that inspiration and prophetic revelation
ceased with Malachi is due partially because there were no other prophetic books written past Malachi, as most devout religious Jews who
are not Messianic believers do not accept as inspired the New Testament books. I find it interesting that today certain Christian groups

accept a teaching of cessation of the vocal gifts of the Spirit listed in 1 Corinthians 12:7–10, which confines the operation of tongues, interpretation of tongues, and prophecy to the first century, the era of the original apostles. The cessationists teach that when the last apostle, John, passed away (somewhere between 96 to 100), both the vocal gifts (tongues, interpretation of tongues, and prophecy) along with certain power gifts (healings and miracles) ceased. Others identify the time of the cessation of particular gifts to the season when the twenty-seven books of the New Testament canon of Scripture was agreed upon, from the middle to the late third century. This view of cessation of divine inspiration seems to mirror the Jewish view, in that it believes that certain supernatural manifestations, including God speaking to individuals, was a past experience and no longer an active event.

This rabbinical idea of God speaking only in a heavenly voice was believed among devout Jews at the time the church was born on the Day of Pentecost. If the rabbis living between Malachi and the Day of Pentecost (Acts 2:1–4) believed it required a heavenly voice as a sign of the *Ruach ha-Kodesh*, then God Himself was about to display in Jerusalem, in the presence of thousands of Jews and devout men out of sixteen named nations (Acts 2:9–11), more than a voice. As the Spirit descended upon the gathering place of these believers, there was a sudden "sound from heaven," as a rushing mighty wind. This sound was a tangible sign to gain the attention of Jewish worshippers gathered in the temple compound. As these uneducated Galilean believers in Christ supernaturally began to speak in the same languages of the nations represented at the feast, this was a visible sign that the prophetic inspiration was being *restored* through this new living organism called *the church*, as the Spirit Himself gave power and authority to these *called-out ones*, identified by the Greek word *ekklesia,* or the *church*. This new prophetic voice was manifest throughout the New Testament and continues to resound around the world through fresh outpourings of the Spirit.

The Spirit of Wisdom

Solomon is believed to have penned the first twenty-nine chapters in Proverbs and wrote Ecclesiastes, books identified by scholars as biblical, wisdom literature. Proverbs consists of thirty-one chapters, the last two added by an unknown person (perhaps King Hezekiah's men). Proverbs teaches practical wisdom principles for daily living. Throughout the book three words are consistently emphasized: *knowledge* is mentioned forty-three times, *understanding* is referred to fifty-five times, and the word *wisdom* is emphasized fifty-four times. These three key words unlock Solomon's wisdom doors for spiritual, emotional, mental, and financial increase and blessing on your life. Following Solomon's three-step pattern will move a person from average to above average. Solomon knew:

- Knowledge is the *accumulation* of facts.

- Understanding is the *arrangement* of facts.

- Wisdom is the *application* of those facts.

Parents, educators, and teachers effectively impart knowledge through reading books, personal example, and by instruction. Knowledge can also be gained through personal life experiences. Knowledge without understanding, however, is like a computer with a hard drive filled with information that is never turned on. We can brag about the gigabytes of information it holds, but until the information is accessed and printed from the laptop, it's just a computer collecting data. You must proceed from information to illumination, or to understanding.

Understanding is the ability to place, in a *proper arrangement*, information (or facts) received through study and personal experience. If we glean information and facts, yet do not put into practice our learning, our knowledge becomes like faith without action and, as it is written, faith without works (action) is dead (James 2:17). One hundred students can sit under the same teacher, gaining knowledge, but not everyone expresses understanding on how to activate the information, making it work in life situations. For example, most smokers have *knowledge* that smoking tobacco can eventually cause cancer. This is medically documented. Yet some smokers don't think cancer through smoking will ever affect *them.* This is not a lack of knowledge, as the facts reveal the knowledge, but it is a lack of understanding.

Christ encountered an understanding deficit among His listeners.

Often those who heard His parables didn't understand their meanings. His personal disciples, after a parabolic discourse, petitioned Christ to explain, or give understanding of the main points concealed within the story. In Matthew 13:13–14 Christ said, "Therefore I speak to them in parables, because seeing they do not see, and hearing they do not hear, nor do they understand." The Greek word for "understand" in this passage means, "to put something together and comprehend it mentally." A person can hear a parable (gain knowledge) but not always comprehend the meaning (the understanding).

Once we have received understanding and can grasp the meaning of a subject or an issue and the purpose of our information, then we must learn to *apply* that information. This leads to Solomon's third key—the necessity of wisdom. True wisdom is the ability to apply these facts, helping people, events, and circumstances to properly function in their natural and divine order. There are two types of wisdom: carnal (human) and spiritual (1 Cor. 2:6). The Holy Spirit is the giver and source of spiritual wisdom, which can provide solutions to practical and complicated problems.

The Feminine Word *Wisdom*

When the name "God" or "Lord" is mentioned in Scripture, masculine personal pronouns such as "He," "Himself," and "Him" are used to describe God from a masculine perspective. However, the Holy Spirit as the *Ruach ha-Kodesh* is in Hebrew in the feminine gender phrase. In English we have three genders: masculine, feminine, and neutral (he, she, and it). In Hebrew (and Aramaic) there is not a neuter gender, as everything is either a "he" or a "she," and the nouns and verbs are also either masculine or feminine. The phrase *Ruach ha-Kodesh* is grammatically feminine, as is *comforter,* a word identifying one of the activities the Holy Spirit performs for a believer (John 14:16, KJV). There are many comments and commentaries that go in depth to explain why the Holy Spirit is in the feminine and not the masculine, although after using the term *Ruach ha-Kodesh,* the same pronouns as "He" and Him" are used. In agreement with this feminine phrase is interesting insight into how wisdom is viewed from a Hebraic perspective.

When Solomon wrote of wisdom in the Book of Proverbs, the gift of wisdom is called a "she" and not a "he." In Proverbs 8 and 9, the pronoun "she" is used (Prov. 8:2–3; 9:2–3). Solomon gave specific benefits and results when wisdom ruled and negative outcomes when wisdom is rejected:

- Wisdom speaks of her children.
- Whoever finds her finds life.
- He who sins against her sins against his own soul.
- She gives instruction in truth, righteousness, and justice.
- By her kings reign.

Now compare these statements on wisdom to the verses revealing the effect of the Holy Spirit in your life. The Holy Spirit bears witness with us that we are the *children of God* (Rom. 8:16). He is also the *giver of life*, as there is life in the Spirit (v. 10). The only sin that cannot be forgiven is blasphemy against the Holy Spirit; thus a blasphemer *sins against his own soul* (Luke 12:10). Notice wisdom instructs in *truth, righteousness,* and *justice,* just as the Holy Spirit reproves the world of sin, righteousness, and judgment (John 16:8). By her, kings reign, and in Revelation we read that we will rule as kings and priests (Rev. 1:6). John wrote that the "Spirit and the bride say, 'Come!'", speaking of the invitation to live in the holy city of New Jerusalem (Rev. 22:17). Thus wisdom is the Holy Spirit, and the Holy Spirit manifests wisdom.

Wisdom is not just a characteristic of an intelligent mind or some mental gift; wisdom is imparted by the Holy Spirit and is often identified as a spirit, as we read in three passages about the "spirit of wisdom" (Exod. 28:3; Deut. 34:9; Isa. 11:2). Maimonides in *Guide of the Perplexed,* 2:45, said wisdom is: "A certain thing that descends upon an individual so that he talks in wise sayings, in words of praise, in useful admonitory dicta, or concerning governmental or divine matters—and all this while he is awake and his senses function as usual." Wisdom was required in Israel's preparation of God's dwelling place.

When Moses was preparing minute details for the wilderness tabernacle and priestly garments, it required a "spirit of wisdom" (Exod. 28:3; 35:31). To this day artisans for the Temple Institute in Jerusalem study the re-creation of the sacred vessels and are amazed at the wisdom required to create such detailed items, including the gold menorah, constructed from one beaten sheet of gold. During the wilderness journey the spirit of prophecy began to operate within the assembly (Num. 11; 24). Before any vocal gift operates (such as the spirit of prophecy), a believer should seek first a spirit of wisdom to discern how to hear the voice of the Lord and when, where, and to whom to speak inspired utterances. When an unwise person attempts to flow in a spiritual gift, it is like placing a burning torch in the hands of a child; they will leave scars upon themselves and others they contact.

The Shekinah Presence

God manifested a phenomenon in the wilderness of a large column of a cloud and a column of fire by night (Exod. 13:21–22). These visible materializations of God's presence were identified by Jewish sages as the *Shekinia*, a word not in the English Bible but used to describe the tangible or visible manifestation of the Lord. God released at times visible manifestations among His people in the wilderness, and when it was seen by the people, it was linked to the tent in the wilderness. When it appeared in cloud form at the tabernacle or later at Solomon's temple, it was called the "glory of the LORD" (Exod. 16:10; 40:34–35). In Hebrew the phrase *Shekinah* means, "He caused to dwell."

The presence of God was visibly seen in the form of a large cloud that "rested" upon the tent of meeting or in the midst of the tabernacle or later the temple (Num. 9:18; 2 Chron. 5:13–14). The Hebrew word for "rested" is *chanah*; thus the glory of God *rested or dwelt in the midst*. In my earlier days our family would attend yearly state conventions conducted under a large metal tabernacle. Called a "camp meeting," the services were centered on singing, preaching, and long, powerful altar services that often continued into the night. I can recall times in which the prayers of fifteen hundred people in unison sounded like a roaring waterfall, and the altar services were charged like an electrical current sending waves throughout the atmosphere. As this divine presence brooded and seemingly hovered over the people, the old-timers would say, "The Shekinah glory is here!"

The idea of these three words—the *Ruach ha-Kodesh*, *Wisdom*, and the *Shekinah* glory of God—being in *feminine* form is unique when we consider that the Holy Spirit is always referred to using the pronouns "He" (John 16:8), "Him" (John 14:17), or "himself" (John 16:13, KJV) throughout the New Testament. He is never identified as an "it" and never a "she." I do believe, however, that the Spirit of God's manifestations, including His gifts and fruits, can be viewed from a *human perspective* in both masculine and feminine characteristics. When a person has muscular arms, is bold, often impatient, easily stirred to anger, likes a conflict, and enjoys a good fight, this is a more masculine series of attributes found in men, who tend to be hunters and aggressive during competition. The feminine characteristics that are found in most females are gentleness, meekness, patience, and tenderness. Now notice in the New Testament there are nine fruit of the Spirit that all believers filled with the Holy Spirit should experience in their daily walk:

> But the fruit of the Spirit is love, joy, peace, longsuffering, kindness, goodness, faithfulness, gentleness, self-control. Against such there is no law.
> —GALATIANS 5:22–23

When God saw Adam, He said, "It is not good that man should be alone" (Gen. 2:18). God created a woman to be a "help meet" (KJV) or, in Hebrew, "one fit for" Adam. Eve was called a *woman*. A woman was created with a womb that a man did not have, providing her the ability of housing within her another living being for nine months, eventually giving birth to an earthly being with an eternal soul. Each woman who has natural affection also has a motherly instinct to care for children who are hurting or in need. This is why the majority of financial giving is by women, as a woman tends to be moved more with compassion toward other's needs, while men are often project oriented.

Not only does the Holy Spirit release the attribute of compassion, but also a mother is gifted and emotionally geared as the *comforter* for her children in their times of distress. This reminds me of the words of Christ where He told His disciples that He would return to heaven but would not leave them comfortless; He would send them "another Comforter...even the Spirit of truth," which is the Holy Spirit (John 14:16–17, KJV). The word "comfortless" in verse 18 is the Greek word *orphanos* and is the word we use to describe a child without living parents, one abandoned by their parents, or more literally, one who has no father.[5] Christ is saying He would not leave us abandoned or alone as an orphan without parents or direction, but He would send us another Comforter! The Greek word for "comforter" is *parakletos,* and this word has been expounded on for generations. The word *parakletos* is derived from two words that mean, "to go along side of to help." It also means, "one who pleads the case for another as an intercessor."[6] As the Comforter, the Spirit is always with us; we are never alone. He stands alongside of you at all times to help and aid you, especially in times of weakness (Rom. 8:26). The Spirit of God does plead our case through using our own voice but by also giving us a prayer language that enables us to communicate directly to God.

The Spirit Brings Inspiration and Wisdom

The Holy Spirit is the wisdom giver to those who seek after wisdom. Wisdom was required in the wilderness when the time arrived to construct the tabernacle and to assemble the sacred gold furnishings required by God to build.

> See, I have called by name Bezalel the son of Uri, the son of Hur, of the tribe of Judah. And I have filled him with the Spirit of God, in wisdom, in understanding, in knowledge, and in all manner of workmanship, to design artistic works, to work in gold, in silver, in bronze, in cutting jewels for setting, in carving wood, and to work in all manner of workmanship.
>
> —Exodus 31:2–5

One of the central pieces of sacred furniture was the seven-branched gold candelabra called the *menorah.* The six-foot-high golden light was beaten out of one sheet of solid gold, and seven branches were forged under the supervision of Bezalel. The artisans at the Temple Institute in Jerusalem have been involved for many years in researching a re-creation of the vessels and furniture from the Jewish temple. They discovered that if the menorah is made from 24-karat gold, the arms, or the seven branches holding the light at the top, are too soft and begin drooping. There are carvings on stones discovered in excavations in Israel that show the second temple menorah with these seven shafts upright and apparently no difficulty with the "drooping effect." Someone suggested running a straight shaft in the middle from branch to branch to cure the problem. However, no straight horizontal shaft connecting the branches can be seen on etchings unearthed on stone or in caves found in Israel. Thus, there was wisdom given to create the original menorah that came from the Holy Spirit, which is somewhat of a mystery to this day.

According to some students at the institute, the ark of the covenant is presently hidden near the Temple Mount area, and thus the only piece of furniture not to be re-created is the ark of the covenant. (Others disagree and say it can be re-created under proper circumstances.) Years ago during a Holy Land tour, we stopped at another Temple Institute housing numerous models and explanations concerning the past and future temples in Jerusalem. A miniature model of the ark of the covenant was on display. With me was a professional electrical engineer who was carefully examining the manner in which the ark was made, according to the written and oral traditions of the Jews. There were actually three separate boxes that were all placed in the one main box. There was wood covered with solid gold on the main box, with a wooden box in the middle and a thin gold box lying inside the solid wood. The lid was wood covered with gold.

My friend looked at me and said, "This is a capacitor that can generate electricity!" He explained how the electricity in the atmosphere amassed on the lid, and if you touched it with your hand, it would shock you, but if you grabbed it with both hands it could send a deadly voltage into your body, causing instant death. The woman directing our tour said, "This is what happened to Uzzah when he reached out to steady the ark with his hands; he was struck dead!" (See 2 Samuel 6:6–8.) I asked my friend Tom how a person could prevent this from happening, and he replied that the staves used to carry the ark would serve as a ground to ground out the electricity buildup. I realized that only God Himself understood this, and He gave specific directions on how to safely transport this sacred box. Again, divine wisdom prepared this sacred artifact.

Consider the holy of holies in Solomon's day. The inside of the most holy chamber was covered in panels of gold. The golden ark sat on a rock in the center of this small room, and in Solomon's time overshadowing the ark were two large, carved olive wood angels, covered with gold. With each angel, one wing touched the wall of the holy of holies and reached out and touched the outspread wing of the other. It was like a wire running from one pole to another pole, but in this case it was wood covered with gold from wall to wall, as their outstretched wings formed an arch over the mercy seat of the ark of the covenant (1 Kings 6:24–27).

Each year the high priest would enter the holy of holies while wearing four linen garments and removing any gold from his person. The idea is that because Israel sinned by worshipping the golden calf (Exod. 32:19–24), the gold crown and breastplate usually worn by the high priest was removed before entering God's presence, so as to prevent the temptation for idolatry. Just as Moses removed his shoes at the burning bush because of God's presence filling the area (Exod. 3:5), the high priest would enter the holy of holies each year without shoes. In Solomon's day, because the area was covered with so much gold, and gold is the best conduit for electricity of any metal (we use copper as it is cheaper), then this place was *charged* with more than just the presence of God and may have actually had an *electrical feel* in the very atmosphere.

Even the garments of the priest were created with the spirit of wisdom:

> So you shall speak to all who are gifted artisans, whom I have filled with the spirit of wisdom, that they may make Aaron's garments, to consecrate him, that he may minister to Me as priest.
>
> —Exodus 28:3

Noise in the Tabernacle

The word *tabernacle* is used 328 times in the King James Version of the Bible. There are several Hebrew words translated as tabernacle. From Exodus 25:9 to Exodus 27:19, God uses the word *mishkan*, which is a tent *dwelling*. There is a sudden change in the word beginning in Exodus 27:21 and going through Exodus 33:11, where the word *tabernacle* becomes *'olel*, which is a word for a *covering* or a tent covering.

There are two ideas with these words. With the *mishkan* God was setting up a place for *Him to dwell* among His people. With the *'olel* this
tent would be a *spiritual covering* and a place of atonement where God
will cover the sins and transgressions of the people.

Both the tabernacle and the temple of Solomon were a place of
noise. The clamor of numerous animals and the chants of the prayers
of priests and people mingled with the smell of burnt sacrifices filling
the air. In the Book of Job a question is asked: "Also can any understand the spreadings of the clouds, or the noise of his tabernacle?" (Job
36:29, KJV). The Hebrew word for "tabernacle" is a different word than
those just mentioned. The word *tabernacle* is mentioned nine times in
Job as the word *'olel* (Job 5:24; 18:6, 14, 15; 19:12; 20:26; 29:4; 31:31). In
Job 36:29, however, the word used for "tabernacle" is *cukkah* (or *sukkot*)
and is the same Hebrew word for "booths," a word used to describe the
huts that the Hebrew people dwell in for seven days during the Feast of
Tabernacles (Lev. 23:42–43; Neh. 8:14–17). The Feast of Sukkot, known
as Tabernacles, was later identified as the greatest festival of rejoicing
of all the seven feasts of Israel.

The seventh feast of Israel, Tabernacles, called Sukkot in Hebrew,
is also identified as "the seasons of our joy." Among devout Jews this
feast is understood to be the most joyous of the seven feasts of Israel.
Both Jews and Gentiles celebrate together during these seven days, and
in the temple days there were numerous offerings and special rituals,
such as the Water Libation Ceremony, which marked this as a joyful
and rather *noisy* occasion!

Since God's first dwelling among His people Israel was in a tent,
then what occurred at this animal skin-covered tabernacle was a picture of things to come. During Sukkot, each family creates a booth
using four types of tree branches, forming a covering above the heads
of those living in these booths for seven days. The noise is the sound
of the singing and people rejoicing.

There is also a link in Judaism between being possessed with the
Ruach ha-Kodesh and ecstasy, or great religious joy, especially in
the water drawing ceremony at the Festival of Tabernacles—a day of
dancing, singing, and music. This was considered the one ceremony in
which the participants drew inspiration directly from the *Ruach ha-
Kodesh*.[7]

The Breathing and Living Tent

Everything about this portable tent-tabernacle was linked to *life* or something that needed to die to provide the materials for constructing the place where death through sin would be replaced by life through God. The lives of countless animals were given to provide the skins and coverings for God's outdoor house.

Fine linen and goat's hair were two primary fabrics used in the tabernacle. The linen provided was Egyptian linen and was the finest in the world in that day, having nearly twice as many threads per inch as the linen made today. The linen was used for the eastern outer gate entrance, the veil leading into the holy of holies, and the holy garments of the priests. Goat's skin was used for the covering of the holy place and most holy place. The goat's skin was laid on top, on the outside with the fine linen underneath (Exod. 35:23). The nomads living in the desert in the Middle East still use goat's skin to construct their tents. When the skins become wet with rainwater, the fibers tighten and make the tent virtually waterproof, which was also needed in the wilderness tabernacle.

The Skins of the Animals

Skins of two other animals were used in the construction of the tabernacle. The ram's skins were dyed red and are a symbol of sacrificial blood and death (Exod. 36:19). The ram was the animal caught in the thicket, replacing Isaac on Abraham's altar (Gen. 22:13). A Jewish tradition states that God chose the ram skins as the covering when He slew the animals to place a covering on the bodies of Adam and Eve (Gen. 3:21). The ram was an important offering, especially related to the priesthood (Exod. 29:15–19). The second animal skin is the badger's skin. There has been a debate as to what the badger skin was. Some teach it was a sea animal, such as a porpoise or a seal. The Hebrew word for "badger" is *tachash* and is of uncertain meaning. There is a small furry animal that can be spotted in parts of the wilderness in Israel called a badger. Others suggest these skins were a type of a wild antelope that lived in the desert regions.

The Trees and the Wood

The wood used for the beams and the furniture was from the acacia tree, which today can be seen growing south of the Dead Sea in the dry Israeli desert. The wood of the tree is a fine grain, darkens with age, and is harder than oak. This tree was used in Egypt for the coffins of the pharaohs. The trees can grow as high as twenty-five feet and survive in the driest climates in the desert. The umbrella shape of the tree allows it to capture water when it rains. The branches are very thorny. However, the flower from the tree has been used for centuries as a fragrance. Some believe that the burning bush God used when speaking to Moses may have been a small acacia tree (Exod. 3:2). The tree needs little water, grows in sand, and survives in dry ground. This strong wood also made up the post holding up the entire tabernacle—a picture of Christ, who is called "a root out of dry ground" (Isa. 53:2).

The wood from this tree was used to construct the sixty posts needed for the outer wall of the tabernacle.

There were five pillars with a curtain on the east entrance of the tabernacle and four posts with a curtain leading into the holy place. According to the Temple Institute, the tall wooden posts were not one piece of wood but were made with two pieces that interconnected, thus making it easier to transport when moving the portable tent. Thus the beams from trees, the skins from animals, and the oil from olives all came from living beings or objects.

The Breath of the Holies

Many years ago, before his passing, I heard a man who was a noted specialist on Hebraic tradition tell of how during the days of the tabernacle, when the presence of the Lord would come down inside of the tent there were two manifestations. The first was the sound of a man breathing, and the second was the sound of the curtains expanding outward and then inward, like a man's lungs. This was known as the "breath of the holies," and since the Hebrew word *ruwach* can mean breath or spirit, the name became the "spirit of the holies." It later emerged into the name the Holy Spirit![8] In the Creation account, the Holy Spirit "moved upon the face of the waters" (Gen. 1:2, KJV). The

Hebrew word for "moved" means, "to flutter, or brood over." God Himself "breathed into his [man's] nostrils the breath of life" (Gen. 2:7). From this moment forward God and the Holy Spirit are always *moving* and *breathing life* into and onto His prophets, His people, and their situations. We read: "The earth shook; the heavens also dropped rain at the presence of God; Sinai itself was moved at the presence of God, the God of Israel" (Ps. 68:8). If a mountain of rock can tremble and shake in God's presence, should we be surprised when the Spirit moves upon men and they too tremble in the presence of the Lord?

This idea of God's breath moving within the tabernacle bears more interest in the story where Christ breathed upon ten of His disciples, instructing them to receive the Holy Spirit:

> And when He had said this, He breathed on them, and said to them, "Receive the Holy Spirit."
>
> —JOHN 20:22

This action from Christ is interesting for three reasons. First, Jesus breathed on them to receive the Holy Spirit, but they did not receive the manifestation of tongues until days later, the morning of the arrival of the Feast of Pentecost (Acts 2:1–4). Second, the disciple Thomas was not present at the time of this significant event. Why didn't Jesus wait until Thomas joined the group before enacting the breathing upon His disciples to receive the Spirit? Third, in John 20:22 there was a total of ten disciples present, as Thomas was missing and Judas was dead. What is the spiritual significance of ten versus eleven or twelve?

First, look at Christ breathing upon His disciples. The word *breathe* simply means, "to puff or to blow out air." When Christ blew air out of His mouth, the disciples would have breathed His air into their own lungs. In the beginning of Creation God breathed out His breath into man, and when the breath entered Adam's being, he became a living, breathing being. Adam did not procreate at that moment until his bride, Eve, was formed and consummated with him to bring forth a family.

The Living Breath of God

Adam, being the first human, was closer to God than any person in history outside of Christ Himself. Adam saw God daily, walking with Him in the cool of the day (Gen. 3:8). The word translated "cool" in this passage is *ruwach*, the word for wind, breath, and spirit. This indicates that God swept into the garden *riding* on a wind, perhaps similar to the type of wind that blew into the Upper Room. This wind was the tangible presence of the Lord Himself. On this one momentous occasion Adam and Eve were missing from their meeting spot and were found hiding (v. 8).

Three distinct marks set Adam apart. First, Adam was not conceived through the normal conception process—the seed of a man and egg of the woman—but was formed out of the earth's dust as a fully grown being. Adam's likeness was God's image (Gen. 1:26), and after breathing the "breath of life," Adam rose to his feet, housing within him an eternal spirit that was the literal breath or spirit of God. This breath of God caused Adam to "become a living soul" (Gen. 2:7, KJV). In Luke 3:38 Adam is called "the son of God." The creation of Adam would also release the image of God in all future human beings, as each living infant has an eternal soul and spirit.

The second distinction was that Adam was created a fully grown man, but the breath of God also imparted a powerful life force liquid in his body called *blood*. With only a spirit and no blood, Adam would have been a creation like an angel, for angels are spirits only without the life force of blood. The blood in Adam provided him physical life. Without a heart pumping blood, a person's physical life ceases (Lev. 17:11). When God breathed into Adam's nostrils, blood was mysteriously created, which filled his clay body. Once this blood ceases to flow, the human body will return to the dust from where it came (Gen. 3:19).

The third aspect of Adam's creation was the fact that he could *communicate* in some form of language between himself and God. We know this because when God completed creating the animal kingdom, He gave Adam an assignment to name the animals throughout the garden. Each animal was named, meaning there were letters of some type of alphabet and verbal forms of communication between Adam and God Himself.

At the fall of Adam in the garden, the *image*, the *blood*, and the *communication* were either altered or lost. We can see this image change as time passed and men began to corrupt the image of the incorruptible God into images of animals, paying homage to the creation instead of the Creator, forming idols, and spreading idol worship. Many scholars believe that if Adam and Eve had not sinned, both would have continued to live as long as they partook of the mysterious tree of life, renewing their bodies and replenishing them—body, soul, and spirit—generation after generation. In some mysterious manner, sin affects the blood of mankind, as "life is in the blood" (Lev. 17:11), and death comes to all men through the bloodline of Adam. It seems that the very cells of man's blood are subject to the power of death through sin. Concerning communication, Adam and Eve were expelled from the garden yet continued to communicate with other humans. However, the intimate one-on-one communication once enjoyed daily at the tree of life was silenced between God and mankind. The bridge linking heaven and earth, man and God, was severed, and God remained in His heavenly temple, occasionally sending angelic messengers to men and women with specific messages or assignments.

The Restoration by the Second Adam

Christ is called the "second Adam," and through His discipline and ministry He succeeded through His atoning process to reverse the threefold losses of the first Adam. First, Christ was the walking image of God: "He is the image of the invisible God, the firstborn over all creation" (Col. 1:15). He told His disciples, "He who has seen Me has seen the Father" (John 14:9). Christ was not just speaking of His physical appearance but also of His miracles, love, compassion, healing, and desire to free mankind from sin's chains.

Christ had an earthly mother (Mary) but not an earthly father, as He was conceived with the seed of the Word through the impartation of the Holy Ghost within the womb of the Virgin Mary. This process, I believe, was necessary to create a blood within Christ that would not be tainted by the normal, natural seed of a man—something required for the blood type in a child. Notice the importance of Christ's blood:

> Not with the blood of bulls and goats and calves, but with His own blood...
>
> —HEBREWS 9:12

> How much more shall the blood of Christ...cleanse your conscience from dead works...
>
> —HEBREWS 9:14

> ...boldness to enter the Holiest by the blood of Jesus...
>
> —HEBREWS 10:19

The third restoration that is often overlooked, seldom taught, and very often misunderstood is the aspect of restoring the direct, face-to-face communication line between God and man. Christians from all nations pray in their native languages, under peaceful circumstances, anywhere and at any time. From Adam to Christ divine revelation was released through inspired words, prophetic warnings, priestly revelations, and godly biblical kings. However, there are times when a person's faith may be weak, and the individual is uncertain what to pray for as he should (Rom. 8:26). This is one primary reason why a more personal, intimate language is needed and provided by the prayer language of the Spirit, as the word is spoken from a direct line from your spirit to God.

The Breath of God

Scholars have debated the spiritual significance of Christ breathing on the disciples and announcing their reception of the Holy Spirit. God's breath formed a living organism called Adam, and Christ's breath initiated a new and living organism on earth called the church. We often teach that the Day of Pentecost was the birth of the church, but every birth requires a moment of conception, and the breath of the resurrected Christ was the breath of life that initiated a "conception moment" that would, several days later, give birth to a living, spiritual organism called the church.

Christ was seen alive after His resurrection for forty days (Acts 1:3). Normally forty is a biblical number of testing, but in this case there is no indication that any of these forty days are linked to the normal biblical patterns of a spiritual test. There is another meaning of forty, in that it requires forty weeks for a normal conception to end in a healthy birth. The church was not a new temple, sanctuary, or a building of stone, but it was actually identified as the mystical body of Christ (1 Cor. 12:27). It requires forty weeks to complete a birth process, and during these forty days Christ was seen alive as He poured into His followers to prepare them to become His body and represent Him on the earth! Christ would take His natural, resurrected body to heaven, yet He would leave a spiritual and mystical body on earth.

Every human body needs a spirit abiding within it to become a living person on earth. James wrote that as the body without the spirit is dead, so faith without works is dead (James 2:26). If a human's heart stops and the blood ceases flowing, the person is not necessarily dead and can at times be revived if the problem was a sudden heart attack. However, once the spirit leaves or is separated from the body, the person is dead, as to be absent from the body is to be present with the Lord (2 Cor. 5:8). This is what occurred when a beggar died and the angels released his spirit from his body and carried his spirit into paradise (Luke 16).

There is a parallel in this thought that *a spirit without a body is dead* for local congregations. If the Holy Spirit is not present, dwelling within the people or manifesting His gifts and fruits in a church, then the body of Christ without the Holy Spirit will be a spiritually dead gathering. I have known of entire denominations whose theology is based on their unbelief toward the supernatural power of God instead of faith in the power of God. I have heard comments from their ministers that the Holy Spirit manifestations in the Pentecostal and charismatic churches are "of the devil," "evil," or "deception." In their own churches they refute and refuse any form of emotional worship or visible manifestations, including any forms of musical instruments. An interesting funeral can be more energetic than what is called a worship experience among some groups. The application here is that if a local congregation, or a denomination for that matter, speaks despairingly or in a derogatory manner concerning the Holy Spirit, they can *grieve, vex,* or go as far as to *blaspheme* the Holy Spirit, and He will not settle and rest where He is not welcomed. If the church body is spiritually dead, it may be because the Holy Spirit is not dwelling and abiding within that body of believers. Thus the breathing of Christ upon the ten chosen disciples was the conception moment of the new body, the church, that would manifest at Pentecost.

Why the Number Ten?

All numbers used in Scripture have a special and distinct meaning. Three is the number of unity; six is the number of man; seven is the number of perfection. The number ten is linked to divine order. For example, there are Ten Commandments given by God to set Israel in order as a nation. There are ten tests in the life of Abraham and ten generations from Adam to the Flood, where Noah's sons survived, reordering, and repopulating the earth with a new order under God's instruction.

Twelve is recognized as a number connected with divine government:

- Twelve patriarchs from Shem to Jacob (1 Chron. 1:24–28)
- Twelve tribes of Israel (Gen. 35:22–26)
- Twelve apostles of the Lamb (Matt. 10:1–5)
- Twelve gates to the New Jerusalem (Rev. 21:21)
- Twelve stones on the city walls (Rev. 21:14)
- Twelve constellations the sun moves through during a solar year

What is the meaning of the number eleven? The number eleven has a rather subversive meaning to it. It is one more than ten and one less than twelve. Thus eleven is out of order with ten and short of order with twelve.

After the death of Judas there were eleven remaining disciples who were living in confusion, fleeing, hiding, and struggling in doubt. A conspiracy caused eleven of Jacob's sons to sell their brother Joseph as a slave. Jehoiakim reigned eleven years before Nebuchadnezzar came and destroyed the city (2 Kings 23:36; 24:1). It was in the eleventh year that Ezekiel prophesied against Tyre that a major judgment was coming (Ezek. 26:1).

Ten—not eleven or twelve—disciples were present when Christ breathed upon them, instructing them to receive the Holy Spirit. Judas was missing after Satan entered his heart, and he took his life. Thomas, whose heart of unbelief is noted in John 20:24–28, was also missing. Notice when Thomas saw Christ later:

> And after eight days His disciples were again inside, and Thomas with them. Jesus came, the doors being shut, and stood in the midst, and said, "Peace to you!"
>
> —JOHN 20:26

Thomas returned and made up the number to eleven. However, before the Holy Spirit was poured out on the Day of Pentecost, the disciples met in an upper room and appointed an apostle to replace Judas. (See Acts 1.) Thus when the Spirit arrived in Acts 2:1–4, there were at that time twelve men appointed as apostles—or divine order reestablished, as the Spirit of God works through order and not confusion! When the Holy Spirit came, He came as the sound of a mighty rushing wind—again a manifestation of the wind or breath of God! All believers were filled with the Spirit and began to "speak with other tongues, as the Spirit gave them utterance" (Acts 2:4).

A common question is, "What is the purpose for speaking with tongues?" The answer is found directly in Scripture but also in patterns formed in the Old Testament. We are told by Paul that our bodies are the temple of the Holy Spirit and that the Spirit dwells within us. The tabernacle of Moses and the temple were both sacred settings in which numerous inspired rituals were set aside for the purpose of appeasing God and drawing men closer to God.

God spoke from three locations: from the *door* of the tent of meeting (Exod. 29:42), from the *holy place* (Exod. 34:34–35), and He communed with the high priest from above the sacred covering of the ark of the covenant, called the *mercy seat* (Exod. 25:22). In each instance it was at or within the tabernacles itself. Today our bodies are the temple of the Holy Spirit, and He dwells in us (1 Cor. 3:16), as a walking, living temple of God. The Holy Spirit also speaks from within our spirit man, which is figuratively the holy of holies. We are a body, soul, and spirit (1 Thess. 5:23). The *door* is the outer entrance of the tent, which represents our body. The holy place is inside the door, representing our soul or mind, and the mercy seat on the ark is the chamber of our spirit, from which the Holy Spirit dwells and speaks to us as we walk in the atoning redemptive covenant and the mercy of God!

The Spirit Is Breath or Wind

Paul wrote to Timothy and said, "All Scripture is given by inspiration of God..." (2 Tim. 3:16). The Greek word for "inspiration" is *theopneustos*, which is from two words, *theos*, meaning "God, and *pneuma*, which comes from the root word *pneu*. The word communicates the idea of the dynamic movement of air, like blowing air through an instrument to give a distinct musical sound. The root word can also allude to a wind blowing over a flower garden and creating a fragrance, or the release of emotions from a person.[9] The Word came when holy men of God spoke as they were "moved by the Holy Spirit" (2 Pet. 1:21). The word *moved* means, "to be borne along or carried along." The imagery is a ship with sails and the wind blowing into the sails, moving the ship according to the wind's direction and not by the hands of the captain. The Spirit breathed, and the prophets spoke and wrote, not by their will but the will of the Spirit! The Spirit moved upon the waters of Creation (Gen. 1:2), and from within our innermost being (belly) flow rivers of living water (John 7:38), which Jesus said was the indwelling of the Spirit.

The Greek word *pneuma* refers to a life force, an energy and power. From the rabbinical thought, this word has the connotation of the life force of God that created all things and the life force within creation itself coming from God's spoken words that hold all created things together. The Bible says that God is "upholding all things [*of creation*] by the word of His power" (Heb. 1:3, emphasis added). The *pneuma* is also the energy enabling a person to perform feats that are beyond his or her own strength, such as when the Spirit came upon Samson and he gripped the jawbone of a donkey and slew a thousand Philistines, or when he ripped the gates off the city. He was enabled with this life-giving supernatural power of God (Judg. 15:16; 16:3).

The word *pneuma* combined with *theos* refers to the breath or special life force of God Himself, thus the word *inspiration*. It refers to how God "breathed upon the prophets" to write the Scriptures under a divine influence. They were the instrument, and God was blowing the wind of His breath into their spirits to produce the sounds or the words flowing through the human instrument. This is what makes the Bible such an amazing book, as it was not written as a novel or some fanciful storybook, but the very words themselves have a life-giving energy concealed within them. This is why, when the Word of God is preached with the unction of the Holy Spirit, believers can actually feel their mortal bodies being quickened or made alive as the message is delivered. Three words describe the revealing and giving of the Scriptures: inspiration, revelation, and illumination.

- Inspiration is how God brought the word to the prophets (2 Tim. 3:16).

- Revelation is how the prophets penned the words on parchment and paper (Rev. 1:1).

- Illumination is how the words on paper are *made alive* to the reader (Heb. 10:32).

The inspiration of God is not the same as an inspired singer, artist, or a secular book that *inspires* a person. This type of inspiration is more emotional or encouraging, an uplifting feeling that brings joy or happiness. God's inspiration, however, reaches beyond the mind and pierces into the depths of a person's spirit to order a transformation and, at times, radical change in their lives. Human inspiration is temporal, but divine inspiration is eternal. This can be observed when comparing secular songs and religious hymns. A secular song can sell ten million records in two years; however, five years from now no one is singing it. However, "Amazing Grace," "It Is Well With My Soul," and other hymns are classics that are still sung decades after being penned. Why? The inspiration for the words originated with the Spirit of God and not the spirit of man.

Inspiration is the breath of God, which in reality is His Holy Spirit. It was Christ who, when speaking about the Holy Spirit in John 3:8, gave an interesting statement comparing the activity of the Holy Spirit to wind. We read:

The wind blows where it wishes, and you hear the sound of it,
but cannot tell where it comes from and where it goes. So is
everyone who is born of the Spirit.

The Greek word for "blows" ("bloweth," KJV) means, to "breathe hard."
Notice the phrase, "You hear the sound of it." There are several Greek
words for "sound," but this word is *phone* (pronounced *fo-nay'*). When
the Holy Spirit came on Pentecost, there was a "sound from heaven,"
which was an outward noise heard in the ears of the people. This word
sound in Acts 2:2 is the Greek word *echos*, and it refers to a roaring
sound or a loud unknown noise. The Greek word *phone* is where we get
our word *phone*—like a telephone, in which you hear the word in your
ear and you carry on a conversation after listening to the words.

The Holy Spirit came in the *echos* sound, with a mighty noise or
an echoing noise from heaven, but once the Spirit entered or filled
the believers that day, they began to "speak in other tongues, as the
Spirit gave them utterance," or we would say they heard the words the
Spirit was speaking to them and began to verbalize them by speaking
out loud with their voices. In John 3:8, when Jesus said you will hear
the *sound*, He was revealing that the Spirit would bring a language
that you would hear and speak. This interpretation of John 3:8 is also
evident when Christ predicted that believers would "speak with new
tongues" (Mark 16:17).

Those who are our ministry partners or have attended our major
conferences and gatherings know that one of my ministry emphases is
the importance of the infilling of the Holy Spirit. I have been blessed
to personally witness more than seventy-four thousand believers being
baptized in the Holy Spirit in altar invitations, with the evidence of
speaking with other tongues. I encourage seekers not to seek "tongues"
but to seek the impartation of the power of God (Acts 1:8). I have
observed from the beginning that the prayer language has always followed the baptism of power (Acts 1:8) given to a believer who accepts
and receives the gift—signs follow believers (Mark 16:17).

The Spirit Manifests Through Our Mouths

Because of certain theological interpretations or other personal reasons, some have difficulty in understanding the reasoning behind the act of speaking in tongues, which accompanies the initial infilling of the Spirit. The Bible uses the phrases "new tongues" (Mark 16:17), "cloven tongues like as of fire" (Acts 2:3, KJV), "speak with tongues" (Acts 10:46), "divers kinds of tongues" (1 Cor. 12:10, KJV), and "tongues of men and of angels" (1 Cor. 13:1). The word *tongues* in Greek is *glossa,* and it can mean "languages," which in context with speaking in tongues are languages not known to the speaker but imparted by the Holy Spirit. The New Testament directly records where the Spirit baptized believers and they all spoke with tongues. In Acts 2:1–4 there were at least one hundred twenty or more, and in Acts 10:46 the first Gentiles—Cornelius and his household—received the gift and spoke with tongues. In Acts 19:6–7 twelve disciples of John the Baptist received the gift of the Holy Ghost, and they spoke with tongues.

The first example of God-imparted *life* in the Bible was when God breathed His breath into the first man, and Adam became a living soul (Gen. 2:7).

Our Threefold Blessings—Restored

God provided Adam three distinct blessings that he lost. Christ, however, gained them back for us, and now we as believers who are aligned with Christ and in covenant with Him can experience these spiritual blessings in our own lives. When we receive Christ's covenant of salvation and redemption, the image of God is restored back to us:

> For whom He foreknew, He also predestined to be conformed to the image of His Son, that He might be the firstborn among many brethren.
> —ROMANS 8:29

> And as we have borne the image of the man of dust, we shall also bear the image of the heavenly Man.
> —1 CORINTHIANS 15:49

Often a person living in bondage of the flesh excuses his or her failure by saying, "I was just born this way…it's just in my blood." I remind them they can be born again and experience a spiritual "blood transfusion" that will create a new person from the inside out (John 3:3, 7). When we have received Christ, we are a "new creation; old things have passed away; behold, all things have become new" (2 Cor. 5:17).

> But we all, with unveiled face, beholding as in a mirror the glory of the Lord, are being transformed into the same image from glory to glory, just as by the Spirit of the Lord.
> —2 CORINTHIANS 3:18

Christ was the first to announce that God was preparing to send the Holy Spirit to those who ask (Luke 11:13) and that believers would "speak with new tongues" (Mark 16:17). When the Holy Spirit filled the believers on Pentecost, they were all filled with the Holy Spirit and began to "speak with other tongues, as the Spirit gave them utterance" (Acts 2:4). These new tongues are, in reality, a prayer language that enables the spirit of a believer to speak directly to God.

Based upon the Scriptures, each human is a tripartite being consisting of body, soul, and spirit. Each part has a particular function. The blood flows through the body (not the spirit), and as long as blood is pumped from the heart to the vital organs, the body will remain warm and the cells will carry oxygen and life-giving minerals to the vital organs to sustain life. When the blood ceases to flow, the body ceases to live. The soul is linked to the brain, the mind, the emotions, and the five senses that bring information and can read the feeling of pain and grow in knowledge. The human spirit is actually the eternal breath of God and has a life force linked with the soul. When it departs from your body, it maintains the same appearance as your physical body, only it does not age in the same manner as your body.

It is unique that your body has the ability to speak using a voice box and vocal cords, and your human spirit also has a voice of its own that uses the same avenue of speaking using the human voice. However, when a human dies, that person is still able to speak and carry on a conversation outside of his or her physical body, as did both the beggar and the rich man who died. After the rich man's spirit was in hell and the beggar's spirit was in Abraham's bosom, both could carry on a normal conversation. (See Luke 16:19–31.) At the Mount of Trans-figuration Elijah and Moses spoke with Christ. Moses had died fifteen hundred years earlier, and the Lord had personally buried the prophet to prevent Israel from finding his tomb (Deut. 34:5–7). Yet when Moses appeared, it was his spirit (not his body, which had deteriorated by then), and he spoke to Christ of His coming death in Jerusalem (Luke 9:30–31). This indicates that the human spirit can speak and be heard outside of the human body. This is why Paul wrote that when he spoke in an unknown tongue, his spirit was praying (1 Cor. 14:14).

When I communicate in my native language, I speak English. Thus, this is the language of my physical body. There is a language, how-ever, of the human soul, and this is identified by Paul as "groanings which cannot be uttered" (Rom. 8:26). The word *groanings* used by Paul means to *sigh*. The Amplified translation says it this way:

> So too the [Holy] Spirit comes to our aid and bears us up in our weakness; for we do not know what prayer to offer nor how to offer it worthily as we ought, but the Spirit Himself goes to meet our supplication and pleads in our behalf with unspeakable yearnings and groanings too deep for utterance.
> —Romans 8:26, amp

I have witnessed this form of sighing and groaning when a person is overwhelmed through grief, sorrow, loss, or disaster, not able to find the words to pray or say, and simply moans or groans.

The third language is the language of the human spirit, which is the language of speaking in other tongues or, as contemporary scholars say, "the prayer language of the Holy Spirit." When I pray in the Eng-lish language, I am praying with my understanding. When I cannot articulate the words and am under a heavy burden, the groaning is the travail of my soul. When I pray in the prayer language of the Holy Spirit, my spirit is praying directly to God, but my understanding is unfruitful.

It may seem like a waste of energy to pray in a language that bypasses the human understanding; however, consider the following. Have you ever encountered an impossible situation, one in which the report was hopeless and so negative that your heart sank, your hands shook, and you felt faint? If so, you know that it is very difficult to have a strong faith and be able to believe in the midst of a terrible situation, unless you can feel the comfort of the Holy Spirit. If you are petitioning God for a special miracle, and all of the evidence around you is negative, if you pray with your *understanding*, it is easier for your intellect to interfere and block your faith, as the voice of the intellect says, "Why are you praying like this? Look at this situation—it is hopeless. This will never change!" However, once a believer begins to pray in the Spirit over the situation, words bypass the mind, and the human spirit is communicating through the Holy Spirit directly to God without human interference.

The Gift of the Language of God

More than four thousand years after Creation, on the Day of Pentecost the rushing wind filled the room and cloven (split) tongues in the form of fire descended upon each believer. Immediately they began to speak with new tongues—or new languages they had never learned (Acts 2:4). Paul received the Holy Spirit when Ananias laid his hands upon him, and later Paul wrote he also spoke with tongues (1 Cor. 14:18). In Acts 8, when Peter and John laid hands upon believers in Samaria, there was a manifestation of some type, as the sorcerer Simon desired to pay for the gift of laying on of hands for people to receive the Spirit. There is no reason to doubt that these believers received the same manifestation at the moment of their infilling that all others were receiving in the first-century church.

There are many reasons given in the New Testament for believers speaking in tongues, or as I like to say, *praying in the prayer language of the Spirit*. Paul taught that your spirit is praying to God when you are speaking in tongues and that when you pray in other tongues you are speaking spiritual mysteries (1 Cor. 14:2). He taught that a believer also edifies himself (v. 4). The word *edify* refers to building a house, which means that a person praying in the Spirit is *building his or her spiritual house*. Jude also conveyed this idea when he wrote, "But you, beloved, building yourselves up on your most holy faith, praying in the Holy Spirit" (Jude 20). The "house" we are building is our inner spirit, as each of our bodies is the temple of the Holy Spirit (1 Cor. 3:16).

In 1 Corinthians 14:14 Paul said that when a believer speaks in other tongues, it is his or her spirit praying. This is interesting when we consider that all humans have a body, soul, and spirit, and vocal organs allowing communication with words that are formed in the mind, flow through exhaled air in the lungs, flow over vibrating vocal cords, and produce sounds—organs that are a part of the physical body. However, when both the rich man and the beggar died, their spirits departed from their bodies, continuing to live in another dimension (hell and paradise); yet they could verbally communicate and reason with others in the next life. (See Luke 16:22–31.) When Moses appeared on the Mount of Transfiguration, he had passed away more than fifteen hundred years prior, yet Moses's spirit came from the other realm and communicated with Christ concerning His future sufferings in Jerusalem (Luke 9:30–31). Moses's body was in the ground (Deut. 34:6–7), yet he could speak and communicate with Christ; this was the soul and spirit of Moses speaking with Him.

The point is that every human has an eternal spirit within his or her physical body. Just as the physical body has organs for communication, the human spirit itself has its own voice, which can communicate. When the Holy Spirit fills a person's spirit, He gives the spirit a supernatural language to communicate directly with God. God is a Spirit, the Holy Spirit is Spirit, and you are a spirit dwelling within a body. Speaking in tongues as a prayer language is a pure form of communication—spirit to Spirit—or your spirit speaking to God. "For he who speaks in a tongue does not speak to men but to God" (1 Cor. 14:2).

Another purpose for speaking in tongues is that when the Spirit manifests in a setting with unbelievers, the Spirit can reveal the secrets of men's hearts and become a sign to the unbeliever of the reality of God and His power (v. 22). I have personally witnessed this manifestation on several occasions, as at times the Holy Spirit would speak through a believer in tongues and a person from a foreign nation would understand each word spoken by the believer who was speaking in tongues.

Tony the Greek

An amazing example of tongues being a sign to an unbeliever happened to my father at the very beginning of his ministry, when he was still a teenager. I take this story from my dad's book, *Fire on the Altar*.

> My first personal experience with the gift of divers tongues happened while I was walking down the street in Welch, West Virginia. A young man named Truman Smith, the son of a Church of God pastor, introduced me to a young man whom he called Tony the Greek. His parents owned a Greek restaurant in the town of Welch.
>
> Tony, Truman, and I were walking down the street, and I was trying my best to talk to Tony. But since he didn't speak English very well, he and I had a language barrier. I knew about the gifts of divers tongues, so I prayed and asked the Lord to let me speak something clearly to Tony.
>
> The Spirit of the Lord said to me, "Do you have the same gift of the Holy Ghost that I gave the church on the Day of Pentecost?"
>
> I replied in my mind, "Yes, Lord, I'm bound to have the same Spirit as the Day of Pentecost."
>
> "What did they do on the Day of Pentecost?"
>
> "They spoke in many languages," I replied in my mind.
>
> "If they spoke many languages, do you think I can give you the power to speak to Tony in any language?"
>
> Faith rose up in my mind. I said, "Yes, Lord, I believe that you can give me the power to speak to Tony in his language."
>
> I took a small Bible out of my shirt pocket, and it fell open to the Twenty-Third Psalm. I stopped Tony and Truman on the street and told Tony I wanted to say something to him. When I opened my mouth, I was speaking in Greek. I continued to read. I went from speaking Greek to German, to speaking Italian. I had no idea at that moment what languages I was speaking.
>
> After I read the Twenty-Third Psalm, Tony took both Truman and me by the arm. He said to Truman in broken English, "You lie. You lie to me."
>
> Truman replied, "Tony, I am your friend. I wouldn't lie to you."

With his heavy accent Tony said, "You tell me this boy no go to school to preach. He go to school! You say he no go to school to learn to preach!"

Truman said to me, "Freddie, have you been to school to learn to preach?" I replied, "No."

Tony said, "That cannot be. You speak to me in Greek. I speak German and Italian, and you speak to me in both languages. You don't wait, you speak to me in other languages like that." He snapped his fingers to indicate that I spoke with a smooth transition from one language to another. "I have to stop and think before I can speak in another language, but you don't wait. How do you do that?"[10]

Dad proceeded to open his Bible and read Acts 2, and he revealed this was the gift of the Spirit. Dad never saw Tony again, but thirty years later I was ministering in Pearisburg, Virginia, and Dad was testifying and telling the story of Tony. Suddenly a woman dressed in black with a heavy accent jumped up yelling, "That was my Tony...that was my Tony." It was his sister, and she related how Tony had told her about the young preacher who spoke to him in three languages and said the Spirit of God had given him the words. She told Dad Tony had given his heart to God and lived as a believer for many years and had died two years prior of a heart attack! This is only one example of how tongues are a sign to the unbeliever. After all, the main goal of the Holy Spirit is to bring people to Christ through the Word of God and by using signs, wonders, and miracles.

I recall years ago during an Israel tour that our group was in the Kidron Valley in Jerusalem. A small group of Arab teens were about fifty yards away, and I could see a mischievous look on their faces. I saw one pick up a rock, and I knew he intended to throw it. I looked at two men and said, "Follow me." I approached the boys and began speaking in other tongues through the Holy Spirit. I was speaking a language they all understood. The leader looked at me, laid down the rock, and walked away. After this, the men said, "What were you saying to them?" The Lord gave me the interpretation. I told them that I said, "The Lord is revealing to me that you boys are planning on throwing rocks at my group. He is telling me that your hearts are unclean, as dirty as the filth and garbage you see in this valley. These are God's people, and if you harm any one of them, God is going to severely punish you, so leave now." This was the operation of the Spirit. The secrets of their hearts were exposed (1 Cor. 14:25).

Christ speaks to us through His *written Word* we call the New Testament. The Father speaks to us through the *inward voice* and divine guidance of His presence in our daily life, and the Holy Spirit can and does speak to us using the *prayer language* of the Holy Spirit, which is given to those who will believe and accept the gift. Thus we have God's Word and illumination with us at all times, allowing the Spirit to guide us into all truth (John 16:13).

Chapter Four

THE HOLY SPIRIT'S
FAVORITE WORD

For God so loved the world that He gave His only begotten Son, that whoever believes in Him should not perish but have everlasting life.

—John 3:16

I F GOD HAD a favorite word, I believe it would be *love*, for "God is love" (1 John 4:16), and He loved the world so much He sent His Son for their redemption (John 3:16). If Christ could reveal to you His favorite word, it would be *believe*, because all new covenant blessings are received through the act of believing and the kingdom is entered through faith (Rom 10:9–10). What would be the one word that would be central to the Holy Spirit—or His favorite word? I believe it is the word *holy*, as He is not just *a* spirit or *God's* Spirit but the *Holy* Spirit! The term *Holy Ghost* is used ninety times in the King James Version of the Bible. The single word *holy* or *holiness* is connected with a word found throughout both Testaments that is seldom mentioned or taught today in the body of Christ, and that word is *sanctification*. Perhaps your impression is that sanctification is an old and outdated word or a subject of traditional theology. To some sanctification is linked to some man-made legalism. However, you need to learn not just the word's meaning, but what this word has to do with your walk with God and your growth in the Holy Spirit.

I grew up in a denomination considered a classical full gospel denomination rooted in the older Holiness movement. In reality, the original Holiness people were not Pentecostals or Baptists but the early Methodists, whose founders, the Wesley brothers, wrote and spoke on the subject of holiness and sanctification. As the Lutherans were the followers of Luther and emphasized justification by faith, then the Methodists were loyal to Wesley and the teaching of a sanctified life. Wesley's teaching created the Holiness movement, which did spread from the Methodists to the early Pentecostals and other smaller Protestant groups. Wesley's emphasis was receiving regeneration through faith with the assurance of salvation by the witness of the Holy Spirit. Entire sanctification was taught as a second definite work of grace, and through the power of the Holy Spirit a person could live a holy life.

I can recall growing up and hearing ministers teach that there were three definite works of God's grace in the New Testament: the primary work was of salvation, which was accompanied by justification; the second work of grace was called sanctification, or being set apart in holiness; and the third was the baptism of power or infilling of the Holy Spirit. Certainly, salvation is the main message of the church for the world, emphasized by all Bible-believing churches. However, in the majority of congregations the Holy Spirit's manifestations are not witnessed, and as far as sanctification is concerned, many contemporary believers know nothing of this work of grace. One reason is that for years the older Holiness churches were often viewed by the younger generation as being "too legalistic" and opinionated, with an emphasis on outward adornment for women, as the outward appearance was often equated to a person's level of sanctification. At times a person could look holy outwardly and be impure inwardly, yet still be perceived holy and sanctified because the congregation judged sanctification from the outward appearance of the hair style, lack of jewelry and makeup, and the fact the women only wore dresses. The weakness was that outward appearances could cover inward weaknesses, and at times the church members ignored or justified bad attitudes and negative comments toward others in the name of just telling it like it is.

God, however, looks at things differently, as we read, "For man looks at the outward appearance, but the LORD looks at the heart" (1 Sam 16:7).

The word *sanctify* is found seventy times; *sanctified*, sixty-two times; and *sanctifieth*, four times in the King James Version of the Bible. In Hebrew the basic word for "sanctify" is *qudash*, which means, "to make something or to announce it as clean, consecrated and hallowed before God." In the New Testament the Greek word for "sanctify" is *hagiazo'*, which is, "to purify and consecrate and separate as holy." The purpose of sanctification was to separate the profane from the things dedicated to God. Sanctification rendered the person or object usable in the tabernacle or temple, the ministry and work of God. In the Old Testament the process of sanctification involved washings and rituals, whereas in the new covenant it is an internal purification accomplished by the cleansing of the body, soul, and spirit through the knowledge of the truth (John 8:32) and the impartation of the Holy Spirit.

The Priestly Cleansing

One cannot read the rules and regulations for the tabernacle and the priesthood without realizing that God demanded a separation between the *holy* and *unholy*, the *clean* and the *unclean*, the *righteous* and the *unrighteous,* and the *sacred* and *profane.* To ensure the sanctity of His dwelling in the tent, the high priest and the thousands of Levitical priests were required to conduct series of washings that separated them from the unclean things.

These ritual washings occurred at the brass laver, which was the first piece of furniture every priest encountered when entering through the only passage into the tabernacle, a set of curtains on the east side of the tent. The priests would wash their hands and feet, wear specifically designed clothes, sprinkle sacrificial blood on the altar, and maintain a continual awareness of God's laws and instructions. In Numbers 19 a special red heifer was burnt and its ashes sprinkled in clean water, called a "water of separation" (vv. 20–21, KJV). The unclean priest was required to be sprinkled with this water to remove his uncleanness. There were specially marked levels of sanctity, as only the Israelites were permitted in the outer court, the Levites and high priest only in the inner court, and the high priest alone was permitted in the holy of holies.

In the New Testament sanctification is imputed by four different substances or methods. In Hebrews 13:12 we are sanctified by the *blood* of Christ. In Ephesians 5:26 Paul informs us we are sanctified by the *Word of God*. The act of sanctification is accomplished by the power of the *Holy Spirit* according to Hebrews 10:29. At other times it is necessary to sanctify *yourself* by separating yourself from the unclean things as admonished in 2 Corinthians 6:17. One may inquire, "How can there be this many forms of sanctification?" The answer is there are levels of sanctification connected with your levels of spiritual growth and maturity.

The first manifestation of sanctification is at the moment of conversion when a person becomes a believer by receiving the redemptive covenant through the blood of Christ. This sanctification is when God receives you as a fallen, sinful being, and upon your confession of faith God "sets you apart" as a son or daughter through the new covenant. This is an *instant* work.

Following our conversion, there is a *progressive* manifestation as we are sanctified by the Word of God. The reason I call this progressive is that a person can only be set apart from the works of the flesh or hidden sins when he or she has knowledge from the Word that certain actions are sinful and need to be dealt with. Even though a new believer experiences a love for God, that person often fights certain attitudes and addictions in the flesh, and the Word of God must separate the soul from the Spirit (Heb. 4:12), or the carnal from the spiritual.

Sanctification by the Holy Spirit is both *instantaneous* and *progressive*. Among the early believers in the full gospel movement, if they struggled with anger, profanity, or a particular habit, they would ask God in intense prayer to sanctify them by freeing them from unclean habits or sinful desires, including a violent temper, cleaning up their language, and their lifestyle. This sanctification wrought through divine power and imparted by the Holy Spirit was at times instantaneous as the person was fully aware *when* the transformation occurred as carnal desires were removed and replaced by spiritual desires. It was also progressive in that the person must *continue to walk* in his or her freedom. This is why Christ emphasized that we must "abide" in

Him (John 15:4, 6–7, 10). The word *abide* means to "continue to remain in a certain place." To remain free we must remain in Christ.

Sanctifying *yourself* is when you consistently live by the Word of God and choose to lay aside every "weight and the sin" that so easily weighs you down. In Hebrews 12:1 the word for "sin" is the common Greek word meaning, "to miss the mark." The Greek word for "weight" refers to something that causes you to bend and bow under a load, slowing down your pace in the race. It is any hindrance that causes distraction to your walk with God. Sins are named in the Bible, but a weight could be a habit, carnal thoughts, or even people who continually pull you away from prayer time and church.

When we sanctify ourselves, we are setting boundaries that protect us from outward forces attempting to make inward assaults. The principle of the boundaries is found in Exodus 19:22–23:

> "Also let the priests who come near the LORD consecrate themselves, lest the LORD break out against them." But Moses said to the LORD, "The people cannot come up to Mount Sinai; for You warned us, saying, 'Set bounds around the mountain and consecrate it.'"

In this setting God was separating Moses from the common people in the camp, as Moses was righteous and the people were very carnal. A boundary was set at the base of Mount Sinai, and the commandment was for the people not to cross a certain line. The New Testament sets spiritual and moral bounds for believers, forbidding them from committing fornication, eating meat sacrificed to idols, and worshipping idols—to name a few (Acts 15:29). The purpose of sanctification is to give a person the strength and ability to set and follow the boundary lines for your body, soul, and spirit of what you allow and what you forbid. Certain negative actions, known or hidden sins, can actually defile the mind and spirit of the one allowing sin to rule in his or her mortal body.

What Is Spiritual Defilement?

The Hebrew word for "defile" means to "do something physically, morally, or spiritually that makes you unholy or unclean," in both a ceremonial or moral sense. The Almighty took very seriously the desecration of those things that were marked or set aside as holy. For example, there was a divine order established for transporting the ark of the covenant, requiring four priests. When this order was broken, Uzzah, who was not a priest, grabbed the ark to steady it during its transportation on a oxcart and was struck dead for breaking divine order (2 Sam. 6:3–7).

When Nadab and Abihu offered strange fire on the altar, both were slain, as only the coals and fire from the brass altar were permitted to be used in the censers (Lev. 10:1). When King Uzziah infringed into the office of the priests, offering his own incense on the golden altar, he did a right thing (offer incense) in an unlawful manner (he was a king and not a priest) and was smitten with leprosy (2 Chron. 26:18–22). God always separated the *clean* from the *unclean*:

> Then the LORD spoke to Aaron, saying: "Do not drink wine or intoxicating drink, you, nor your sons with you, when you go into the tabernacle of meeting, lest you die. It shall be a statute forever throughout your generations, that you may distinguish between holy and unholy, and between unclean and clean."
> —LEVITICUS 10:8–10

The spiritual defilement of the body involves the sins of adultery, fornication, and various dangerous and addictive habits. The soul defilements include unclean thoughts, and the defilement of the Spirit includes bitterness, jealousy, unforgiveness, and negative feelings and emotions. In the New Testament there are five types of defilements:

1. The conscience

> However, there is not in everyone that knowledge; for some, with consciousness of the idol, until now eat it as a thing offered to an idol; and their conscience, being weak, is defiled.
> —1 CORINTHIANS 8:7

The conscience is the inner voice of perception that speaks to us through our mind and is used by the Holy Spirit to reveal when something is right or wrong. It is also that gnawing sensation within, that feeling in the pit of your stomach you cannot ignore that serves as an internal alarm when wrong or evil is present. If your conscience says, "Don't do this," and you do it anyway, you defile the conscience as you override the spiritual conviction from within.

2. The mind

> To the pure all things are pure, but to those who are defiled and unbelieving nothing is pure; but even their mind and conscience are defiled.
> —Titus 1:15

Here the mind refers to the intellect, which reasons facts and processes information. A pure mind means a pure conscience, but a defiled mind creates a defiled conscience. The mind can either be all carnal, all spiritual, or a mix of both. However, fleshly lust and sins will bring defilement to the mind. Eventually dwelling on wrong thoughts can build a mental stronghold, which becomes difficult to penetrate (2 Cor. 10:3–6).

3. Bitterness in your spirit

> Looking diligently lest anyone fall short of the grace of God; lest any root of bitterness springing up cause trouble, and by this many become defiled.
> —Hebrews 12:15

Bitterness begins as a root. The Greek word for "root" is *rhiza* and refers to a root of a tree that goes down deep into the earth. Once a root is deep, the tree is firmly established in its place. The Greek word for "bitterness" is *pikria*, and it paints the imagery of a person whose bitterness is so deep that it shows on his or her facial expressions.[1] The root of bitterness produces the fruit of bitterness, and bitter people are always unhappy people. Something tasting bitter is sharp, acidic, and unpleasant. Bitter people spit distasteful and acidic words from their mouths, which exposes their inner hostility. They are often sarcastic and critical and quite unpleasant to be around. Bitterness will totally defile a believer from within, producing sour fruit from without.

4. Defilement with women

> These are the ones who were not defiled with women, for they are virgins. These are the ones who follow the Lamb wherever He goes.
> —REVELATION 14:4

When a single person commits fornication and a married person commits adultery, they become spiritually defiled in body, mind, and spirit. Remaining faithful to your marital engagement and covenant protects a man and woman from defilement of their flesh and spirit. There is a special blessing in remaining undefiled in this area, as seen in Revelation 14, when 144,000 Jewish men are sealed with God's protective seal during the tribulation.

5. Garments are defiled

> You have a few names even in Sardis who have not defiled their garments; and they shall walk with Me in white, for they are worthy. He who overcomes shall be clothed in white garments, and I will not blot out his name from the Book of Life.
> —REVELATION 3:4–5

The word *garments* here is not natural clothes but is the righteousness God imparts to believers who have been justified and delivered from their sins, which is described as "white raiment" (Rev. 3:5, KJV; see also Rev. 19:8). Outward and inward sin will place spots on your garments of righteousness and defile your fellowship with God. Any form of these defilements brings spiritual uncleanness and pollution. When a believer has been defiled, there is a sense of grieving and vexation in his or her spirit as the Holy Spirit uses these emotions as a fuel to spark a return back to righteousness.

The Secret Was in David's Prayer in Psalm 51:6–12

Growing up there was a split opinion as to whether sanctification was instantaneous or progressive. One denomination taught sanctification as an instantaneous work and a second work of grace, while another taught it as a progressive work, a work from God made available as a person continued learning to walk in and act upon spiritual knowledge. David was a man after God's own heart, a true worshipper, and yet in midlife he fell into a terrible series of sins—adultery and premeditated murder. In Psalm 51:6–12 he writes a very moving, heartfelt psalm that holds the keys to a life of cleansing. This passage reveals *initial* freedom, *progressive* freedom, and *continual* freedom.

> Behold, You desire truth in the inward parts,
> And in the hidden part You will make me to know wisdom.
>
> Purge me with hyssop, and I shall be clean;
> Wash me, and I shall be whiter than snow.
> Make me to hear joy and gladness,
> That the bones You have broken may rejoice.
> Hide Your face from my sins,
> And blot out all my iniquities.
>
> Create in me a clean heart, O God,
> And renew a steadfast spirit within me.
> Do not cast me away from Your presence,
> And do not take Your Holy Spirit from me.
>
> Restore to me the joy of Your salvation,
> And uphold me by Your generous Spirit.
>
> —PSALM 51:6–12

It is one thing to *receive* a deliverance from sin, bondage, addiction, spiritual weaknesses, and other hindrances, but it's quite another thing to *maintain* that freedom. If you bought a new car with a lifetime warranty, the car would still require an oil change, new tires, bad lights replaced in the signals and headlights, and occasional maintenance. Thus, we as believers must maintain all spiritual blessings.

David had sinned and was seeking for God's cleansing and forgiveness when he petitioned God to "purge me," "hide my sins," and to "blot out my iniquities." David, knowing that sin separated him from God's presence, sought earnestly for spiritual forgiveness and restoration when he prayed for God not to take away His presence from him and to restore the joy of his salvation. When believers walk in freedom from sins, there is a consistent presence of God with them, and the joy of the Lord becomes their strength (Neh. 8:10), enabling them to daily remain free and rise above the pressure of temptation.

To continually remain free David prayed, "Restore a right spirit within me."

When seeking the grace of sanctification as an inner force that separates you from unclean thoughts, words, or habits, the first principle is to ask in prayer, which is what Christ did in John 17:15–17: "I do not pray that You should take them out of the world, but that You should keep them from the evil one. They are not of the world, just as I am not of the world. Sanctify them by Your truth. Your word is truth." Notice that sanctification has a preserving power, as Christ pointed out when He prayed to "keep them" from the evil one. The Greek word for "keep" is *tereo* and means, "to keep an eye upon and guard from a loss or injury." God assists in preserving you through sanctification. By Christ sanctifying Himself (v. 19), He provided the grace to bring the power of sanctification to His followers. The "truth" is the foundation of sanctification (v. 17). Paul wrote:

> Husbands, love your wives, just as Christ also loved the church and gave Himself for her, that He might sanctify and cleanse her with the washing of water by the word, that He might present her to Himself a glorious church, not having spot or wrinkle or any such thing, but that she should be holy and without blemish. So husbands ought to love their own wives as their own bodies; he who loves his wife loves himself.
>
> —EPHESIANS 5:25–28

Years ago I heard the old-timers talk about "entire sanctification." The noted verse for this was 1 Thessalonians 5:23 (KJV):

> And the very God of peace sanctify you wholly; and I pray God your whole spirit and soul and body be preserved blameless unto the coming of our Lord Jesus Christ.

Notice the word *wholly*; in this verse the Greek word means, "completely, or to complete to the end." When Christ healed certain individuals, the Gospel writer said they were made "whole." There are numerous Greek words translated as "whole" in the healing narratives of Christ. The woman with an issue of blood touched Christ and was made whole (Matt. 9:20–22). This word is *sozo* and has a wide variety of meanings, including being saved, delivered, healed, protected, and made well. *Sozo* is the common word translated as "saved" in the New Testament. Thus when someone is "saved by faith and grace in Christ," we are saying they have been forgiven, delivered, and are in the process of being made whole or complete. When the man with a withered hand was healed and made whole, the Greek word for "whole" in this case is to *be made well* or made sound (Matt. 12:13). In Matthew 14:36, where those who touched Christ's garment were made "perfectly whole" (KJV), the Greek word is *diasozo*. The Greek prefix *dia* in the front of *sozo* means, to "pass through, across or over," or in this case the process of passing though a healing.

The will of God is for sanctification for your body, your soul (mind), and your spirit. Truth is found in the person of Christ and in the written Word of God. The word *truth* in Greek is *aletheia* and conveys the thought of "unclosedness, or disclosure, meaning a state of not being hidden or being evident." People often say that "facts are truth," and basically this is correct—except in the spirit realm. For example, it is a fact that the devil is a fallen angel and exists; however, Jesus said, "There is no truth in him" (John 8:44). Christ is a *fact*—He is real and alive at this moment—and He is also *truth*. At times it requires truth to conquer the fact, as Christ our truth has the power to change the evidence against us and transform every negative situation. In Christ's ministry the truth (Christ) met the facts (the evil, sickness, and death—all facts) and conquered the facts!

It is fact that all men are born into sin, but when Christ, who is truth, steps in, the truth defeats the fact and the sin nature is defeated. It may be a fact that you are diagnosed with an incurable disease, confirmed by X-rays and doctors' reports. You are told not to deny the facts. It is not faith to deny the facts; that would be presumption. It is, however, possible to have the truth (Christ) enter into the situation and meet the facts head-on and alter the facts, for Christ who is truth can overpower the facts, making you whole—thus truth conquers the fact. The Word of God does not just contain truth—it is truth, and

God Himself confirms His Word with visible evidence, called in the New Testament "signs and wonders, with…miracles" (Heb. 2:4).

Asking God for the grace of sanctification is the first step. Then there must be a willful choosing and willingness to separate yourself from places, people, or habits that form unhealthy or spiritually dangerous ties to you. Just as in the Old Testament there was a law of separating the clean and unclean, the profane and the sacred, the sanctification process is not intended to make you live the life of a monk in isolation, shielded from temptation because you never see a woman, or to cause a wife to look and dress like a Victorian housewife. Jesus did not pray for us to be taken *out* of the world but to be preserved from evil while living *in* the world (John 17:15).

The third process is to be continually in a state of cleansing and *renewal.* Temptation is present on this earth, and believers cannot escape the presence of the tempter. But believers can have power over the temptation.

The Man in the White Suit

Many years ago a great revival broke out in an Assembly of God church in Louisville, Kentucky, with the McDuff brothers from Houston, Texas, and it continued for many weeks. As word of the revival spread, one night a man in a white suit walked into the service to hear the "good Gospel music." Everyone in the church knew this man, as he sat down on the front row. That night when the altar service was given, the man stepped out and knelt down at the altar. The pastor knelt beside him and asked, "Would you like to get born again?"

With tears in his eyes, the old gentleman replied, "I really would. Do you think that Jesus could save me to the point that He could take away all of my cussing?"

Pastor Rodgers answered, "God is going to save you tonight, and you will not cuss again!" The man prayed and from that moment was a changed man. He was Colonel Sanders, the founder of the Kentucky Fried Chicken fame. He was not just seeking a born-again experience, but to the old-timers, he was asking for sanctification, which he did receive.[2]

My father was raised in McDowell County in the coalfields of West

Virginia, where in the late 1940s at times it looked somewhat like the wild, wild West! Men were continually drunk on weekends, unfaithful to their wives, and used profanity during normal conversations. When Dad's brother Morgan was converted in the great Coalfield Revival in the late 1940s, he ceased from cursing, which amazed my father. Later, when my father was converted to Christ, he noticed an immediate change in his conversation and his attitude. A peace was with him, and the hot temper was cooled by the living waters of the Holy Spirit flowing in him (John 7:37–39). He had experienced the grace of sanctification.

My father once told me about a man who was a friend with his father, William Stone, named Grover Hatfield (yes, of the Hatfield/McCoy fame). Mr. Hatfield had a very hot temper (it was in the DNA) and tended to be one whom you did not mess with when he was angry. He could, as they would say, "cuss like a sailor or peel the paint off the wall with his language." On one occasion, Dad's brother Morgan was hunting at night and accidentally shot Hatfield's cat in a tree. (Remember, a war started over a pig years earlier.) Seeing eyes in the dark, they shot, and when the animal fell, it was the Persian cat belonging to Grover Hatfield. The boys hunting with Morgan agreed with him not to say anything for fear of Hatfield's violent temper. Days later someone found the cat and took it to Grover. Instead of cussing and making threats, he said, "Well, boys, better find a place to give it a decent burial." Morgan returned home and told his family, "Something has happened to Hatfield. They say he got saved. Man, he really got saved…he really did. He is a changed man!" That's what justification and sanctification will do! The Holy Spirit loves sanctification.

Chapter Five

THE CODE OF THE DOVE
AND THE HOLY SPIRIT

When He had been baptized, Jesus came up immediately
from the water; and behold, the heavens were opened to
Him, and He saw the Spirit of God descending like a
dove and alighting upon Him.

—MATTHEW 3:16

IN BIBLICAL THEOLOGY there is a concept known as *the law of first
mention*. It basically teaches that when a person, animal, color, metal,
or number is first mentioned in a Scripture reference, it often sets
the theme of that particular item throughout Scripture. This is why
the serpent that appeared in Genesis 3 in the garden as the tempter of
Eve became the symbol of Satan or sin throughout the Bible, even in
the Apocalypse where the seven-headed *dragon* (in Greek) is actually a
seven-headed *serpent* (Rev. 12:3–9). The symbol of a lamb based on the
Passover narrative in Exodus 12 and in the New Testament becomes
the symbol of Christ, who is identified as the "Lamb of God" (John
1:29) and is referred to as the Lamb twenty-six out of twenty-seven
times in the Book of Revelation. Another significant symbol is the
dove, the gentle creature that represents the Holy Spirit.

In the law of first mention, the dove is one of the two birds mentioned in the story of Noah's flood. Most believers have read Moses's account of righteous Noah and his three sons building a floating zoo and riding out a universal deluge (Gen. 6–7). As the waters begin to slowly recede, Noah sent two birds out of the ark: a raven and a dove. Not only are these two birds totally opposite in nature, in color, and in their eating habits, but also there is prophetic insight encoded within the story.

Noah sent a raven from the window in the ark, and the raven flew back and forth until the waters were dried up. He later sent a dove, but the dove returned to the ark after finding no place to rest its feet (Gen. 8:7–9). A raven will eat carrion (the bodies of animals killed by other animals), but dove will not. It has been said that ravens will often follow packs of wolves to have access to the meat that the wolves will tear apart. When the dove went forth from the ark, he returned, because a dove will not rest on a carcass or eat decaying flesh, as 99 percent of their diet is seeds. There are, however, certain types of doves that are fruit eaters.

Eventually the dove brought an olive leaf into the ark (v. 11). This is unique because the olive became a sacred fruit for the priestly ministry. Crushed olives produced olive oil, and the first pressing of oil was used in the temple menorah. Olive oil was also used in the ceremonial anointing of kings, priests, and prophets (Exod. 30:25, 31). The olive leaf in the mouth of the dove speaks to us that out of the crises and storms (floods) of life, the Holy Spirit will bring an olive branch, which today is a universal symbol of *peace*, in the midst of our conflict.

Jesus and the Dove

At age thirty (Luke 3:23) Christ was baptized at the Jordan River by his cousin John. We read:

> When He had been baptized, Jesus came up immediately from the water; and behold, the heavens were opened to Him, and He saw the Spirit of God descending like a dove and alighting upon Him.
>
> —MATTHEW 3:16

This account of the Holy Spirit descending as a dove was so important that it is referred to in all four Gospels (Matt. 3:16; Mark 1:10; Luke 3:22; John 1:32). Having been to Israel numerous times and having conducted pilgrim baptisms in the Jordan River, I have seen many doves in the area resting in trees and occasionally swooping down over the chilly waters. The present tourist baptismal site is located in the Galilee, surrounded by many trees. Jesus's baptism, however, was in the area of the Judean wilderness where the only green plant life is around Jericho or tall green reeds growing on the banks of the Jordan River. This was not a *natural dove*, but the Holy Spirit in the shape of a dove (Luke 3:22).

I believe one of the reasons that the Holy Spirit used the form of a dove is because a dove has natural characteristics similar to the spiritual characteristics of the Holy Spirit. There is a dove that is white in color, and white in the Scripture represents purity or righteousness (Rev. 19:8). A dove expresses its affection by stroking its young and cooing in a soft tone. Spiritually the Holy Spirit causes believers to be caring and loving for one another and even for those who are lost without a covenant. The dove is a gentle creature and never retaliates against its enemies. Believers are told to turn the other cheek and pray for our enemies and those who spitefully use us (Matt. 5:39–44), and never retaliate. When the young of a dove are attacked, the dove will not attack, but instead it cries out in distress. This concept is also seen in the words of Romans 8, as Paul wrote that when a believer does not know how to pray, then the Holy Spirit will make intercession with groanings (Rom. 8:26–28).

The parallels between a dove and the Holy Spirit continue when we understand that a dove can easily be *spooked* by strange noises. It is said that a dove will return to the same spot a couple of times when hearing a strange noise, but it will not return the third time to the same location. God had said to Noah, "My Spirit shall not strive with man forever" (Gen. 6:3). The Holy Spirit can be vexed, grieved, and even blasphemed (Eph. 4:30; Mark 3:29). When the Holy Spirit is purposely offended, He can be grieved and eventually can depart from a person, as He did with King Saul (1 Sam. 16:14).[1]

It is also interesting to note that the when birds hover in the air, their wingtips point toward the back in the direction of the tail feathers. On a dove, the wingtips point toward the head and not the tail. This is unique when considering how the anointing oil was poured upon the heads of the kings and priests in Israel. The oil was poured on the head of the priest from one ear across the front of the head to the other ear. It was in the form of a Hebrew letter *kuf.* The letter *kuf* has a similar form of a dove's wings when a dove is hovering and the wings are opened. At Christ's baptism the Holy Spirit manifested as a dove above Christ and descended upon Him.

Years ago the great evangelist Leonard Ravenhill noted that there are nine main feathers on the left and right wings of the dove. He pointed out that there were nine gifts of the Holy Spirit (1 Cor. 12:7–10) and nine fruit of the Spirit (Gal. 5:22–23). There are also five main tail feathers, which can represent the fivefold ministry gifts of apostles, prophets, pastors, evangelists, and teachers (Eph. 4:11). The tail feathers of a dove are like the rudder of a ship—they assist in balance and direction in flight, just as the fivefold ministry gifts in the church bring balance to the body of Christ.

Jonah—the Dove

The Book of Jonah is the story of a prophet who resisted the calling of God to warn a wicked Gentile city that judgment was coming. The name *Jonah* in Hebrew is *Yonah* (pronounced *yo-naw*), which is the same Hebrew word for "dove," spelled *yownah,* found in fourteen references in the Old Testament. This Hebrew word *yownah* translated as "dove" is used to indicate the warmth of their mating.[2] There is a Hebrew root word *yayin,* which is the Hebrew word used for "wine" or "intoxication." Thus the Spirit of God being like a dove indicates the Spirit's warmth and intimacy, and the experience of being filled with the Spirit can be similar to being intoxicated, as evident on the Day of Pentecost when the believers were accused of being filled with new wine (Acts 2:1–4, 13). Paul's admonition was that believers were not to be drunk with wine but to be filled with the Spirit (Eph. 5:18). The total joy released though a Spirit-filled life has an exhilarating and almost intoxicating effect.

The first mention of the dove is in the story of Noah, and Christ reminded His followers that, "As it was in the days of Noah, so it will also be in the days of the Son of Man" (Luke 17:26). There are many different end-time signs encoded in the days of Noah. What is often overlooked is the parallel of the original Creation (Gen. 1–2) and how following the Flood a new creation was established.

At the first Creation, "the Spirit of God moved upon the face of the waters" (Gen. 1:2, KJV). At the re-creation after the Flood, "The ark went upon the face of the waters" (Gen. 7:18, KJV), where eventually a dove brought an olive branch. In Eden, God blessed the first couple and commanded them to be fruitful and multiply and replenish the earth (Gen. 1:28). After the Flood, "God blessed Noah and his sons, and said to them: 'Be fruitful and multiply, and fill the earth'" (Gen. 9:1). In the Garden of Eden Creation, "God made the beast of the earth according to its kind, cattle according to its kind, and everything that creeps on the earth according to its kind" (Gen. 1:25). In the Noah account, in Genesis 8:17 it reads, "Bring out with you every living thing of all flesh that is with you: birds and cattle and every creeping thing." God instructed Adam to, "Have dominion over the fish of the sea, over the birds of the air, and over the cattle, over all the earth, and over every creeping thing" (Gen 1:26). God gave a similar promise to Noah after the Flood: "The fear of you and the dread of you shall be on every beast of earth, on every bird of the air, on all that move on the earth, and on all the fish of the sea" (Gen. 9:2). When Adam was removed from the garden, God Himself cut the skins of two animals to cover the bodies of Adam and Eve. When Noah left the ark, he built an altar and offered sacrifices (Gen. 8:20). The Flood was a re-creation of the original Creation.

The "End-Time Floods"

Rain and water were the central features in the flood story of Noah. The outpouring of the Holy Spirit is compared to rain being poured out (Joel 2:28–29). There are three types of floods that will be unleashed according to Scripture. Daniel 8:23 indicates that the future Antichrist will arise when "the transgressors have reached their fullness." Daniel also taught that the end will be like a flood, and in Daniel 9:26 the context is that terrible wars will be a sign of the time of the end. The prophet Habakkuk predicted a flood of spiritual knowledge of God's glory covering the earth as the waters cover the sea (Hab. 2:14). The outpouring of the Spirit is never compared to a flood, although the idea of a pouring out can imply a downpour of water from heaven in the form of rain. James predicted:

> Be patient, then, brothers, until the Lord's coming. See how the farmer waits for the land to yield its valuable crop and how patient he is for the autumn and spring rains.
>
> —JAMES 5:7, NIV

A Code in the Covering

I am a strong believer that the major stories of the Bible that have end-time parallels can hold prophetic layers. The ark of Noah was prepared with a special upper window. This window is mentioned twice in the Flood narrative: once before the Flood and once after the Flood when the waters were settling. Two different Hebrew words are used that are translated as "window." Before the Flood the "window" is called *tsohar* in Hebrew, a word meaning, "light or illumination." This was a literal window where eventually light could come from the outside and Noah could see out. It was not glass but would have been an opening in the ark on the top level, covered most likely by wooden coverings.

After the flood, Noah opened the same *window*; however, the word here is *challown*, which is the *covering* over the actual window (Gen. 8:6). The *challown* would have been wood and covered the window during the storms, thus designed to keep the rain out. Studying this many years ago I realized the ark was a picture of the place of safety and security in time of distress and trouble. This was a man-made window that not only kept the rain from getting *in*, but it also prevented or withheld the dove from being free to *get out* and fly.

I compare this to some churches that have placed man-made barriers intended to protect the people inside the congregation. However, these traditions often lead to man-made control, such as when the rain of the Holy Spirit is falling in locations other than their church, the leadership closes the window to prevent anyone from seeing or experiencing these outpourings. These barriers also prevent the Dove, the Holy Spirit, from free access over the face of the waters where the new life will soon begin to burst in the light of the Son of God. It seems too many men attempt to control the Dove and limit His ability to freely move over the waters of our spirit.

Time to Free the Dove

In the New Testament there were men who served as money changers at the temple. In Christ's time the Roman government was in charge of the currency. Only Hebrew coins were permissible to pay the temple tax—thus the need for money changers who set up tables in the court of the Gentiles and exchanged the Roman coins for local coins. Those attending worship from other nations often brought with them coins with the faces of men, gods, or animals, which also were exchanged before entering the temple. These exchanges provided oil, salt, wine, and animals for the various sacrifices—all purchasable for a price. Money changing had become a very profitable business, as the exchange rates went as high as 300 percent.[3]

On this particular day Christ entered the temple and would have first passed by the court of the Gentiles, where the tables of the money changers were set. Christ observed doves. According to Leviticus 12:5–6, the doves were a special offering after a woman gave birth to a child, and the offering was for "purification." At that moment Christ set His heart on purifying the temple compound, and He suddenly began overturning the tables of the money changers and those who sold doves:

> Then Jesus went into the temple of God and drove out all those who bought and sold in the temple, and overturned the tables of the money changers and the seats of those who sold doves. And He said to them, "It is written, 'My house shall be called a house of prayer,' but you have made it a 'den of thieves.'"
> —MATTHEW 21:12–13

We can assume that when the fragile wooden cages of the doves struck the floor, they broke, and suddenly the doves were loosed and began to fly. The freed white birds would be seen by casual observers from any high hills, such as the Mount of Olives. In my mind I can see many individuals who needed healing or a miracle watching the commotion from afar, knowing there was some unusual and uncommon movements at the temple. As they came to the temple to see or perhaps were carried there by others, notice what occurred *after* Jesus *loosed the doves*:

> Then the blind and the lame came to Him in the temple, and
> He healed them.
> —MATTHEW 21:14

When the house of God is cleansed from the selfish, greedy, and carnal leaders and the church no longer sits in their seats and attempts to control the movement of the Dove (the Holy Spirit) but releases Him within the body of Christ for ministry, then sinners will be converted, the depressed released, the sick cured, and the people rejoice.

When Noah opened the window, the light and illumination poured into a dim ark, and the dove had an opening to flow in and out. There are so many spiritual hindrances, including the traditions of men, that can stop the flow of the Spirit. We must remove denominational coverings that have separated the outpouring on the outside from the people on the inside. Spiritual veils must melt from the eyes of our understanding, and this is accomplished through the deeper illumination and understanding from the Word. According to Paul, when these spiritual veils are removed, then the Spirit is free to work, and "where the Spirit of the Lord is, there is liberty" (2 Cor. 3:17).

Just as the dove was sent from the hands of Noah to hover over the waters of a new creation, the Holy Spirit is the first person we encounter as we seek forgiveness of sins and request to enter into a covenant of eternal life with Christ.

> And when He has come, He will convict the world of sin, and
> of righteousness, and of judgment: of sin, because they do not
> believe in Me; of righteousness, because I go to My Father and
> you see Me no more; of judgment, because the ruler of this
> world is judged.
> —JOHN 16:8–11

Out of the water the dove returned with an olive leaf in its mouth. Of the hundreds of possible tree leaves to reappear after the earth was covered with water, the dove found the leaf of the tree created by

God to produce olives. When crushed, the olives from the olive trees produce thick yellow oil, which was used to anoint the national and spiritual leaders of Israel. The leaf was in the mouth of the dove. The anointing of the Holy Spirit is not a cloud, or a fire, or even a dove, but it is a divine presence whose authority is released through the mouth—through preaching, teaching, singing, and prophetic utterances flowing like oil from the lips of those upon whom the Spirit has rested. The prophet Zechariah described two olive trees on the left and right side of the menorah, whose olive branches are like pipes pouring out golden (olive) oil out of them. They are identified as the two anointed ones standing by the Lord (Zech. 4:11–14). Thus, the dove represents the Holy Spirit, and the olive leaf the anointing flowing through the spoken word He gives. He is still like unto a dove!

Chapter Six

THE CHEMISTRY OF
THE ANOINTING

Then Samuel took the horn of oil and anointed him in
the midst of his brothers; and the Spirit of the LORD
came upon David from that day forward.

—1 SAMUEL 16:13

H E WAS ONLY a teenager and was standing before thousands
of older ordained ministers from around the world who gathered for an assembly held every two years. An eyewitness of
that moment in 1939 told me that the skinny teenage preacher, Thea
Jones, stood flat-footed behind a microphone and began preaching like
a seasoned minister of fifty years, quoting hundreds of scriptures from
memory. Suddenly the glory of God fell like a blanket over the entire
audience of believers as grown men were suddenly overwhelmed by
the divine presence of God, falling to the floor weeping. Years later
my father heard this same man preach in a big tent in War, West Virginia, and said he never heard a more powerful or eloquent man in
his lifetime. In the 1950s Thea eventually pastored a church in Philadelphia with more than ten thousand members—the largest church
at that time anywhere in America. One of my former board members

was related by marriage to Thea. I asked him, "What made this man's preaching so powerful?" The answer was always the same, "He was remarkably *anointed* by the Holy Spirit!"

The words *anoint, anointing,* and *anointed* are known, understood, and common phrases among Pentecostal-charismatic and Spirit-filled believers in various denominations. The word *anoint* is penned thirty-five times in the King James Version of the Bible, while *anointed* is recorded ninety-eight times and *anointing* twenty-eight times.

There is an interesting point to bear out concerning the word *anointed*, which in Hebrew is *mashach*. Devout Jews use a term for their coming Messiah, calling Him the *anointed one*, and use the name *Messiah*, which is found twice in Daniel (Dan. 9:25–26). The Hebrew word "Messiah" is *mashiyach* and means, "the anointed one" or "the consecrated one." The New Testament reveals that Christ was that anointed one, when at the Jordan River the Spirit came upon Him in the form of a dove and God's voice confirmed Christ as His Son before all of the people (Matt. 3:16–17). Christ was anointed with the Holy Spirit and power, and He delivered all who were oppressed of the devil (Acts 10:38). The anointing gives authority for preaching, inspiration for singing, revelation in biblical study, energy to your prayers, joy to your daily walk, and it breaks bondages in lives.

When describing the *feeling* accompanying the anointing, some say it is like an inner energy, a spiritual electricity or a physical quickening within and upon the body, a life force that makes your mind and spirit alert. This anointing is what causes preaching to move from the mundane to the motivating, from lifeless to lively, and from boring to anticipation. When this divine energy works within you, faith rises and you can believe for the impossible.

What Is the Anointing?

All traditional Christian churches and denominations, whether Baptist, Methodist, Pentecostal, or Catholic, have their own theological terminology, or "spiritual lingo," which becomes an "inner circle code" among the people associated with that group but is often not understood or is misunderstood by outsiders. A Catholic will speak of *Mass*, which is the sacrament of the Eucharist, known among Protestants as the Lord's Supper. An uninformed unbeliever could overhear a Catholic say, "We were at Mass," and he may think to himself, "What in the world is *mass*?" No group, however, had more inner circle code words than early Pentecostals. Imagine (which happened at times) sitting in a restaurant after Sunday night, and a Baptist overhears a Pentecostal say, "Yeah, she got slain tonight and they had to carry her out of the church." To the secular mind, someone being slain means they were murdered, but to the Pentecostal it indicated being overwhelmed by the presence of God. Then speaking of people being intoxicated by the Spirit, another charismatic believer may say, "Man, he got drunk in church tonight, and someone had to drive him home!" Those nominal folks would look around thinking, "They must have had a drunkard disrupt their service tonight!" Someone else may refer to people "falling under the power of God," saying it this way, "Did you see all the people who got decked out? They were stacked up like cord wood." The interpretation is, "Many people could not physically stand on their feet as they felt the power of God." Another may comment, "The place was on fire," speaking of the burning presence and zeal of the Holy Spirit. However, the imagery the outsiders received was, "Did they say their building was on fire? I wonder if it burnt down. Did you hear any fire trucks? I didn't."

I still laugh when remembering these were common phrases when I grew up, but as I traveled and our ministry expanded with more nominal people from non-charismatic backgrounds, I discovered my perception was not their perception and my definition of the anointing was not theirs, which brings me back to the question: "What is the anointing?" Is it an emotional high or an inner energy that inspires a minister to preach louder, harder, or longer? Is the anointing an invisible, mystical power like an energy that shoots through the human body? To answer this question we must refer to the Old Testament where the words *anoint* and *anointing* originated.

The word *anoint* is first used when Aaron and his sons were anointed with oil. In ancient Israel the act of anointing a person was a visible ritual to initiate that person into the spiritual realm of consecration, as is recorded in Exodus 28:41. God spoke of Aaron and his sons: "You shall anoint them, consecrate them, and sanctify them." In the Old Testament the Hebrew word for "anoint" is *mashach*, meaning, "to smear over with oil." This spiritual consecration through anointing was not confined to a person, as shields were anointed (Isa. 21:5). Sacred furniture such as the altar was also anointed (Exod. 29:36), along with sacred stone pillars marking visitations from God (Gen. 31:13).

The priestly code required sacred oil to be poured upon the high priest and his sons (Exod. 29:7; Lev. 6:13; 8:12), and later all priests from the family of the Levites were set apart for ministry service when anointed with oil prior to their public ministry service at the tabernacle and temple. Later the kings of Israel and Judah were set apart in holy consecration with the oil. According to rabbinical thought, anointing stands for greatness as it signifies God's hand and blessing upon that which has been consecrated back to Him. In early Israel, when a person was anointed with oil, it was not a small drop pressed on their forehead by the thumb of the person performing the anointing, but it was poured out in its entirety over the head of the person, often using an animal horn filled with oil (1 Sam. 16:13). When the golden oil ran down the beard and the garment of the recipient (Ps. 133:2), often the Holy Spirit Himself would come upon the anointed one. We read in 1 Samuel 16:13:

> Then Samuel took the horn of oil and anointed him in the midst of his brothers; and the Spirit of the LORD came upon David from that day forward.

According to the Jewish Talmud, when the oil was poured upon the head of the king, he was anointed in the shape of a wreath, as the king would wear a special crown. The priests, however, were anointed in the shape of what we know today as the Greek letter *chi*, which is in the shape of the letter *x*. The one doing the anointing simply had oil poured upon his head at times from a horn of an animal.[1] The oil used was always from olives.

One of the early rabbinical traditions is that the olive tree was the original tree of life in the Garden of Eden. The Hebrew word for "olive tree" is *es shemen*, which is literally, "tree of oil." The word *shemen* comes from a primitive root word meaning, "to shine." It is also related to the word *shemesh*, a word meaning, "to be brilliant," and is also the Hebrew word in the Bible for "sun," because of its brightness.[2] The olive oil rubbed over the body causes a glistening effect in the sun, and an anointed person always stands out brighter than others! This tradition of the olive tree being the tree of life (and it is only a tradition) may be why some of the books of the Apocrypha carry the concept that the ointment used to anoint Adam when he was sick and used to anoint certain sects centuries after the early church was called the "ointment from the tree of life," and that the ointment used to anoint Aaron was called the "heavenly ointment of the tree of life." It was also called the ointment of incorruption and was considered a mysterious ointment among some of the Gnostic books.[3]

The Need for Fresh Oil

David wrote, "I have been anointed with fresh oil" (Ps. 92:10). The word *fresh* can mean something that is new and probably refers to the first pressing of the oil, which is the best. The term *fresh oil* is also linked with the new wine from the grape harvest. An abundance of the oil and wine was a sign of God's blessing upon the land (Joel 2:19, 24). Any loss of oil and wine was considered a sign of the judgment or disfavor of God upon the land (Deut. 28:51). Most kings, priests, or prophets were only anointed with the sacred oil *once* in their lifetime. Only two individuals were anointed on numerous occasions—King David and Christ, both anointed on three different occasions, as the following list demonstrates:

David was anointed three times	**Christ was anointed three times**
1. Anointed as a teenager (1 Sam. 16:13)	1. Anointed at His baptism (John 1:32)
2. Anointed as king of Judah (2 Sam. 2:4)	2. Anointed by Mary (John 12:3)
3. Anointed as king of Israel (2 Sam. 5:3)	3. Anointed by Nicodemus (John 19:39–41)

The anointing of a king, priest, or prophet released a special gifting of the Holy Spirit needed for that person to function in his specific office. The inauguration of a king (such as David) released the *ruach* (Spirit) to come upon him for the purpose of illumination, as the king needed abundant wisdom from the Spirit to rule an often unruly people. A high priest and the Levites were to be set apart by spiritual consecration to bring the *quodesh,* or the quality of *holiness* into their lives as holiness was required when ministering in God's house. This level of holiness was necessary for the priest to walk in spiritual insight and sensitivity to God as he performed the daily rituals by following the revelation of the Holy Spirit. The third person in Israel was the prophet, and the oil set him apart with the *n'shama,* which is the *inspiration* to speak the words of God with authority. The wisdom of the king, the holiness of the priest, and the inspiration of the prophet formed a threefold cord to direct the political, spiritual, and economic direction of the nation.

King David was a king, but he is also called a prophet (Acts 2:30). We read: "The Holy Spirit spoke before by the mouth of David" (Acts 1:16), and "therefore, [David] being a prophet..." (Acts 2:30). David also *infringed* upon the office of the priesthood when on one occasion he ate from the table of showbread, which was the bread in the holy place reserved only for active priests (1 Sam. 21:4–6). When the disciples plucked corn on the Sabbath, the Pharisees rebuked Christ, and Christ shot back at them, reminding these hypocrites of David eating the holy bread, which was forbidden in the Law for him to eat; yet the priest fed him the bread, and neither David nor the priest was struck dead (Matt. 12:3–4). The Messiah is the "son of David" (or through the lineage of David), and Christ was a prophet (Matt. 21:11), is presently the High Priest presiding over our confession of faith (Heb. 9:11), and will in the future be the King of kings and Lord of lords (Rev. 19:16). David was a prophet, a king, and ate the bread as a priest—thus a picture of the threefold ministry of the Messiah.

With each new position, from his pre-kingly anointing as a teenager to his anointing over Judah and finally as king of Israel, fresh oil was poured over David to consecrate him into the higher level of responsibility. When God exalts a person to a higher level of ministry, he or she often encounters a new devil with a new level. As a teen David fought bears, lions, and a giant. As king of Judah he dealt with fighting armies of the Philistines, and as king of Israel his ultimate battle was with his own lust of the flesh. A fresh anointing can be released when we renew our spirit and mind in God's presence and come apart for a season to be restored. When David wrote the Twenty-Third Psalm, he spoke of God "restoring his soul," and later he said God would anoint his *head* with oil. From a shepherd's perspective, this anointing upon the head of the sheep was necessary for the sheep to be comfortable in their daily routine.

Fly Eggs on Your Head

David was a shepherd and penned the Twenty-Third Psalm, a wonderful poetic masterpiece illustrating the care of a shepherd for his sheep. David said the great shepherd (God) would "anoint my [David's] head with oil" (Ps. 23:5). The imagery is a caring shepherd rubbing the head of his precious sheep with oil. This statement is not just a spiritual metaphor, but it is a literal process in the life cycle of the ancient sheep. I discovered the reason for David's statement years ago on a tour of Bethlehem, when an Arab Christian began dissecting the practical aspects of the Twenty-Third Psalm for my tour group. It is common for flies to lay their eggs on the top of the head and on the inside of the nose of a sheep. This causes an agitation for the little animals, and when this occurs, the sheep can be observed shaking its head and gritting its teeth. It can also cause a loss of appetite. It is possible for an adult female fly, in the summer and fall months, to deposit up to five hundred larvae in the damp nasal membranes of sheep, where they can remain in the nasal passages for eight to ten months.[4] Lice and other small insects could also remain in the sheep's wool or burrow into the sheep's ear, eventually killing the sheep. Sheep must deal with the warble flies, the deer flies, nasal flies, and even the agitation of the tiny gnats and mosquitoes. In reality, sheep are easily distracted with little agitations, just as believers are often distracted with small distractions that consume much of their valuable time.

The remedy for fly eggs in the time of David was for a shepherd to provide a mixture of oil and, when available, a dark, natural tarlike substance mixed with the oil (including olive or linseed oil) that was smeared on the sheep's head or rubbed around the nose. This provided relief for the sheep and made it impossible for insects to occupy the slippery wool on the anointed sheep. If this was not done, fly eggs and insects on the sheep's head, if not eliminated, would eventually cause frustration, harm, and in a few cases, death, as the sheep could beat its head against a wall or a tree.

It is interesting that one of the names of the adversary is Beel-zebub, actually called *Baal-Zebub*, a name meaning the lord of flies (Luke 11:15–19). According to Jewish sources, this was the name of an ancient Philistine god worshipped in the city of Ekron in southern Israel. Sources differ on the purpose of this idol, as some suggest he controlled the flies and others suggest he was allegedly the god that drove away plagues on behalf of his followers.[5] This idol god is men-tioned in 2 Kings 1:2, when a dying king, Ahaziah, fell through the upper lattice of his chamber in Samaria and requested that his mes-sengers go inquire of Baal-Zebub if he would live or die. This story indicated that this idol was somehow believed to be linked to a med-ical idol or one that could determine if a person was healed or not.

This is perhaps the reason that the Pharisees accused Jesus of casting out evil spirits (curing people) by Beelzebub, the prince of devils (Matt. 12:24). To certain unbelieving Pharisees, Christ's miracles were being inspired by the power of this idol. What is so bizarre about this idea is that the Pharisees knew that there was no power in any idol, as they were made of images of wood and stone, unable to see, hear, speak, walk, or answer any prayers. Notice they called the prince of devils Baal-Zebub, which in this case suggested they believed this demon was able to heal people through Christ. This was blasphemy. (See chapter 13, "Can a True Christian Commit the Unpardonable Sin?")

The battle always begins in the mind, and there is a continual need to renew the attitude of the mind (called "the spirit of your mind," Eph. 4:23). Because believers struggle between two natures—the carnal and the spiritual—the mind must be renewed to override the thoughts and actions of the carnal nature. The renewal process means to be renovated by an inward reformation, meaning renewal is a spiritual work from the Holy Spirit, which begins inside and affects the outside. Greek scholars point out that by the construction of the Greek lan-guage, this renewing process is a transitional and a *continual* one. It is not a one-time transformation, but a continual process of keeping the mind clear of the clutter and refreshed with the fresh oil of the Spirit! The fly eggs represent those fiery thoughts that bombard your mind, including negative seeds that begin to build up—and add up—causing mental stress, discouragement, and temptation.

Dead Flies and Stinking Oil

Solomon built the most magnificent temple in the history of Israel. Besides the sacred building housing the outer court, inner court, and holy of holies, special rooms were constructed for storing wood, oil, financial gifts, spoons, shovels, vessels, and various offerings, including items needed for the daily rituals. Throughout the year there were thousands of sacrifices offered on the brass altar. The bloody flesh of these sacrifices of animals could attract flies to the sacred area. We read where Solomon wrote:

> Dead flies cause the ointment of the apothecary to send forth a stinking savour; so doth a little folly him that is in reputation for wisdom and honour.
> —ECCLESIASTES 10:1, KJV

The word *apothecary* is used four times in the King James Version: Exodus 30:25, 35; 37:29; and here in Ecclesiastes. In Exodus the apothecary was the art of combining the spices for the sacred anointing oil (Exod. 30:35) and the incense that was mixed and burnt on the golden altar (Exod. 37:29). Flies are attracted to scents, and in this passage they are attracted to the fragrances of the apothecary. But when they make contact with the oil, they are stuck and cannot escape, eventually dying. Thus the oil becomes ruined, and the fragrance is corrupted by the dead flies. In the context of this passage Solomon wrote that when a person with a good reputation does foolish things (a little folly), it ruins their image and reputation among people like dead flies in oil. The Hebrew word for "folly" here can also be translated as "silliness."

This would be an excellent time to comment that those who are entrusted with the anointing must at all times be on guard against the *dead flies* that will cause you to *stink* in the eyes of your brethren. It takes many years for a minister or a business leader and even a politician to build up a reputation for having wisdom and honor. Unwise decisions have cost a man his ministry, his business, and his position of authority. With this in mind, Solomon also wrote:

> Let your garments always be white,
> And let your head lack no oil.
> —ECCLESIASTES 9:8

This is a beautiful picture of the necessity of believers to keep their garments spotless from sin (2 Pet. 3:14) and their minds (heads) anointed by the Holy Spirit. Jews wore white garments in times of celebration and black garments in times of mourning and sorrow. According to rabbinical thought, white is also a color representing innocence; thus white linen is a symbol for the righteousness of the saints (Rev. 19:8). We are not to defile our garments (Rev. 3:4) and are to *keep* our garments—meaning to keep an eye upon them to prevent spots and defilement (Rev. 16:15). When mourning, Jews refuse to anoint themselves with oil, as a lack of oil was a symbol of grief and carrying a burden (2 Sam. 14:2; Dan. 10:3). The Holy Spirit is the power given that renews the mind continually.

The Oil and the Olive

The Mount of Olives has been called by rabbis the *Mount of the Anointing*, because throughout history the mount was known and recognized for its olive trees. The olive tree is one of the world's most unique trees for the following reasons. Olive trees grow, living up to a thousand years if grown under the proper conditions. The trees grow naturally in the Jerusalem-Bethlehem region, and they grow wild in the region of Galilee. Olive trees are known to tolerate long droughts and can survive dry spells quite well. In the Garden of Gethsemane in Jerusalem, tourists see many old trees near the Church of All Nations that have become hollow in their trunks, but these older trees actually can grow thicker, up to twenty feet in circumference. The olive tree is also an evergreen and keeps its leaves in hot, warm, and cold weather— all year long. Even when an olive tree is cut down, you will eventually see smaller green shoots growing up around the edges of the root of the tree, ensuring the tree will grow again. There is an olive fly that attacks the fruit but not the leaves of the tree, and the leaves endure and actually have a slightly bitter taste that helps repel insects. The apostle Paul also used the natural and wild olive trees as an analogy for both Jews (Israel) and Gentiles. (See Romans 11.)

It is the *fruit* of the tree, the *olive*, that holds such significance in the Bible. The olive fruit blossoms at the beginning of summer and ripens during the early October rains. The olive is at first green in color but turns black as it matures. At harvest time the olive trees must be shaken and the branches beaten for the olives to fall to the ground and be gathered, either for eating purposes or to produce the golden oil and many other oil-based items in Israel.[6]

In the time of the Jewish temples there were four major pressings from the olive harvest, and each pressing was used for a different purpose.

1. The first pressing was used for the temple's menorah or for the oil of anointing.

2. The second pressing was oil used for oil lamps to give light in the homes.

3. The third pressing was used for cooking purposes.

4. The fourth pressing was for medical purposes.

There is much Middle East history and varied scriptures related to the oil or the olive trees. However, one of the great prophetic verses written in Isaiah was used by Paul when speaking about natural Israel and the Gentiles who were grafted into the covenant.

> There shall come forth a Rod from the stem of Jesse,
> And a Branch shall grow out of his roots.
> —ISAIAH 11:1

This verse is considered a Messianic prophecy. In the Hebrew the word "branch" is *netzer*, and the word for "rod" is *choter*, which means a small shoot. Years ago in Israel my tour guide, Gideon Shor, had heard a lecture that amazed him. It was a study on what the Hebrew believers in Christ (his Hebrew name is *Yeshua*), were called in the early period of Christianity. We know that among the Gentiles, believers were first called Christians at Antioch (Acts 11:26). *Christian* is the Greek word *Christianos*, meaning, "follower of Christ." But in the Hebrew they were called *Netzarim*, which comes from the word *netzer* for the "branch," as believers were considered to be cut out of the branch of the stem of Jesse (Isa. 11:1), and according to Paul, Gentiles were the "wild branches" grafted by the Lord into the natural tree of Israel. (See Romans 11.) The tree of Isaiah's prophecy was the olive tree as indicated in Paul's analogy in Romans 11.

It is the olive, however, that reveals the high *price* of receiving and maintaining a powerful anointing to minister. There are hundreds of individual olives on any olive tree. Yet each olive is important when making up the olive oil that, for example, was used in the temple menorah. To ensure being a part of the process, the olive must abide on the branch in order to mature in growth, just as believers are instructed to abide on the vine to mature in Christ (John 15:4–7). Once mature, the olive must then encounter a shaking process to be separated from its comfort zone and closeness to the other olives. In ancient times a stick was taken and the branches were beaten until the olive would lose control and find itself in the basket of the olive picker. Our shakings we experience are not for evil, but they are for our good to get what is in us out of us!

The most difficult part is when the little olive is placed in the olive press, where a massive round wooden circle is pressed over the olive several times to crush the oil out of the olive. This process is repeated until there is nothing left of the olive, but the oil has been released. We no longer see the olive, as the tiny bits are now mixed with the fragments of other olives in the olive press, but we do see the oil that drips into the vat, used as a first pressing for the light in the menorah and the oil at the temple. The olives in the press can actually endure four pressings and still get the oil out of the olives. Thus, if you want to know the cost of the oil, then ask the olive who laid down its life to release the oil within it. Christ poured out Himself on the cross to bring His followers the gift of the Holy Spirit!

Releasing the Anointing

The anointing is not given for a believer to sit in a rocking chair and feel "goose bumps" rising as he prays. The anointing provides the inner power to defeat the enemy in every area of your life and bring wholeness. When praying for the sick in a local assembly of believers, James instructed the elders to anoint the sick person with oil in the name of the Lord (James 5:14). However, when believers of the New Testament era and today receive the baptism of the Holy Spirit, an anointing is imparted within them. This anointing is called "an unction." John wrote:

> But ye have an unction from the Holy One, and ye know all things.
> —1 JOHN 2:20, KJV

The Greek word for "unction" is *chrisma*, which is a special endowment for the Holy Spirit. I have often said that the Holy Spirit will give you an *unction to function*. There are different levels of the anointing of the Spirit, just as there can be different levels of faith and joy. There is a measure of faith (Rom. 12:3), great faith (Matt. 8:10), and Christ said on two occasions there was "such great faith" (Matt. 8:10; Luke 7:9). Joy is a fruit of the Holy Spirit (Gal. 5:22) and also flows in levels. There is joy (Luke 6:23), great joy (Acts 8:8), and joy unspeakable and full of glory (1 Pet. 1:8). With the Holy Spirit there is an infilling of the Holy Spirit available for all believers. However, there can be different levels of the anointing. Elisha received a double portion of the Holy Spirit that was upon Elijah (2 Kings 2). Christ, however, received the Spirit "without measure" or an unlimited level of the anointing of the Spirit (John 3:34). To walk in a deep and consistent level of the anointing requires a price of personal sacrifice—spending more time with God than with people, fasting, and separating yourself in prayer and study of the Word. The anointing activates the presence of God, mixing it with a person's faith, and brings deliverance to the body, mind, and spirit.

Gifting or Anointing?

One of the dangers among individual believers who understand and operate in the unction of the Holy Spirit is a lack of discernment to distinguish between a person's *gift* and their *anointing*. When comparing the difference, a person can be born with a certain gift in their family's DNA, but an anointing can only be imparted by God. A gift will remain in you despite your moral character, but the anointing can be removed by continual sin, as was the case with Samson (Judg. 16:20). A special gift will bring attention to *you*, but the anointing will always bring attention and point people back to *God*. With your gift people will give *you* honor, but with an anointing people will give *God* honor. A person can have a *gift* without an *anointing*, and there are men and women who are anointed but who have no natural gifts outside of the ability to communicate or pray anointed prayers. When you have a gift, then people will follow *you*, but when you are anointed, people will become hungry for and follow *God.*

In the ministry there have been singers and ministers who could inspire through their vocal range and their ability to communicate. Many years ago I knew of a male singer who could, as the expression says, "raise the roof" and "turn a crowd on" with his vocal range. People would leave, saying, "Wasn't he anointed?", and they judged this "anointing" by the vocal range and an occasional "goose bump feeling" they received during the high point of the concert. For some time, after his concerts the man would get drunk and party wild, and he had a woman he was seeing who was not his wife. In those situations, without repentance and turning, the Lord will permit the exposing of the iniquity. Believers, however, were confusing the gift with the anointing.

Remember this: *gifts bless people, but the anointing will break yokes*, as it is written in Isaiah 10:27: "And the yoke will be destroyed because of the anointing oil." When the true anointing rests upon a singer, that person may have little or no voice training and be incapable of reading music. Or as a minister, that person may have no formal academic training in public speaking. But as they wax warm and eloquent in the Spirit, the unction begins to stir the embers of fire as their message or song penetrates the veil of darkness and breaks yokes. When the Holy Spirit came upon King Saul, he was "turned into another man" (1 Sam. 10:6)!

Christ Must Be Anointed

Luke records the words of Peter in Acts 10:38–39:

> How God anointed Jesus of Nazareth with the Holy Spirit and
> with power, who went about doing good and healing all who
> were oppressed by the devil, for God was with Him.

Christ's ministry consisted of two major parts: teaching and healing.
The miracles often followed the teaching. Here, Luke reveals that "God
anointed Jesus." The Greek word for "anointed" is *chrio* and carries
the idea of rubbing or smearing something with oil. There is no record
of Christ having literal oil poured over Him at the beginning of His
ministry; however, the Spirit came upon Him at the Jordan River. This
anointing was the inner power that attacked and defeated sickness and
death in those to whom He ministered "with power." The word for
"power" here is *dunamis* and is the word for miraculous ability and
inner power, which produces the supernatural.

I can recall the first time I felt the tangible presence of the Holy
Spirit. I was eleven years of age, and the event was the state church
camp meeting under a large metal tabernacle in Roanoke, Virginia.
Dr. T. L. Lowery was praying for a man paralyzed in one leg. When
he touched the man, the fellow fell backward and like a rubber ball
bounced up, shaking his limp leg. TL threw the man's cane in the
air in my direction, and the man began running at full speed without
assistance. At that moment I felt a warm tingling over my body, and
my hair rose up on my arms. I felt a peaceful sensation and began to
cry. This was the first moment I sensed God's presence upon me, but
it was certainly not the last.

If Christ required the anointing for teaching and ministry, and the
apostles were instructed to tarry in Jerusalem to receive power from
on high (Luke 24:49), and both Peter and Paul emphasized the Holy
Spirit baptism (Acts 8; 19), then who are we to escape the need to
experience the same baptism of power in our own lives?

Chapter Seven

GETTING SOAKED
ON THE JOEL 2 ROAD

And it shall come to pass afterward
That I will pour out My Spirit on all flesh;
Your sons and your daughters shall prophesy,
Your old men shall dream dreams,
Your young men shall see visions.
And also on My menservants and on My maidservants
I will pour out My Spirit in those days.

—JOEL 2:28–29

THE BOOK OF Joel promised an outpouring of the Spirit in the last days. The term "pour out" (Joel 2:28) paints the imagery of a vessel filled with a liquid slowly being poured out over something. However, the "outpouring" is also a term used when a sudden rain gushes from the cloud, filling the fields and streets and covering the land. In the South I have witnessed a storm dump up to eight inches of rain in a few hours. In the Deep South the old-timers called this a "gully washer," as the water would fill the gullies and wash out anything lying in its path. I believe we are the generation walking on the Joel 2 road, and we will be soaked in the presence of the Holy Spirit!

In North America the early signs of this "pouring out" began in the 1960s and was termed the *Charismatic Renewal*. In the 1960s a reporter from *Look* magazine wrote about a Charismatic Renewal of the Holy Spirit that was breaking out among some in the Church of the Brethren. During their prayer time a prophetic utterance was given and the words were recorded and reported as follows:

> This which you now see, and that which you now hear, shall spread the length and breadth of not only this land, but around the world: and every remnant of faith shall taste of that which I am doing and this remuneration and this restoration of My Spirit shall cause men to fall before their God and cause men to melt together and they shall forget their differences and recognize the true and living God.[1]

This prediction certainly came to pass and continues to be fulfilled. However, if I were to assemble hundreds of ministers in one building, pastors from various denominations, and ask the question, "Will there be a major outpouring of the Spirit in the future prior to Christ's return?", the answer would be a split opinion based upon each minister's own denominational traditions, theological background, or personal experience. From my early evangelistic travels at age eighteen to my personal ministry to thousands in major conferences, praying with men and women from ten major denominational backgrounds, the perception of the Holy Spirit and especially any form of a physical or visible manifestation divides church attendees into two main groups—"I believe in the spiritual manifestations" or "I don't believe in the spiritual manifestations." Some would remain neutral. Please note that this division is not *caused* by the Holy Spirit but is created by individual *perceptions* of the Holy Spirit.

Among many believers throughout the world there is a strong belief of a unique revival among sons and daughters prior to Christ's return, which is initiated through the global preaching of the gospel (Matt. 24:14) and accompanied with an outpouring of the Spirit (Joel 2:28–29). Among the more nominal churches their theology stresses that the Holy Spirit's outpouring was strictly for the Day of Pentecost (Acts 2:1–4) to assist in the growth and maturity of the first-century believers. The theory is based upon the concept that now that we have the complete canon of Scripture (the sixty-six books of the Bible) and the church has grown from 120 (Acts 1:15) into possibly billions around the world. There is no need for miraculous gifts, only the teaching of the Scriptures.

We must not look to opinion or tradition but to the prophecies and promises concerning this subject. Here are a series of scriptures from both Testaments indicating the pouring out of the Holy Spirit, some linking the timing to the last days:

> Turn at my rebuke;
> Surely I will pour out my spirit on you;
> I will make my words known to you.
>
> —PROVERBS 1:23

> For I will pour water on him who is thirsty,
> And floods on the dry ground;
> I will pour My Spirit on your descendants,
> And My blessing on your offspring.
>
> —ISAIAH 44:3

> And it shall come to pass afterward
> That I will pour out My Spirit on all flesh;
> Your sons and your daughters shall prophesy,
> Your old men shall dream dreams,
> Your young men shall see visions.
> And also on My menservants and on My maidservants
> I will pour out My Spirit in those days.
>
> —JOEL 2:28–29

> Therefore be patient, brethren, until the coming of the Lord. See how the farmer waits for the precious fruit of the earth, waiting patiently for it until it receives the early and latter rain.
>
> —JAMES 5:7–8

Without question, prophets and apostles foresaw an outpouring of the Holy Spirit, including "all flesh" (all nations) along with "sons and…daughters…servants and… handmaids" (Joel 2:28–29, KJV). Hundreds of years after Joel, when the Holy Spirit filled believers on Pentecost, Peter stood before a multitude of Jews and quoted Joel's prophecy as a fulfillment of the pouring out of the Spirit (Acts 2:17–18).

After the disciples began speaking with tongues, Peter stood up before the Jews gathered at the temple for the festival of Pentecost and began his discourse by saying, "Men of Israel" and "Men and brethren" (vv. 22, 29). This phrase has caused some scholars to teach that the outpouring was only intended for the original apostles and only *men* received the gift, and no women were present in this section of the temple. This may be taught with a slight prejudice toward women, as some denominations believe that a woman cannot receive the anointing of the Spirit like men, or teach and preach.

This cannot be possible for several reasons. First, when the Holy Spirit is poured out, both men and women (servants and handmaids), sons and daughters will receive (Joel 2:28–29). If the Spirit baptized only *men* at Pentecost, then the *daughters and handmaids* part of Joel's prediction did not see fulfillment in Acts 2. Second, in the previous chapter (Acts 1), several days before the Feast of Pentecost the apostles and select disciples were meeting together in an upper room. Included in the group were women:

> And when they had entered, they went up into the upper room where they were staying: Peter, James, John, and Andrew; Philip and Thomas; Bartholomew and Matthew; James the son of Alphaeus and Simon the Zealot; and Judas the son of James. These all continued with one accord in prayer and supplication, with the women and Mary the mother of Jesus, and with His brothers.
>
> —ACTS 1:13–14

In an ancient Jewish synagogue the men sat on the main floor, and a balcony was provided for the women to observe the services. At the temple in Jerusalem there was a court of the women, dividing the women from the men. The room where the 120 people met to await the promised Spirit was believed to be the possible upper room of a wealthy Jewish family, possibly the family of John Mark. Some among the Orthodox Christians suggests it may have been at the home of Nicodemus.[2] In Luke 22 and Mark 14 the writers record Christ seeking out a furnished upper room to celebrate the Last Supper and to wash the disciples' feet. While normally men and women were separated in public Jewish prayers, here the men and women were waiting and praying together.

Throughout my ministry I have heard radio and television ministers proclaim that the outpouring on Pentecost was the "complete fulfillment" of Joel's prophecy. To this I would disagree for several reasons. The first is that the prophecy predicts that when the Spirit is poured out, visions and dreams will accompany this pouring out (Joel 2:28–29). Dreams and visions were a common method of spiritual revelation in the Old Testament. There is no recorded dream after Acts 2:1–4 in the New Testament, and six visions are reported: Ananias was told by an angel to pray for Saul (Acts 9:10–12); Peter saw a vision of an angel and a sheet (Acts 10:10–17); Cornelius had a vision of an angel with a message (Acts 10:3); Paul experienced a vision of a man petitioning him to come to Macedonia and minister (Acts 16:9–10); later the Lord appeared in a vision telling Paul to not be afraid, that no man would harm him (Acts 18:9–10); and John experienced a vision of the Apocalypse (Rev. 1–22). When the final outpouring flashes across the globe, dreams will be seen by old men and visions by young men on a global scale. This is not a metaphor but literal.

The second reason is one word difference in the Joel and Acts quotes.

A Code in the Text

The prophetic promise penned in Joel 2 is repeated in Acts 2, with the exception of one word that can change the *timing* of the outpouring based upon the verses before and after, or the context of each prophecy. When Peter quoted from Joel, he changed one word. Joel spoke this way, "It shall come to pass *afterward* that I will pour out My Spirit..." (Joel 2:28, emphasis added), whereas Peter said it this way: "It shall come to pass in the *last days*..." (Acts 2:17, emphasis added). Some would suggest that there is no difference between "afterward" and "the last days." However, there is a difference when comparing the *timing* and context of both passages.

When Peter spoke of the "last days," we assume from our eschatology that the last days in Peter's mind were the last days for Jerusalem, Israel, and the Jewish people, for Peter knew that Christ had predicted the coming destruction of Jerusalem and the temple to occur within one generation—which did occur in AD 70 (Matt. 24:1–2; Luke 21:5–6, 12–23). In the *initial* outpouring time frame Christ predicted that God was going to pour out His Spirit in Jerusalem, Judea, Samaria, and the uttermost parts of the earth (Acts 1:8). This outpouring began in about 32 at Pentecost and continued until the destruction of the temple in 70. The date 70 was not the climax and conclusion of the outpouring, as numerous early fathers continued to mention exorcism of evil spirits, speaking with tongues, and prophecy long past 70.[3]

Now look at the context of Joel's prophecy when he wrote, "It shall come to pass afterward." I have read many times the prophecies in Joel, and the prophet's three chapters can be divided up into three themes:

1. Chapter 1 is Israel's *ruin*.

2. Chapter 2 is Israel's *restoration*.

3. Chapter 3 is Israel's *revival*.

Joel predicted how God would bring about a complete restoration of Israel as a nation and restore agricultural blessing throughout the land. In Joel 2:28–29 is the prediction of the outpouring of the Spirit. Just three verses prior is the announcement of a future restoration:

> Be glad then, you children of Zion,
> And rejoice in the LORD your God;
> For He has given you the former rain faithfully,
> And He will cause the rain to come down for you—
> The former rain,
> And the latter rain in the first month.
> The threshing floors shall be full of wheat,
> And the vats shall overflow with new wine and oil.
> "So I will restore to you the years that the swarming locust
> has eaten,
> The crawling locust,
> The consuming locust,
> And the chewing locust,
> My great army which I sent among you."
>
> —JOEL 2:23–25

The context of the prediction centers upon the *future restoration of Israel*! When Joel said the Holy Spirit would be poured out "afterward," he was referring to *after* Israel experiences her greatest last days of restoration. Israel was brought back from Babylonian captivity, but there is no biblical or historical record of any form of Holy Spirit outpouring after the Jews returned from Babylon to Jerusalem, even up to the writings of Malachi. This time frame was the first major restoration of Israel from captivity, and there was no outpouring—just physical rebuilding that occurred. (See Ezra and Nehemiah.) The Joel prediction was set for the time when Israel is a nation and the Jews return to their land, which in this setting was initiated in 1948, when, after being scattered to the Gentile nations for 1,878 years, Israel was reborn in a day, at midnight on May 14, 1948, and the restoration of the people and the agricultural blessing began from this point forward. In the same year the Holy Spirit initiated a great revival on the North American continent.

At the same time in 1948, America entered a most amazing spiritual awakening, stirring all major full gospel denominations from coast to coast. Evangelists blazed the trail, setting up tents with the most noted ministers seeing five to twenty thousand seekers each night who heard the messages and watched men minister to the lost and pray for the sick. This became known as *the Healing Revival* and continued for seven years, beginning the year of Israel's national restoration in 1948 and continuing until about 1955. This was the revival in which my mentor, Dr. T. L. Lowery, was a part of, and my father as a young man sat under numerous ministers who blazed the trail in their gospel tents.

It was nineteen years later, in 1967, that the Six-Day War erupted with Israel and her neighbors, including Egypt, Jordan, and Syria, in which Israel crushed the opposition and seized East Jerusalem from the nation of Jordan, annexing it into Israel and uniting the old city of Jerusalem under Jewish control. This occurred on the third day of the Six-Day War. One verse that came alive to prophetic scholars was Psalm 102:16:

> For the LORD shall build up Zion;
> He shall appear in His glory.

The year 1967 is marked as the year of the reunification of the city of Jerusalem. Prior to June of 1967, the city was divided between two nations: Israel and Jordan. The division was political and visible, as a huge concrete wall topped with barbed wire stood at the borders, and armed soldiers guarded both sides of this man-made border and prevented movement from either side, except for tourists. When East Jerusalem fell into Israeli's hands, the Israelis began dismantling the concrete divider and annexed east with west, thereby uniting the city. The man-made barriers were removed to create a united city under one head.

The 1967 date is also significant as it related to an amazing outpouring of the Holy Spirit. It was in the early 1960s that an unexpected and rather dramatic outpouring of the Spirit occurred, accompanied by speaking in tongues and various charismatic gifts. The amazing fact of this event was that it was not among the traditional Pentecostal-charismatic or full gospel movements, but it was happening among Catholics and nominal denominational groups. The date 1967 is given as the beginning of the noted Charismatic Renewal, where tens of thousands of men and women accepted the gift of the Holy Spirit and the various biblical manifestations in their home prayer groups and local congregations. A renewed interest in the Holy Spirit and the spiritual manifestations also spread among the men and women in the business community through two organizations formed during the Charismatic Renewal, the Full Gospel Businessmen's Fellowship International (FGBMFI) and the women's Aglow International.

I can recall the late 1960s as a child. My father pastored a small red brick church in Big Stone Gap, Virginia, and taught his small flock about the Holy Spirit and His gifts. I can recall the perception of our simple and humble church members in our rural town, and how these small congregations were often maligned, persecuted, and misunderstood because of two main beliefs: the belief that the Holy Spirit baptism is available today, accompanied by a prayer language, and the belief that God has never ceased to heal the spiritually and physically sick but can and will do so today. Because both beliefs required faith in the supernatural and brought the invisible world of spiritual manifestations into the human realm, we soon discovered that most folks would rather resist this type of belief than switch from their unbelief.

The charismatic outpouring among many mainline groups, including businessmen and women, was a significant event and brought some relief to the rural churches, as it created the perception that believers were not some *cult* or *fringe element* of Christianity but a part of a coming river in the mainstream of Christianity.

Joel's predictions reveal that after Israel's restoration God would pour out His Spirit. It is not a coincidence that the same year Israel was restored as a nation, a great coast-to-coast revival of healing was manifested to believers, neither was it some odd chance that in the same year that Jerusalem was reunited, the Charismatic Renewal was released by the Holy Spirit. Just as a man-made barrier separating two nations, Israel and Jordan, was removed in Jerusalem in 1967, the denominational barriers began to crumble in 1967 with the initial outpouring of the Spirit that began in North America and spread around the world.

To teach that the statement of Peter on the Day of Pentecost was the final and total fulfillment of Joel's prediction is to ignore the significance between the "last days" and the "afterward"—meaning the final days for Jerusalem, Israel, and Jewish control of the city in Peter's time and Joel's restoration of Israel accompanied by an outpouring to emerge at the time of the end. To relegate the Holy Spirit's outpouring to a one-time initial event in Acts chapter 2 misses another important portion of Joel's prophecy, where Joel speaks of the "former [early] rain, and the latter rain" (Joel 2:23).

James alluded to this early and latter rain when he was speaking about the coming of the Lord:

> Therefore be patient, brethren, until the coming of the Lord. See how the farmer waits for the precious fruit of the earth, waiting patiently for it until it receives the early and latter rain.
> —James 5:7

This verse reveals the purpose of the early and latter rains: to ripen the fruit—a metaphor for preparing the souls of men and women prior to the return of Christ. In the New Testament the parables speak of *wheat* being the children of the kingdom and the *tares* being the children of Satan, with the angels being the reapers. (See Matthew

13.) It is rain that causes a productive and full harvest of both grains (barley and wheat) and fruit-bearing trees in Israel. The outpouring water and rain verses that are in some cases used as a metaphor for the outpouring of the Holy Spirit are important, as the early and latter rain indicate two distinct outpourings of the Holy Spirit. In Israel I discovered the difference between these two types of rains.

In ancient Israel Jews were familiar with the terms "early and latter rain." The early rain fell in order to prepare the ground for the seed, and the latter rain fell at a time prior to and up until the grain harvest (Deut. 11:14). Historically and biblically the first major outpouring of the Holy Spirit occurred on the Day of Pentecost, in Acts 2:1–4, to introduce the Christian church and impart spiritual power to the individual disciples. This Pentecostal outpouring was the *rain* season when the *seed* of the new covenant was planted throughout the world. As the time of the end approaches, with the climax of the gospel being preached from nation to nation, another outpouring, identified with the "latter rain" of the Holy Spirit, can be expected to help ripen the condition of the hearts of humanity and bring in the final *full harvest* of the lost into the kingdom of God. Water always softens hard soil, and the rain of the Spirit has similar effects on the hearts of humanity, melting the callous hearts and minds to receive God's love and His Word.

The early rains begin during the fall months of late October and early November, never suddenly, but by varying degrees. Usually the rains continue for two or three days at a time, especially at night. This enables the farmer to plow his fields, planting wheat and barley. Once the seed is planted, under normal circumstances the rains become steady during the late winter months. This early rain prepared the dry ground to receive the seed, and the latter rain, which peaks around March or April, helps mature and ripen the barley and the wheat for the harvest. Historically the spiritual application is that the *early rain* occurred at the birth of the church, and the *latter rain* will occur before the catching away of the church and begins to manifest after the restoration of Israel (Joel 2:28). Both outpourings of the Holy Spirit are for the maturing of the spiritual harvest of souls, bringing the good "wheat" into the kingdom (Matt. 13:30). Peter also predicted that God would *pour out His Spirit upon all flesh* in the last days (Acts 2:17–18). The first outpouring of the Spirit came upon mature men and women who gathered in an upper room to seek God and wait for the "Promise of My Father" (Acts 1:13; Luke 24:49). The latter rain outpouring will come upon our "sons and our daughters" (Acts 2:17–18), and "all flesh," which refers to people of all nations.

The early rain fell upon the dry, barren hearts of the Hebrew nation as the seed of God's Word was planted in Jerusalem, Judea, Samaria, and the uttermost parts of the earth (Acts 1:8). The latter rain will help ripen the hearts of people around the world and prepare the final great harvest of souls for the kingdom of God (James 5:7).

The Third-Day Blessings

One of the great outpouring *codes* is found in the writings of Hosea the prophet. Hosea's name means, "salvation." His prophetic ministry occurred at the time when the ten northern tribes of Israel were still in the land. Hosea lived a long life as indicated by the fact he prophesied in the time of four kings—Uzziah, Jotham, Ahaz, and Hezekiah, all were kings of Judah—and also during the reign of Jeroboam, king of Israel. This time period spans about seventy-two years!

The prophecy begins in Hosea 5:15 and continues through Hosea 6:3. It has been carefully examined by prophetic scholars and students since Israel was restored as a nation in 1948. There is no indication in Israel's past history that the key passages of Hosea 6:1–3 have been fulfilled:

> Come, and let us return to the LORD;
> For He has torn, but He will heal us;
> He has stricken, but He will bind us up.
> After two days He will revive us;
> On the third day He will raise us up,
> That we may live in His sight.
> Let us know,
> Let us pursue the knowledge of the LORD.
> His going forth is established as the morning;
> He will come to us like the rain,
> Like the latter and former rain to the earth.

Because Hosea mentions the "latter and former rain" (v. 3), the same terms used in James 5:7 as a sign to occur prior to the return of the Lord, this marks the Hosea prediction as an *end-time prophecy* related to Israel.

In his prophecy Hosea predicted Ephraim (the northern kingdom) and Judah (the southern kingdom) would eventually be torn and taken away (led into captivity, Hosea 5:13–14), which occurred during the Assyrian invasion, the Babylonian captivity, and was repeated hundreds of years later during the occupation and the destruction of Jerusalem by the Romans in AD 70. The Lord spoke to Hosea indicating that He would "return again to [His] place" until they acknowledged their offense (Hosea 5:15). If we interpret this as a prophetic message for a future generation, then it agrees with Christ's promise that He would "go and prepare a place for [us]" (John 14:3). Forty days after His resurrection Christ ascended from the Mount of Olives back to His heavenly Father (Acts 1:10–11). He is now seated in the heavenly temple, ever living to make intercession for us (Heb. 7:25). He is preparing *a place* to receive us in heaven when He returns. Hosea said the Lord would remain at His place until "they acknowledge their offense" (Hosea 5:15). Who in this text will acknowledge their offense? In the verses prior to this statement God is speaking to three distinct groups: the house of *Israel, Ephraim*, and *Judah* (v. 5). Since this prophecy can also allude to the Messiah returning, then who are these three groups today?

1. The house of Israel consists of both the natural and the spiritual houses of Israel, or the natural and spiritual seed of Abraham. This would be the natural Jew and the spiritual Jew, the spiritual Jew being believers who have received Christ as their Messiah. (See Romans 9; 11.)

2. Ephraim represents the many Gentile nations, as Moses said that the sons of Joseph, Ephraim and Manasseh, would push people to the ends of the earth (Deut. 33:17).

3. Judah is a name given to the Jews who lived in the area of Judea.

According to Hosea there must be repentance and acknowledging of offenses among these three groups.

Presently the gospel is being proclaimed to the Gentile nations of the earth (Matt. 24:14). After years of distrust and animosity, the body of Christ is now witnessing a mutual understanding and friendship emerge between the numerous Jewish leaders and Jewish people in Israel and the many Christian denominations and organizations, many who have apologized for the atrocities committed to the Jews in the "name of Christ" through centuries of anti-Semitic teaching. The church is acknowledging their offenses, and this is forging a new relationship between Jews and Christians.

The Promise of Healing and Reviving

As we continue to examine the marvelous Hosea prophecy, the Lord promises that after the return of Israel there would be a healing and a reviving. This prophecy has several possible interpretations. Based on numerous Old Testament prophecies, the words *torn* and *smitten* allude to Israel's separation from God and being torn out of their land, led into captivity, and living among the Gentile nations (Ezek. 33:21; 40:1; Amos 4:9–11). The ultimate affliction for the Jews came during the Holocaust, during which the Nazis led a mass extermination of the Jews, literally tearing and forcing them from their homes, businesses, and cities, and smiting them in the labor camps and leading them to the gas chambers as sheep going to the slaughter.

This unimaginable event began in 1939 and continued for seven years until Hitler's suicide on April 30, 1945. Three years later in May of 1948, God began to heal the Jewish people by giving them a homeland in the very territory they once possessed more than 1,878 years prior. The Hebrew word for "return" in Hosea 6:1 is *shuwb*, and it means, "to turn or to repent." It is also used when referring to the Jews' return to the land of Israel after the Babylonian captivity (Jer. 29:10) and when the Jews return to their land from other nations (Jer. 30:10)! Thus the *return* (Hosea 6:1) can refer to the Jews returning to the land, both during the Babylonian captivity and their return to the land after 1,878 years of being scattered among the Gentile nations around the earth.

The most interesting and often difficult part of this prophecy to interpret is when Hosea said, "After two days He [God] will revive us; on the third day He will raise us up, that we may live in His sight" (Hosea 6:2). Since the return of the Messiah is connected to the return of the Jews to Israel and the rebuilding and expansion of Jerusalem (see Psalm 102:16), this prediction may cryptically signify an event in 1967 linked to the amazing Six-Day War.

From 1948 to 1967 Israel had been a Jewish state for nineteen years. However, the sacred city of Jerusalem was divided between the country of Jordan (East Jerusalem) and Israel (West Jerusalem). All major Old Testament prophecies concerning the return and reign of the Messiah reveal that Jerusalem will be in Jewish hands and the capital of Israel when the King-Messiah returns (Ps. 102:16; Zech. 12:2–9; 13:1–5; 14:2–8). Thus, the greatest sign of the return of the King-Messiah would be when Jerusalem was in the hands of the Jewish people.

In June of 1967 Israel launched an air strike against Egypt, initiating a major war. On the *second day* of the war Israel had the upper hand against Egypt, Jordan, and Syria through Israel's air superiority and their ground forces. On the *third day* of the war, at ten o'clock in the morning, the Israeli paratroopers moved into the Old City of Jerusalem, liberating the entire Western Wall area and announcing they had taken East Jerusalem from the Jordanians. Rabbi Shlomo Goren announced that Israel had entered the Messianic age. This dramatic prophetic event occurred on the third day, early in the morning. Hosea mentioned living again in God's sight on the *third day* and how the Lord's "going forth is established as the *morning*" (Hosea 6:3, emphasis added). At ten o'clock in the morning on the third day of the Six-Day War, Jerusalem was united and in Jewish hands for the first time in more than eighteen hundred years—once again living in God's sight!

Another clue that this two-day to three-day resurrection alludes to God's favor coming on Jerusalem is the next verse that predicts the "latter [early] and former rain" (v. 3). This phrase is also referenced in Joel 2:23 and in James 5:7. In both passages the "early and latter rain" refers to the outpouring of the Holy Spirit in the last days and after a restoration. Hosea said that on the "third day," the Lord will "come...like the rain." Using the date of 1967 and the Six-Day War as a possible time frame of this prophetic prediction being fulfilled, it was also in 1967, as previously stated, that a leading spiritual event—the Charismatic Renewal—was the main thrust to alignment for the return of the Messiah.

Thus in 1967 not only was Jerusalem reunited and the walls of separation between the east and west divisions of the city were removed, but also the Holy Spirit suddenly began falling upon the nominal mainline denominations, breaking down the man-made barriers that had prevented spiritual unity among the Christian churches. The combination of Jerusalem's reunification and the fresh outpouring of the Spirit was the beginning of a season of restoration and the beginning of a "latter rain outpouring." This type of restoration was predicted in Acts 3:20–21 (KJV):

> And he shall send Jesus Christ, which before was preached unto you: Whom the heaven must receive until the times of restitution of all things, which God hath spoken by the mouth of all his holy prophets since the world began.

The classical Greek word here for "restitution" has several meanings, including "repairing a broken bone, balancing accounts, repairing a hole in the road, and restoring something back to its original condition and returning an estate to its original owner."[4] When the major restitution of Israel and Jerusalem begins to occur, it becomes another indicator that Christ will soon return (Acts 3:20). The restitution began with the return of the Jews to their homeland and continued with the reunification of Jerusalem as the biblically, undisputed capital of Israel. The final phase of completing the final restoration will be when Israel enters the redemptive covenant with the Messiah, Christ Jesus. When Israel acknowledges its offense, then the Lord will return from His place, meaning He will return from heaven to earth (Acts 3:20). For centuries the understanding of Christ as Messiah has been veiled from the understanding of the natural seed of Abraham (2 Cor. 3:13–16). However, at the very end of days, this spiritual veil will be lifted. Jesus gave a prediction concerning His return and said:

> For I say to you, you shall see Me no more till you say, "Blessed is He who comes in the name of the LORD!"
>
> —MATTHEW 23:39

The above statement is a prophecy originally found in Psalm 118:22–26:

> The stone which the builders rejected
> Has become the chief cornerstone.
> This was the LORD's doing;
> It is marvelous in our eyes.
> This is the day the LORD has made;
> We will rejoice and be glad in it.
> Save now, I pray, O LORD;
> O LORD, I pray, send now prosperity.
> Blessed is he who comes in the name of the LORD!
> We have blessed you from the house of the LORD.

Today in Israel, at the Western Wall, devout Jews use this prayer from Psalms to speak blessing to the one (the Messiah) who will come in the name of the Lord. While the vast majority of these religious Jewish men do not believe that Christ is the Messiah for the Jews, Christ taught that when they pray these words, they would see Him again! Several Hebraic-prophetic scholars believe that 1948 was the early beginning of the last days and that 1967 initiated the era of the Messiah. Certainly the events of 1967 have a parallel to the prediction on Hosea 6:1–3.

This generation is living in the season of prophetic fulfillment, which includes the outpouring of the Spirit. It will be up to each individual Christian to determine if he or she will choose to follow the Holy Spirit or simply remain in a comfort zone behind the four walls of their local congregation.

Several years ago I was meditating on what I call the third phase of my ministry. I knew if Christ called me home at that moment, I had thirty-five wonderful years of traveling, preaching, and ministering and could depart happy knowing I did God's will. However, if many more years remained, then I wanted to know God's plan for the future. As I was praying, I heard that still small voice that had guided me over the years say, "Son, do you wish to go where I am going?"

I immediately replied verbally, "Yes, Lord!"

Then I heard, "I am going to the sons and the daughters to pour out My Spirit!" From this moment of inspiration my heart was turned toward this generation and the end result of a major gathering place for large meetings, a youth camp, and a mentoring center for youth who are called into the ministry. I suggest you go where God is going— He is traveling the Joel 2 road to pour out His Spirit on all flesh.

Chapter Eight

THE LAST DAYS—BETWEEN PENTECOST AND TRUMPETS

...the testimony of Christ was confirmed in you, so
that you come short in no gift, eagerly waiting for the
revelation of our Lord Jesus Christ.

—1 CORINTHIANS 1:6–7

THERE ARE SEVEN major biblical feasts for Israel listed in the
Torah. They are Passover, Unleavened Bread, Firstfruits, Pentecost, Trumpets, the Day of Atonement, and Tabernacles. (See
Leviticus 23.) Of these seven there are three—Passover, Pentecost, and
Tabernacles—where all men over twenty years of age were commanded
by the Lord to attend in Jerusalem (Exod. 34:22–23). The feasts have a
practical purpose and a prophetic application.

Based upon the New Testament, Christ's first appearing fulfilled
the first three spring feasts: He was *crucified* near Passover, *in the
tomb* during Unleavened Bread, and *raised from the grave*, being seen
alive by His disciples, during the season of the Feast of Firstfruits. The
fourth feast that follows Firstfruits is Pentecost, and this is clearly
the feast established for the church, as it was the very day the body
of Christ was recognized at the Jewish temple with three thousand

new converts and a group freshly baptized with the power of the Holy
Spirit. (See Acts 2.)

The fifth feast in order after Pentecost is the Feast of Trumpets
(called *Rosh Hashanah*, meaning the head of the year). Its various rituals and more than one hundred trumpet blasts paint the imagery to
many prophetic teachers of the return of Christ for the overcoming
believers, or those who have walked in purity and righteousness.
When discussing the prophetic times, I am often asked this question:
"Where do you believe we now are on God's prophetic calendar?" The
answer most people expect is a comparison of recent events with biblical signs, or current events in Israel and the Middle East with various biblical prophecies. However, several years ago I realized there
was a unique pattern concealed in the *time gap* between Pentecost
and Trumpets. Understanding this will explain the theological theory
that various spiritual gifts and manifestations of the Holy Spirit have
ceased.

The Dry Season

It is commonly taught among more liberal nominal churches that the
various scriptural manifestations of the Holy Spirit recorded in the
New Testament, chiefly speaking with other tongues, have ceased. I
have heard the theory that the miraculous gifts ceased with the death
of the apostle John, or with the completion of the New Testament
canon in the fourth century. Based upon Acts 2:1–4, I can tell you the
month (Pentecost is in the fifth month of the Jewish calendar), the day
(the Day of Pentecost), the hour (about the ninth hour), and the place
(Jerusalem) when the Holy Spirit first baptized believers. However, no
one who teaches the cessation of the spiritual gifts can give you the
year, month, day, or hour when the Holy Spirit abruptly and suddenly
lifted His charismata from off the church and carried the miraculous
back to the heaven.

The fact is that no gift of the Holy Spirit was ever removed from the
church by the Holy Spirit, but certain gifts were suppressed through
unbelief and removed from operation by the Holy Spirit because the
negative and critical words of men grieved the Holy Spirit, and He
withdrew His presence. Throughout church history the carnal lives of

unspiritual men—or flagrant sin—prevented the Holy Spirit from gloriously manifesting His presence.

The natural world often reflects spiritual truths. Historically there was a decline of certain spiritual manifestations and gifts around the time of the completion of the New Testament Canon. Some scholars mark this occasion as the point where God slowly lifted the gifts of prophecy, tongues, healings, and miracles. Their reasoning is that once men had the Word of God (the church had now been given a complete Bible of sixty-six books), there was no necessity of dramatic manifestations of the Spirit.

Think about this theology. Men can now hold in their hands a book with sixty-six individual books of history, prophecy, wisdom, and divine instruction. The Bible is a book that reveals four thousand years of human history, including the rise and fall of empires and the past, present, and future history of Israel and the Jews. This divine collection contains the narratives of hundreds of signs, wonders, and miracles, including healings—from the mass healing of the Hebrews departing Egypt to the miracles of the apostles in Acts. Yet some ministers teach that for four thousand years God activated the miracles so men could compile it in one big book and future generations could read stories of how powerful God *used to be—and not believe He can repeat His miracles in our day!*

One of the main theological stances concerning the miraculous gifts of the Holy Spirit is that from about the fourth century onward there was a ceasing of the miraculous spiritual gifts. It is also noted that there were few manifestations in history until the late 1800s and early 1900s when in America in Murphy, North Carolina (1896), Kansas City, Kansas (1901), and Los Angeles, California (1906, the Azusa Street Revival) reports emerged where many began to speak with tongues and experience a reviving of the miraculous. This would imply that for about thirteen hundred to fourteen hundred years the Spirit of the Lord was silent, working, perhaps, in the massive stone cathedrals of Europe or moving occasionally by choice upon some chosen monk living as a recluse in a musty monastery in Italy. This would be a very long dry spell for the Lord to remove His Spirit from the presence of His people.

One of many problems with this theory of cessation of certain gifts is that the Bible was not permitted in the hands of the common people for hundreds of years. If the Lord was to withdraw certain gifts once the Bible was compiled, then He should have removed the gifts after the translation and printing of the 1611 King James English Bibles or after Bible companies were established, which finally allowed common people to own a Bible without being burned at the stake or beheaded. It is utter human rationalization to suggest that by the fifth century the spiritual gifts ceased due to a lack of written records indicating otherwise. The fact is there was a long spiritual dry spell in the traditional Christian church and in the Roman and Orthodox groups, as for hundreds of years the emphasis was upon building a physical kingdom upon earth through crusades and wars, and not building a spiritual kingdom that delivered souls from sin and spiritual death. It was actually the printing and release of the Bible to the commoners that initiated a renewal in the belief of Christ's return and the outpouring of the Holy Spirit prior to the appearing of Christ.

The Clue Is in the Feasts

The clue as to why a long, spiritual dry spell stretched through history and how it is broken with the return of the latter spiritual rain is to understand the gap between the Feasts of Pentecost and Trumpets. Each of the seven feasts has a distinct function and a practical and a prophetic application. Pentecost is a feast God designed to be the birthday of the church, and we have been living in the dispensation of the grace of God or, as some scholars identify it, the church age (Eph. 3:2). The assignment of the church is to preach the gospel to all nations as a witness, and then the end shall come (Matt. 24:14). I believe this assignment climaxes with the return of Christ for the overcomers. (See Revelation 2–3.) This event is identified as the *gathering together* of the saints and the resurrection of the dead in Christ (1 Cor. 15:52; Eph. 1:9–10; 1 Thess. 4:16–17). The imagery of this great ingathering of saints (some call it the catching away or the Rapture) is pictured in the feast that follows Pentecost, the Feast of Trumpets.

There are about four months between Pentecost and Trumpets, which is quite a time gap considering that the three spring feasts all occur within one week, and the three fall feasts all fall within a twenty-one-day time frame. There are fifty days from Passover to Pentecost, but four months between Pentecost and Trumpets. There are seasons of rain in the spring and in the fall. However, Pentecost occurs in May or June, and this is the beginning of a very hot and dry summer in Israel, meaning no rain! This dry season usually runs for the entire summer until the fall feasts begin and the atmosphere begins to change, and by November the winter rains can begin.

The entire, universal body of Christ has been living at Pentecost, preaching to the Jews and the Gentiles, and also preaching the importance of the Holy Spirit baptism and the outpouring upon all men. The Spirit arrived to impart life and comfort to the believers and has been active on the planet since He exploded upon the scene in the Upper Room. As the church prophetically approaches the return of Christ, the greatest outpouring of the Spirit will occur at that season—or, prophetically, prior to the blast of the *shofar*, since the Feast of Trumpets has more than one hundred blasts of the shofar, giving the imagery of the trump of God raising the dead in this feast.

Here is the prophetic application. The closer the body of Christ moves toward the Feast of Trumpets, or the catching away of the church, the four months of dryness will break and the atmosphere will change, causing the spiritual clouds to form and send the rain—a fresh outpouring of the Spirit—to cover the world. This is what occurs in Israel in the natural and what will occur to the church in the spiritual realm. Understanding this concept explains why there was such a long dry spell from the fifth century to the early 1800s, when the atmosphere began to slowly change, and now the global rain of the Spirit is raining down over entire nations.

What About the Nine Spiritual Gifts?

Many people hear so much about speaking in tongues they believe that is the only gift that the full gospel folks know anything about! There are nine gifts of the Holy Spirit according to 1 Corinthians 12:7–10:

> But the manifestation of the Spirit is given to each one for the profit of all: for to one is given the word of wisdom through the Spirit, to another the word of knowledge through the same

Spirit, to another faith by the same Spirit, to another gifts of healings by the same Spirit, to another the working of miracles, to another prophecy, to another discerning of spirits, to another different kinds of tongues, to another the interpretation of tongues.

Paul called these nine manifestations "spiritual gifts." The Greek word for "gifts" here is *charismata*, which refers to a special endowment freely given by the Holy Spirit. This Greek word for "gifts" is used five times in 1 Corinthians 12 (vv. 4, 9, 28, 30, 31), and each reference refers to the nine gifts mentioned in the same chapter. Over time theologians have conducted a "hack job" and cut out the gifts they chose to omit and left intact such gifts as wisdom, knowledge, and faith. These gifts require little emotion or demonstrative display by the recipient when operating in the flow of the Spirit.

Without engaging in a long written debate, there are two verses in the New Testament—Romans 11:29 and 1 Corinthians 1:7–8, both written by Paul—that indicate the duration of these gifts and the time when they are no longer necessary.

> For the gifts and the calling of God are irrevocable.
> —ROMANS 11:29

In the context of Romans 11 Paul was speaking of God's election and Israel's unbelief. Some in his day (and our time) believed that God was finished with national Israel and had replaced them with the Gentile church. Paul made it clear that the gifts and calling cannot be revoked. The calling was His calling on Israel, and the word for "gifts" here is *charismata*, the same word used for the gifts of the Holy Spirit. Thus God does not give the church any of His spiritual *charismata* and then do a recall and take back what is so needed to edify the body of Christ.

The New Testament lists many spiritual blessings and classifies them as gifts. These are available to those who will believe on the Lord and follow Him by faith:

- The gift of *salvation* (Eph. 2:8)

- The gift of the *grace of God* (Eph. 3:7)

- The gift of *righteousness* (Rom. 5:17)

- The gift of *eternal life* (Rom. 6:23)

- The gift called *the unspeakable gift* (2 Cor. 9:15, KJV)

- The gift of *giving finances* (Phil. 4:17)

- The gift of the *Holy Spirit* (Acts 2:38)

- The *spiritual gift* (Rom. 1:11)

- The *gifts of the Spirit* (1 Cor. 12:7–10)

Look at this list and ask yourself, "How many of these gifts have ceased since the time of the New Testament?" Has the grace of God, His righteousness, eternal life, or salvation ceased? Do churches reject your tithe or offering because the gift of giving ceased after the death of Paul? Then who gave human men the permission to tell the body of Christ that the spiritual gifts or *charismata* have been removed from the church? I think I have discovered over the years that church members should never judge God's ability based upon the spiritual activity or the lack thereof in their local congregations. Some churches never support missionaries, so based on their inactivity shall we assume that souls no longer need salvation on the mission fields? I have ministered in congregations that are self-centered and have no outreach for feeding the poor in other nations. Should we now suggest that the world must have plenty of food now and feeding the poor is no longer necessary with the invention of the massive combines on farms?

Suppose you have never personally seen a manifestation of the Holy Spirit in your congregation. Would this suggest to you that the gifts have ceased, or otherwise they would be active in your church? Or could it mean that there is little or no interest in spiritual gifts among the members in your church, and they would not be receptive to their operation if spiritual manifestations were made visible? The fact is the gifts were never *revoked* by God but were and still are *rejected* by unbelieving and uninterested Christians.

Look at this powerful promise recorded in 1 Corinthians 1:7–8:

> So that you come short in no gift, eagerly waiting for the revelation of our Lord Jesus Christ, who will also confirm you to

the end, that you may be blameless in the day of our Lord Jesus
Christ.

The Greek word for "gift" is *charisma*, the singular word for a specific gift versus the combination of all nine gifts (plural). The church
at Corinth was overloaded with spiritual gifts, and Paul wrote three
chapters—1 Corinthians 12, 13, and 14—to correct errors and instruct
in the operation of vocal gifts within the church. Yet he makes it clear
that he desires the church to excel (not to come behind) in any gift!
Paul then states that the gifts will "confirm you to the end." The word
confirm here means, to "stabilize and establish" a person. Note that
according to Paul, a spiritual gift will continue unto the day of the Lord
Jesus, and God wills for you to be stabilized spiritually until the end.

The Reasons for No Gifts

After many years of full-time evangelism and meeting tens of thousands of people from ten major denominations, I have pinpointed the
main reasons why there is a shortage or a drought of spiritual rain
and spiritual manifestations in many churches. Any spiritual gift
must operate through a human vessel; it does not supernaturally float
through the atmosphere in some mystical type of fog. The need for a
human vessel brings me to the first common reason for lack of gifts:
they have been neglected by the vessels (people) themselves.

Timothy was a young minister whom Paul appointed as pastor over
a large congregation in Ephesus (1 Tim. 1:3). Some of the elders were
upset to have such a young man, whom they considered to be too
immature for ministry. Paul instructed his spiritual son not to rebuke
an elder (1 Tim. 5:1). He also spoke to Timothy about the gift that had
been imparted to him:

> Do not neglect the gift that is in you, which was given to you
> by prophecy with the laying on of the hands of the eldership.
> —1 TIMOTHY 4:14

The gifts can be *neglected.* In Greek the word for "neglect" means to
be careless, make light of, or have no regard for. We will neglect what
is not important to us. Just as a muscle on the body that is never used

will, if neglected, eventually cease to do what it was created for, then spiritual gifts can be neglected and thus deactivated. The danger is that something can be neglected so long that eventually you will not miss it. To prevent being neglected, the gifts must be "stirred up":

> Therefore I remind you to stir up the gift of God which is in you through the laying on of my hands. For God has not given us a spirit of fear, but of power and of love and of a sound mind.
> —2 TIMOTHY 1:6–7

To *stir up* is to *rekindle a fire with the remaining embers.* All it takes are a few burning embers and some fuel to cause flames to leap again and burn brightly. If people neglect spiritual gifts and allow the flames of zeal and desire to die, then there will be a dearth in the operation of gifts. God works though people, which leads to the second reason gifts have appeared to cease: *people cease to flow in the Spirit.*

When the clear voice of the Spirit becomes muffled in the spirit of a person and there is no clarity that the Lord is speaking, then the person says, "Is this the Lord directing me, or is this just me?" The Holy Spirit would never tell you to function outside of the boundaries of the Bible, so judge what you hear by what is revealed in the Word. Do you think the adversary would tell you to go witness to a man who was sitting on a park bench about Christ? Should you question if it is the Lord or just you to give a poor person a meal to eat or some money? When you have an open door to minister to orphans or widows, why should you think, "The Lord may not want me to do that"? The same is true when you have an inner desire to give an offering for ministry. God's voice agrees with His Word, and the Holy Spirit always agrees with God.

On a more humorous note, a few times when God could not find a person to speak, He used what was available—including animals! The prophet Balaam was stubborn, ignoring God's will, so God opened the mouth of his donkey to rebuke him. The odd part is that instead of realizing the supernatural element of a talking animal, Balaam began to argue with the dumb beast (Num. 22:25–30). In the New Testament a rooster crowed three times, and Peter came under conviction and repented for denying the Lord (Mark 14:72). God will use whom and what is available to enact His purposes and lay out His will.

The third reason gifts can be neglected is that *if these manifestations are not permitted by the leadership in the local congregations, then the members are to be under their leaders' authority and follow the instruction of those who are over them in the Lord* (1 Thess. 5:12–13). A person who believes in the gifts should avoid sitting in a congregation where gifts are publicly discouraged and rejected and then attempt to jump up in the crowd and give a message in tongues or initiate a prayer line to lay hands upon people for prayer. Such action would create confusion and be rejected from the beginning. As another example, I preach on the Hebraic roots of the Christian faith, and often good-hearted and sincere people will bring a ram's horn (*shofar*) into the building and begin blowing it without permission from the pastor. For churches unfamiliar with the blowing of a shofar, they have numerous questions that cannot be answered in a single worship gathering. Also, there are some sincere believers who haven't really learned how to perfect the different sounds emitting from the shofar, and the noise sounds like a factory horn that loses steam in the middle of blowing. You should know the setting, the belief of the church, and never exercise your own authority over top of the leadership for the congregation.

Even in the New Testament believers were removed from synagogues because their teachings on Christ clashed with the synagogue members' Jewish traditions and theology on the Messiah. For leadership of a ministry or in a church to maintain a spiritual walk and sensitivity to the Holy Spirit, it requires a continual hunger and determination. It is far easier to have a great worship service, teach for thirty minutes with a feel-good message, and have some exciting basic spiritual programs believed to meet needs in a local congregation. In reality, it is *easier* to maintain a church through the flesh-appealing routines than through convicting spiritual manifestations.

My father, Fred Stone, was the most spiritually minded man I have ever known. He walked with the Lord every day and maintained a mind of prayer and sensitivity to Christ. He spent hours in prayer and days in fasting, and on a few occasions in local church services I witnessed all nine gifts of the Spirit operate through his ministry. I was present in the services and witnessed this firsthand, including two unforgettable services in Louisville, Kentucky, and another in Brooksville, Florida. I know that hours of prayer and fasting fine-tune the human spirit to sharpen the hearing to recognize God's voice. In our Western culture it is far easier to please the flesh than to discipline the human spirit. Once the spiritual gifts operate, the life of the receiver must be maintained through discipline and prayer. It is easier to have a pizza party than a prayer meeting, and the pizza draws more eaters than the prayer does seekers. But pizza cannot accomplish what one spiritual gift can!

The fourth and very common reason that gifts cannot operate is because of *the atmosphere of unbelief and skepticism in the church.* I remember showing a "Christian" man, a church member for more than fifty years, certain verses in the Bible that crushed his theology of unbelief. He looked at me and said, "I don't care what the Bible says; I don't believe it, and I will believe it my way!" I was thinking at that moment that I had officially met a Pharisee of Pharisees, as this was the same attitude among the elite Jewish Pharisees in the time of Christ—"if it doesn't fit my theology, *it's not of God.*"

In Nazareth Christ could do no mighty miracles because of their unbelief (Mark 6:5–6). Yet He could leave the upper Galilee in Nazareth and descend to the lower Galilee at Capernaum and perform numerous miracles in the cities around the Sea of Galilee, where the Gospels record His exciting ministry being received by the common people. In Matthew 17 a father brought his epileptic son to the disciples, who, after prayer, were unable to expel a spirit possessing the lad. Christ appeared on the scene, rebuked the spirit, and delivered the boy. When the disciples inquired of the reason why they had failed in their prayer, Jesus answered, "Because of your unbelief" (v. 20). Unbelief is such a strong force that the spirit world can sense if a person has faith or a lack thereof. On another occasion, when Christ was preparing to raise a young girl from the dead, He removed everyone out of the room, as their lack of faith was stagnating the atmosphere and could have prevented a miracle from occurring (Mark 5:39–40). If you refuse to believe, the Holy Spirit will refuse to operate.

Another important point is that according to the apostle Paul, we are to "covet earnestly the best gifts" (1 Cor. 12:31, KJV). It seems odd for Paul to teach that we should "covet" the best gifts, when in Romans 7:7 we read that, "You shall not covet," which is also one of the Ten Commandments (Exod. 20:17). The definition of coveting in Exodus

20:17 and Romans 7:7 is to set your heart upon something that is forbidden. However, the Greek word Paul used in 1 Corinthians 12:31 for "covet" is a different Greek word that means, "to have a warm feeling for and to have a zeal for." Thus if we have no strong desire for spiritual gifts, there will be a lack of any spiritual gift in manifestation.

When Paul said, "the best gifts," the question becomes, what are the *best* gifts? I believe the best gift is what is needed at that particular moment to meet the spiritual need of a seeker. When I was a young teenager, I was blessed to see a great man of God, T. L. Lowery, ministering under the large metal tabernacle during what was called "camp meeting," and I personally watched as he laid his hands upon the sick. Right before my eyes I saw men and women instantly cured by the power of the Lord. These miracles stirred my own spirit into studying books on the great healing revival and gave me the faith to begin praying for people in our own revivals.

As an example, there were believers in Christ who saw the disciples praying and getting results, and they themselves began to minister to others, seeing the same results. The disciples were somewhat concerned that these new believers were not a part of their group and set out to set them down. Jesus, however, stopped this action and said that if they were not working against Him, then they were working for Him and that He had other sheep that were not of the disciples' flock (John 10:16).

The fifth observation is that *gifts cannot operate when people have no knowledge of their availability.* In America Christians often assume that about everyone born in America has already heard the gospel at least once, which is a total misconception. Among full gospel people many assume that everyone sitting in a full gospel church has heard of or experienced the infilling of the Spirit based upon Acts 2:4. This is also a misconception.

In the Book of Acts, many years after the outpouring at Pentecost, Paul came to Ephesus, and we read:

> And it happened, while Apollos was at Corinth, that Paul, having passed through the upper regions, came to Ephesus. And finding some disciples he said to them, "Did you receive

the Holy Spirit when you believed?" So they said to him, "We have not so much as heard whether there is a Holy Spirit."

—Acts 19:1–2

Apollos became one of the main leaders in the early church. Paul was in Ephesus and found disciples of John the Baptist, whose emphasis was baptism in water unto repentance. These disciples were followers of John, and even though the Spirit had been poured out, these sincere men had heard nothing about it. In this narrative Paul laid his hands upon these twelve, and they were all filled with the Holy Spirit and spoke with tongues (vv. 3–7).

When desiring a spiritual gift, we must keep in mind that the gift is not given to show we are more superior to others or more spiritual, and certainly must not be operated with pride. The gifts are for the edification, exhortation, and comfort of the church, and to assist in ministering to the unsaved, revealing the living God. We are presently living in the church age, or prophetically the four months from Pentecost to Trumpets. In Israel as one got closer to the fall Feast of Trumpets, the atmosphere began to change as the rain prepared to fall. As we move closer to the coming of Christ, the world will be engulfed in the latter rain outpouring of the Spirit! The dry spells will be broken.

Chapter Nine

THE IMPORTANCE
OF TESTING SPIRITS

Beloved, do not believe every spirit, but test the spirits, whether they are of God; because many false prophets have gone out into the world.

—1 JOHN 4:1

URING MY MANY years of ministry, only three times did I ever ask a pastor if I could minister in his church. On one occasion I was strongly burdened in my spirit to call a particular pastor and request to minister several nights in his church—a congregation of about seventy people. My wife and I stayed with the minister and his family in their home located next to the church.

For three days when I went into the sanctuary to pray for the night services, I was troubled and restless in my spirit. Finally on Sunday night, the final night, the Lord impressed me to say, "This is a warning for this church. Someone is committing adultery, and if you do not repent and forsake this sin tonight, it will be exposed and the church's reputation will be harmed in the community." A few weeks later the pastor stepped down after confessing to having an affair with a woman in the church. I was sad, but at the same time I believed the Lord had sent me to him as a final warning. Without any knowledge of the situation, the Holy Spirit used the gift of *discerning of spirits* and *word of knowledge* to detect the conflict and relate it.

There are three spirits in operation at any given time of the day: the spirit of man, the Spirit of God, and the spirits of evil. The conflicts, strategies, and operation of these spirits bring about the need for believers to learn how to discern the spirits and test which voice they are hearing.

The necessity of trying (or testing) a spirit is to determine the *truth* or *deception* behind the voice. The spirits operating in the kingdom of God include the voices of God, Christ, angels, and the Holy Spirit. The opposing kingdom of Satan includes the voices of Satan, demonic spirits, evil spirits, foul spirits, and spiritual rebels divided into principalities, powers, rulers of the darkness of this world, and wicked spirits in high places (Eph. 6:12). All humans are tripartite beings—a body, soul, and a spirit (1 Thess. 5:23). Thus, the human spirit communicates with the human soul, which in return is interpreted in the mind.

In the Old Testament era in Israel true prophets were challenged by false prophets, confusing the people as to who was speaking the truth. Was the vision or dream from the Lord or from the imagination of a self-acclaimed seer? Anyone could stand and prophesy in the name of the Lord, and some did so through the direction of lying spirits. (See 2 Chronicles 18.) In the New Testament Christ taught from the inspiration of the Holy Spirit, while the majority of Pharisees were teaching the traditions of men out of their own spirits (Mark 7:13). The confusion that can be caused by such a mixture of voices requires a level of *discerning of spirits*, one of the nine gifts of the Holy Spirit listed by Paul (1 Cor. 12:10).

There are spirits assigned to influence sinners and possess their spirits. Spirits can also send darts into the minds of believers, attempting to pervert their choices, and mentally or physically attack believers. On one occasion the disciples asked Christ to call down fire from heaven on the Samaritans. Elijah called fire down upon Mount Carmel, a mountain range positioned on the edge of ancient Samaria. Christ's disciples were envious and even bitter toward the Samaritans, whose ethnic mix was part Jew and part Gentile. Christ rebuked His disciples and said, "You do not know what manner of spirit you are of"

(Luke 9:55). After the ascension of Christ Phillip conducted a major revival in Samaria, converting much of the city! The apostles Peter and John were sent to lay hands upon the new converts to receive the Holy Spirit baptism. (See Acts 8.) The disciples demanded judgment fire, but Christ's plan was to bring Holy Spirit fire. Thankfully Christ tested the voices and rebuked the wrong spirit.

Three Ways to Test a Spirit

There are three primary ways to test a spirit to see if it is from God. The first is to test it by the Word of God and to test it by the Holy Spirit bearing witness, including the spirit behind the words or actions. There is a prime example in Malachi 4:5–6. The prophet revealed that God would send Elijah to earth before the great and terrible day of the Lord to turn the hearts of the fathers to the children. When John the Baptist was baptizing in the wilderness, some suggested he was Elijah, although John did no miracles. John was baptizing in the Jordan not far from the valley where Elijah was translated to heaven, just outside of Jericho (2 Kings 2). The close proximity to the area and the anticipation of a coming Messiah created this speculation concerning John the Baptist. John's father Zacharias was told by Gabriel that John would come "in the spirit and power of Elijah" (Luke 1:17), yet John said he was not Elijah but the voice of one crying in the wilderness (John 1:21–23). John knew who he was and was not deceived into believing he was someone that he wasn't.

In the past there have been outstanding men of God with widespread influence who were somehow deceived into believing they were the fulfillment of Malachi 4:5, the Elijah that should come. One such man was a minister named John Alexander Dowie, who witnessed thousands of miracles through his prayers and eventually formed a Christian city. Dowie later dressed in a Jewish high priest's garment and called himself *Elijah*. Shortly after this "Elijah deception" spread, he died as a result of a stroke.[1]

Another man, named William Branham, had some of the most remarkable operations of spiritual gifts that people had seen for many years. Branham was uneducated, and in his later years some followers attempted to convince him that he was one of the two witnesses in Revelation 11, and that he might even be Elijah. I am personally acquainted with a man who played the organ in Branham's meetings. Weeks before Branham's death he told this man and another minister that God was going to take him to heaven because people were beginning to worship him, and the Lord was not going to permit it. Word was out that Branham said he was Elijah, but his closest ministry friends said this was not true. Branham believed there was a spirit of Elijah upon him (like John experienced), but it was people who admired him to the level of believing he was Elijah. A few weeks later Branham was killed in an automobile accident.

If a person knows the Scripture, he or she understands that Elijah the prophet, who was translated to heaven (2 Kings 2), will return to Jerusalem for forty-two months as one of the two witnesses in Revelation 11. He will reappear as a full-grown man and will not be a man who is born on earth and who grows from infancy into manhood. He will appear in Israel—not in America, and he is not incarcerated in prison right now for dealing drugs and about to be released (as indicated by one letter I received from a man who was incarcerated).

Another example is that of small groups in rural mountain churches who teach snake handling as a "sign" of their faith. In Mark 16:18 the Bible does say, "They will take up serpents." However, a closer look at the phrase "take up" reveals no indication of parading around with a rattlesnake hanging from your neck. The Greek word for "take up" is *airo* (pronounced *ah'ee-ro*) and can mean, to "take up or to take away." It can also mean, "do away with, gear up, put away and remove."[2] The actual intent of the verse indicates to do as Paul did when he was accidentally bitten by a deadly viper on an island—he shook the snake off into the fire and felt no harm (Acts 28:5).

Missionaries and evangelists from Christ's day until today often travel through rugged and dangerous terrain to reach the lost, encountering serpents, scorpions, and wild beasts in their travels. Christ was giving a promise of protection from danger, not an opportunity for a show of the flesh to demonstrate one's faith. Based upon the Word of God and common sense, snake handling only scares unbelievers, so there is no edification. However, if in traveling in a foreign field someone is accidentally bitten and does not die, then this becomes a *sign* to those who witness it.

When judging the spirit of a thing, we must remember that there is the *letter* of the law and the *spirit* of the law. The letter is the exact wording of the law, and the spirit of the law reveals the reason God gave the law. The letter says, "You shall not commit adultery" (Deut. 5:18), and the letter says clearly that if you do so, you will be stoned to death under Mosaic Law (Lev. 20:10). However, Jesus revealed the spirit of the law when He forgave a woman caught in adultery and told her to sin no more (John 8:1–11). I have seen ministers preach in an almost hateful way, calling other ministers' names to "expose" their teachings to others. However, the letter brings the judgment, but the spirit brings the mercy.

Believers must try the spirits because in the time of the end there will be a strong spirit of deception that will turn people from the truth. People are actually being clearly *deceived* and at the same time are making a justification for their deceptions.

One of the most noted examples was when a woman on a church staff was having a fifteen-year affair with the pastor of a large church. She confronted him as to how he could encourage this when it was contrary to the Bible. His alleged response was that he was in the highest position of an archbishop, and the archbishop was not under the biblical restrictions of other bishops. Such "activity" was permitted as she was "ministering to the needs of the man of God." Their actions were totally contrary to both Testaments, and both were breaking covenants, yet the deception justified the actions. Another pastor would have certain staff members over to his home after the Sunday evening service, where they would eat and "fellowship." After eating, the pastor would say, "Are you all ready for some fun?" The group would go into the basement and either watch XXX-rated movies or, at times, swap wives and have sexual relations.

A stunning example has been seen when ministers of large churches have publicly stood before their congregations and confessed they were living a bisexual lifestyle. Others confessed they were closet homosexuals or, in some cases, lesbians. It would seem that if a person has read and studied Romans chapter 1, he or she would ask for prayer and step down from ministry for counseling. However, in most cases they simply split the church and captivate a following who accept their lifestyle, joining them in the new church that is *released from legalistic traditional Christian views.*

Common Deceptions

There are more common deceptions being accepted in the name of Christian liberty, when, in reality, they are appealing to the fleshly desires of the persons. Below is a list of some common deceptions impacting Christians and churches.

"God told me to leave my wife for this more spiritual woman."

There have been ministers in churches who have literally moved from one wife to another and eventually to a third wife, using the excuse that "God had not put me with my previous wife." He was seeking out a woman who would be more spiritual and could be a better helper in the ministry. However, according to the New Testament, the only scriptural grounds for a divorce for believers is if one of the partners commits fornication or adultery (Matt. 5:32). Marital unfaithfulness is not to be used as an excuse just to get rid of your companion, whom you really didn't care about to begin with, so you can now have a legal right to replace him or her for someone you have been looking at for some time. The highest level of spirituality is not to divorce and replace, but to be able to forgive, if the offending person is humble and desires to remain in the marriage.

"God told me tithing is wrong and under the Law, and we are not under the Law."

There are entire Internet blogs that are designed to discourage believers from tithing to their local church. The reason they give is that according to their "in-depth research," tithing is under the Law, and we are not under the Law. Therefore we are not required to tithe. These individuals don't know the Scriptures. The tithe is the tenth, and Abraham paid the tithe to Melchizedek more than four hundred years before the Law was given. (See Genesis 14.) It was about three hundred years before the Law that Jacob also promised to give the tithe to the Lord if the Lord would bring him back safely in the land (Gen. 28:22).

In the New Testament Christ instructed people that tithing was a good thing (Matt. 23:23). Long after Christ was resurrected from the dead, the writer of the Book of Hebrews said, "Here mortal men receive tithes, but there he receives them, of whom it is witnessed that he lives" (Heb. 7:8). Thus tithing is also a part of the new covenant practice and not just part of the Law.

"God told me to stay home and not go to church."

More Americans today than ever before no longer attend church. I have heard people say how they drink their coffee and watch their favorite minister on Sunday morning or log on to the Internet, as through this is the same as being in God's house. There are some who are physically unable to attend church because of infirmities or age, and at times older believers may not be able to drive; thus gospel programming serves them well. However, for those in good health and with a car and fuel, your lack of attending a local gathering may be a spiritual issue of laziness, because to say, "God told me not to go," is contrary to Hebrews 10:24–25:

> And let us consider one another in order to stir up love and good works, not forsaking the assembling of ourselves together, as is the manner of some, but exhorting one another, and so much the more as you see the Day approaching.

If we believe that the Lord is coming soon, then this passage indicates we should not forsake the assembling of ourselves together. The Greek word for "assembling" is *episunagoge*, which refers to a complete collection, especially of Christians who meet together for worship. The word *forsaking* means, "to leave behind in some place, let remain over, or to desert." It means don't leave others behind in an assembly and desert them!

This is why a person's words, actions, and even statements that "God said to them…" must be in line with the revealed Word of God. Remember these three facts:

1. The Holy Spirit will never contradict the written Word of God, especially the instruction and revelation in the New Testament.

2. Those whose spirits have been redeemed will bear witness that what is being heard is from the Lord.

3. The Holy Spirit is not the author of confusion and division, so any type of words or actions that cause a split or run people away is usually the flesh of others rising up.

We need the community of fellowship found in a local body of believers.

"God told me that that music was not of God."

I cannot tell you the number of times I have heard a person comment that someone or something was "not of God." What I have also learned is that this can be a cop-out for spiritual laziness. Instead of the accuser taking the time to study and research the alleged information, it is easier to shout out, "That teaching is not of God." I once saw a young man on television judging the style of music in the local churches today. His traditional upbringing was in older, Southern Gospel music and many of the old hymns. He began, in "his" terms, "exposing" a major youth ministry whose music was "worldly, demonic, and was not of God!"

I happened to know and work closely with the youth ministry he proclaimed was not of God, and in reality, that ministry has seen more youth born again and filled with the Holy Spirit in one year than the screaming young man has witnessed in his lifetime. Thus, the *fruit* is what counts and is evidence of God's blessing—not the *method* or *style*. He was judging what he personally liked or didn't like. If it fit his traditions, it was "of God," and if it didn't, it was "not of God." Anyone with the gift of discerning of spirits could detect that his tone, attitude, and spirit behind his statements were expressed in the wrong manner and wrong attitude.

Never judge others by the opinions of others, and never determine what is and is not from God upon the twisted or biased comments of self-appointed watchdogs of Christianity. Many good ministers have been labeled false prophets by men who simply have a theological disagreement with another person's teaching. I once saw another minister on television calling out names of men and women who had impacted entire nations with the gospel. He was like a raging pit bull, screaming at the camera and telling the world that, "These so-called ministers are not of God!" When I heard this, I was reminded of James and

John, who demanded that Christ call fire down upon the Samaritans. Christ replied, "You do not know what manner of spirit you are of" (Luke 9:55). James and John had a political-social disagreement with the Samaritans that historically dated back to the time of Nehemiah. Christ saw a spirit of *revenge* and not one of *revival* in the hearts of two of His disciples, whom He rebuked.

When we think of *testing a spirit*, we often think of evil entities— the types of spirits possessing a person. However, we must also discern and test the statements of ministers. Are their comments coming from their own spirits instead of the Spirit of God? Are they speaking out of their own bitterness in order to retaliate against a person with whom they have an offense? Never fall for the deception of offense, as dwelling in an offense will bring open the door to a spirit that is truly not of God.

Chapter Ten

WHAT DOES GOD THINK ABOUT WOMEN PREACHERS?

Let your women keep silent in the churches, for they are not permitted to speak; but they are to be submissive, as the law also says.

—1 Corinthians 14:34

BEFORE DELVING INTO this rather controversial subject, let me, from the outset, make three important points. First, the Scripture has taught that in the last days sons and daughters would prophecy (Joel 2:28). *Daughters*, in Hebrew, is *bath*, and is simply, "a daughter." In Acts 2:17 the Greek word for "daughters" refers to a female child. Both words are clear references to females. Both sons (males) and daughters (females) will prophesy. In Acts 2:18 Peter mentions "handmaidens" (KJV), which in Greek is *doulos* and refers to a female servant or slave, or one who involuntarily or voluntarily serves a master. In Acts 2:18 the word refers to a female who willfully serves and worships God. These daughters and handmaidens will prophesy. In the King James Version of the Old Testament, the word *prophesy* is found seventy-five times; it is a word used for a person, especially a prophet, who speaks under divine utterance or inspiration. It can include speaking, preaching, teaching, and singing. Thus, daughters will prophesy, or speak under divine utterance in the final outpouring.

The second point is that my own father, Fred Stone, was converted to Christ in the late 1940s in what was marked as the *Great Coalfield Revival*, a revival that continued for about forty-two months, going from church to church with the featured speaker, a woman named Mildred Collins. Out of this extraordinary revival, under Mildred's ministry, three hundred souls were converted to Christ, and seventy young men were called into the gospel ministry as missionaries, pastors, and evangelists. Dad always maintained a respect for women who served as evangelists, because his own life and ministry was impacted by "Sister Mildred."

The third point is that I was raised in a denomination that acknowledged that men and women could receive the gift of the Holy Spirit (as the prediction says, "all flesh"), and women could also be used in the teaching and preaching gift. In fact, when I was growing up, my father pastored in a rural town, and one of the prominent nominal ministers taught from his pulpit that if the full gospel churches would sit the women down and make them keep silent the way the Scripture instructed, then, "All those tongues would cease." My father reminded him that this spiritual gift didn't originate with women and would not end with women, but it began with God and would conclude when God's kingdom and Christ returned to earth, or when the perfect one would come (1 Cor. 13:8–10). Being raised around powerful female teachers in Sunday school classes and female evangelists, I have witnessed the unction of the Spirit upon their words and instructions from my earliest days.

Scripture and Women Ministers

Because of my early family link with women ministers, some may suggest I cannot deal with this subject in a balanced or fair manner. However, my opinions matter little, as it is the Scriptures that must be properly understood and interpreted to give us proper understanding.

One of the two main passages used to teach that a woman must never speak in a public church setting is penned in 1 Corinthians 14:34–35:

> Let your women keep silent in the churches, for they are not permitted to speak; but they are to be submissive, as the law also says. And if they want to learn something, let them ask their own husbands at home; for it is shameful for women to speak in church.

The second passage used in connection with the above is 1 Timothy 2:11–12:

> Let a woman learn in silence with all submission. And I do not permit a woman to teach or to have authority over a man, but to be in silence.

The Book of Acts is the earliest record of the actions of the Holy Spirit in the lives of the apostles and the first-generation Christian converts. Peter, at Pentecost, quoted Joel, announcing that sons and daughters would prophesy. In Acts 21:9 we read where Phillip had four daughters who prophesied. In the epistles we read where God used husband and wife couples to assist in organizing churches in their homes, and the husband and wife team are both listed working together teaching and instructing. One such couple was Priscilla and Aquila, a dynamic couple who assisted Apollos in understanding the Holy Spirit (Acts 18:24–28). In the Scripture it reads, "They took him aside and explained to him the way of God more accurately"— *they* meaning Aquila and his wife (Acts 18:26). This couple formed a church in their house (Rom. 16:3–5). Paul, in Romans 16:1, lists a woman named Phoebe as a "deaconess" (AMP) and a "servant" (NKJV).

When ministers publicly state that Paul forbade any women to speak in the church, they will have difficulty explaining another instruction that Paul gave in 1 Corinthians 11:5:

> But every woman who prays or prophesies with her head uncovered dishonors her head, for that is one and the same as if her head were shaved.

In this reference Paul acknowledges that women both prayed and prophesied in the church. Is this a clear contradiction that a woman should *never speak in a church* and yet they are permitted to *pray and prophesy* in the church? Going back to the "let the woman keep silent" passage, Paul followed this injunction with these words, "And if they want to learn something, let them ask their own husbands at home" (1 Cor. 14:35). This is actually the second half of the verse that explains the keep silent admonition. In the Jewish culture, at the temple there was a court of the women where the women were permitted to watch the procedures of the temple, and there was also a Gentile partition restricting Gentiles from entering past a certain point. In the Jewish synagogues men sat on the main floor, and the women were permitted in the balconies. Today in Israel at the famous Western Wall, the men pray on the left and the women pray on the right, with a stone wall separating the two. Thus in the Jewish culture, the man and woman sit separate.

Many scholars believe that the passage on women keeping silent was not related to praying or prophesying, but it was written to prevent the occurrence that when a speaker was speaking, the women sitting in a separate area from their husbands would disrupt the service by asking their husbands for further explanations *right then*, thus creating confusion. Paul instructed the women to learn from their husbands when they were at home in order to prevent a public disruption and confusion. Greek scholars have pointed out that in that culture the men attended the synagogues and were educated, while the women had children and performed the task of being a wife and mother. Thus the educated men taught their wives in private. Paul is not dealing with the subject of women preachers but of discipline during a religious service.[1]

The theme of Paul's admonition is women speaking in the church. There are two important words for "speak" and "speaking" that must be understood in relation to a woman not speaking in the church. They are the Greek verbs *laleo* and *lego*. The word *laleo* refers to the ability or use of the organs of speech, giving a sound, utterance, or expressing words with your voice. *Lego* means to speak in the sense of declaring an intelligible message. According to Greek scholars, *laleo* emphasizes the outward form of speech, and *lego* refers to the substance and meaning of what has been spoken. In brief, *laleo* refers to the act of speaking, while *lego* declares what the speaker actually says.[2]

The Greek word *laleo* is also used for the sounds made by birds, insects, bees, and even the sound of a trumpet (Rev. 4:1), the sound of thunder (Rev. 10:3–4), voice of the dragon speaking (Rev. 13:11), and the speaking voice given to image of the beast (Rev. 13:15). The word was also used by Greeks when infants would jabber before they could actually articulate words. The root of the word *laleo* is *lal*, illustrating the effort of a child to make its first sounds—"la, la, la."

To understand the context of a woman keeping silent, Paul does not use the word for a woman making intelligent words or speech, but the word for making sounds. He was saying they should not be "la-laing" around in the church. It was about disturbing the service and not about teaching and instructing with an intelligent sound and voice. Obviously women were permitted to pray and prophesy and were active in ministry. (See Acts 21:9; Acts 18:24–28; Romans 16:1–6; 1 Corinthians 11:5.)

In 1 Timothy 2:11–12 Paul wrote that the women were not to "usurp authority over the man" (KJV). The Greek word for "usurp" is *authenteo* and means, "to act upon your own, or to dominate over." Look at the word "silence." In 1 Corinthians 14:28, if a person speaks out loud in tongues in a church service and no one interprets, then they are to "keep silence" (KJV). This Greek word is *sigao* and means, "to hold your peace and say nothing else." It is used when the multitude kept silent while Paul and Barnabas were speaking (Acts 15:12) and when Paul gave a speech before a group of men (Acts 21:40). In 1 Corinthians 14:34 Paul said for the women to keep silent, and he used this word, *sigao*—to say nothing—as they were disturbing the speaker by interrupting. As the minister spoke, they were to listen and not ask at that time for explanations.

A great example of this occurs to this day on the mission fields. In the large outdoor meetings where numerous unbelievers are attending, it is common that while the speaker is speaking, men and women in attendance will begin talking out loud, either to counter a statement made by the speaker or to begin asking questions of others sitting near them. Many missionaries, who minister in nations such as India, have witnessed this firsthand. Because they are speaking by using a large public address system, they are not disturbed by this activity as much as when it occurs in a small rural area where hundreds are packing out a small building. This type of interruption of the speaker by individuals in the congregation was what many scholars believe Paul was addressing, especially in his letter to the Corinthians.

However, in 1 Timothy 2:11, when women are told to keep silence, the Greek word for "silence" is different from the word used in 1 Corinthians 14:34. This Greek word, *hesuchia*, is a word meaning, "more of being still and in quietness, or figuratively away from the bustle and the noise." Paul is saying, "Let them be at peace and not attempt to rise up against the spiritual authority of the men in the church." If men were teaching, then women were to be subject to the male teachers, and not rise up and challenge their authority.

When a person reads 1 Corinthians 14:34 and 1 Timothy 2:11 without researching textual and historical context, it would seem Paul was very much against women saying or doing anything in a church setting. However, the Greek words, the context, and the cultural traditions of the day have a bearing upon understanding the intent of Paul's instructions. Paul was blessed to have many co-laborers, including numerous women, who assisted him in ministry. We read:

> I implore Euodia and I implore Syntyche to be of the same mind in the Lord. And I urge you also, true companion, help these women who labored with me in the gospel, with Clement also, and the rest of my fellow workers, whose names are in the Book of Life.
> —PHILIPPIANS 4:2–3

Consider also the numerous women linked with Christ's ministry. When Mary presented the infant Christ at the temple, a female prophetess named Anna saw the Christ child and gave a wonderful prophecy under the inspiration of the Holy Spirit (Luke 2:36–38). One man suggested that Anna was living under the old covenant and not during the church age, where God demanded silence from the women. How strange is that? A woman could prophesy for four thousand years, but after Pentecost and the birth of the church God only used men and made the women sit down! Miriam (Exod. 15:20), Deborah (Judg. 4:4), Huldah (2 Kings 22:14), Naodiah (Neh. 6:14), and Isaiah's wife (Isa. 8:3) were all specifically called *prophetesses* in the Old Testament. Philip had four virgin daughters who operated in the prophetic gift under the new covenant (Acts 21:9). The evidence is that God permits men and women to participate in His spiritual charismata. In Luke 8:1–2 several wealthy women ministered to Christ of their substance:

> And the twelve were with Him, and certain women who had been healed of evil spirits and infirmities—Mary called Magdalene, out of whom had come seven demons, and Joanna the wife of Chuza, Herod's steward, and Susanna, and many others who provided for Him from their substance.
>
> —LUKE 8:1–3

If we move from the ministry of Christ to the time of His sufferings, all of His chosen eleven disciples fled the scene except the apostle John (Mark 14; John 19). However, dedicated women were present, including Mary, the mother of Christ, who was given into the care of the apostle John. When the disciples were hiding behind locked doors and windows for fear of their lives, it was two women with the same name, Mary, who journeyed to the tomb at about sunrise to anoint Christ's body (Matt. 28:1). After Christ's ascension to heaven there were women, including Mary, the mother of Christ, present during the early meetings in Jerusalem prior to the outpouring of the Holy Spirit (Acts 1:14). While the men ran away, the women remained and became the first to announce the good news that Christ was resurrected (Matt. 28:7). Today they would be termed an *evangelist*, or one who bring good news.

The Deaconess

Most churches are familiar with male deacons, but few know about female deaconesses. The earliest biblical mention of a female deacon was when Paul wrote in Romans 16:1, "I commend to you Phoebe our sister, who is a servant of the church in Cenchrea." The Greek word for "servant" in this verse is not the normal Greek word *doulos*, used in the New Testament for a slave or servant, but it is the Greek word *diakonos*, which is an attendant in ministry, one who assists or is a teacher or pastor.

When the Christian church split between the West (Catholic) and the East (Byzantine, later termed the Orthodox), the Eastern church permitted women to serve in the position of deaconess. A deaconess was a female who served to help in the work of the ministry. The ministry of a deaconess was mentioned by the early fathers Clement of Alexandria and Origen.[3] The deaconess was generally a widow who had been married only once, although sometimes the position was filled by virgins. Their ministry functions included certain pastoral duties, including baptizing the women converts in the congregation, caring for those who were imprisoned, and assisting in comforting the persecuted. The deaconess also assisted the women who had given birth to children and visited with members of their own sex.[4]

In the third century, in Syria, a document called *Apostolorum Didascalia*, expressed that the bishop, "Appoint…a woman for the ministry of women. For there are homes to which you cannot send a male deacon to their women, on the account of the heathen, but you may send a deaconess. Also, because in many other matters the office of a woman deacon is required."[5] In the fifth century the Apostolic Constitutions recorded the instance of a bishop laying hands upon the women and calling down the Holy Spirit for the ministry of the diaconate.[6]

No one would read the New Testament and deny that the women were actively involved in the ministry and support of the church. However, the issue has been a woman who teaches or is a pastor of a congregation. One of the significant changes that occurred under the new covenant when the Gentiles were grafted into the Abrahamic blessing was the change in how God viewed both men and women in the body of Christ. The Jewish tradition was that women were less significant than men and had no spiritual authority except a few rare instances where the Spirit of God moved upon them (as the case of Deborah in Judges 4–5).

One of the significant passages that may give the best summary of men and women, Jews and Gentiles in the body of Christ is the following:

> There is neither Jew nor Greek, there is neither slave nor free, there is neither male nor female; for you are all one in Christ Jesus. And if you are Christ's, then you are Abraham's seed, and heirs according to the promise.
> —GALATIANS 3:28–29

Under the new covenant the blood of Christ makes all believers one in faith and one family of God. There are no racial or ethnic divisions, and all men and women are formed in God's image. The covenant gives each individual access to the fullness of God's spiritual blessings.

The Fried Pie People

Some of my fondest and clearest memories are from age five to nine when my father pastored a small rural church in the town of Big Stone Gap, in the mountains of southwestern Virginia. I can recall that the church attendance averaged about sixty, and on special occasions more than one hundred would attend. At that time the church consisted mostly of older women and just a few men and a few young couples. In order to pay the expenses of the church mortgage, the heating and light bills, and parsonage payment, the precious older women would take one day a week and bake the best fruit pies or chicken dinners in the community, selling them at bake sales and businesses in the community. My dad and mom both said many times that without the dedicated work of the women, the church and ministry could have closed, unable to pay expenses. With a shortage of men to teach, women were needed to teach the children, teens, and the young couple's classes.

In the first century the church met in homes, and many of the church gatherings were hosted by godly women who opened their doors for the converts to break bread and be taught the Scriptures. In the last chapter of Romans (chapter 16) Paul lists numerous individuals, including women, who assisted him in the ministry.

With the global harvest so ripe, and Christ saying we should pray laborers into the harvest (Matt. 9:38), we must acknowledge that the sons and daughters will be the key to the final outpouring and be instrumental in reaping souls from around the world. God will use sons and daughters, servants and handmaidens, and men and women to bring in the harvest that ripens after the rain of the Spirit prepares the souls for harvesting.

Chapter Eleven

THE CODE CONCEALED
IN THE MENORAH

> He also made the lampstand of pure gold; of hammered
> work he made the lampstand. Its shaft, its branches, its
> bowls, its ornamental knobs, and its flowers were of
> the same piece. And six branches came out of its sides:
> three branches of the lampstand out of one side, and
> three branches of the lampstand out of the other side.
>
> —Exodus 37:17–18

SPIRITUAL MYSTERIES ARE concealed in the cycles, patterns, symbols, and types and shadows penned in the Torah and throughout the prophetic Scriptures. A powerful mystery is concealed in one of the sacred pieces of furniture created for the wilderness tabernacle. Moses was instructed to take a sheet of gold and create a seven-branched candlestick—one central shaft and three shafts on the left and right side. In Hebrew this golden lampstand is called the *menorah*.

In Exodus 37:19 the bowls of the menorah are shaped like almonds. The almond was considered a sacred fruit among the priesthood of Israel, as Aaron was divinely selected as high priest after his rod began producing leaves and almonds overnight. The menorah was created out of one sheet of pure gold with three branches facing west of the center shaft and three branches facing east. The center shaft was called the *ner Elohim*, or the *lamp of God* and the *shamash*, the *servant's lamp*. It is also called the western lamp as it was positioned west of the three eastern lamps. Each lamp held six eggs of olive oil, and when burning, the oil lasted for about one day and had to be replenished each morning by a priest serving at the tabernacle and later the temple.[1]

According to Philo, the menorah was a symbol of the heavens, with the center shaft being the sun and the side branches symbolizing the three months of the four seasons (winter, spring, summer, and fall). The lamps remained lit night and day like the stars.[2] The Jewish historian Josephus wrote of the menorah and the seven branches representing the seven lights of heaven—five planets (Mercury, Venus, Mars, Jupiter, and Saturn) and the sun and moon.[3] It can also be noted that the servant lamp or center shaft is the fourth lamp when counting the lamps from both the left and right side of the menorah. This is significant, as this lamp is the most significant of the others. The sun, which gives light to the entire earth, was created on the fourth day of creation (Gen. 1:16–19), thus the idea that this center lamp represented the sun.

The Seven Feasts and the Menorah

The temple menorah had seven branches. The number seven is the most spiritually significant number. The ancient nations named seven planets. The week was divided into seven days, and the seventh day was a rest cycle. Every seventh year and every seven times seven years was marked as a season of jubilee. There is a count of seven weeks between Passover and Pentecost. Thus, the seven arms of the menorah can also represent seven days of the week, with the center shaft representing the Sabbath.

Another amazing code is found in how the seven branches on the menorah can also match the seven appointed feasts of Israel. The chart below reveals this parallel between the seven lamps and the order of the seven feasts celebrated yearly in Israel:

Israel's Feasts and the Menorah

First branch	Passover
Second branch	Unleavened Bread
Third branch	Firstfruits
Fourth branch	PENTECOST
Fifth branch	Trumpets
Sixth branch	Atonement
Seventh branch	Tabernacles

The Feast of Pentecost is the fourth feast in the order of the seven. Pentecost would be linked with the servant branch or the lamp of God on the menorah! The three spring feasts—Passover, Unleavened Bread, and Firstfruits (first through third branches)—all lead up to the servant branch of Pentecost. Then we see that following Pentecost, the next three branches (fifth, sixth, and seventh) lead into the three fall feasts of Trumpets, Atonement, and Tabernacles.

The bowls on the top of the seven shafts holding the oil were in the shape of almonds (Exod. 25:33–34; 37:19–20), which is a reminder of the human tongue. The almond-shaped bowls with the sacred oil were lit by a wick being placed in the narrow opening of each bowl, positioned on top of the shafts. Thus the seven lights on the menorah were like small *tongues of fire* glowing with light and fueled by oil. On the Day of Pentecost, tongues like fire fell upon the believers, baptizing them with the Holy Spirit and with fire (Matt. 3:11), as the oil (anointing) of the Holy Spirit was placed within these human lamps. The light of the gospel would be spread to the nations as these early believers opened their mouths and began to speak God's Word! Their words of fire pierced the darkness of the world and brought illumination and light.

Thus, Pentecost and the menorah speak to us that as the menorah served to light the holy place, the Spirit of Pentecost is to bring the light of the gospel to the nations, just as it did in Acts 2 when the Spirit baptized believers, enabling them to go into all the world and preach the gospel (Mark 16:15).

The menorah held oil that needed to be *replenished*. In Acts 2:1–4 the disciples were all filled with the Holy Spirit on the Day of Pentecost.

However, in Acts chapters 3–4, persecution began to break out against the church. In Acts 4:31 they were all filled with the Spirit and spoke the Word of God with boldness. These were some of the same people who received in Acts 2. Many believe that the stressful level of persecution required a fresh *refilling* of the Holy Spirit. Just as the menorah required fresh oil, all believers need to continually be filled and refilled with the Spirit.

Another observation is that all other branches (six) are aligned around the center shaft. In Isaiah 11:2 the prophet identifies six major manifestations of the Holy Spirit that are also linked with the Messiah:

> The Spirit of the LORD shall rest upon Him,
> The Spirit of wisdom and understanding,
> The Spirit of counsel and might,
> The Spirit of knowledge and of the fear of the LORD.

The central branch on the menorah is the servant branch or a picture of the "Spirit of the Lord." Three manifestations are wisdom, understanding, and counsel, and the three others are might, knowledge, and fear of the Lord. Thus the six manifestations of the Spirit in Isaiah 11:2 are parallel with the six branches of the menorah, three on either side of the servant branch.

The Menorah Is a Him

Moses constructed six major pieces of sacred furniture: the brass altar, brass laver, menorah, table of showbread, golden altar, and the ark of the covenant. Some say there were seven items when counting the lid of the ark of the covenant, called the mercy seat (Exod. 25:17–22). This seat was the gold lid and the two cherubim beaten out of pure gold that were placed as the covering on the top of the ark of the covenant. God said that on the Day of Atonement He would come down and commune with the high priest from between the wings of the cherubim (v. 22). Thus the covering was similar to a seat as God descended upon the ark to extend His mercy to His people.

Something rather odd is observed in Exodus chapter 25. The sacred furniture is neither male nor female, and the ark, the veil, the atonement, the laver, and the oil are all called "it," a word that is considered neuter, meaning neither male nor female. It is a piece of furniture, thus an object. Notice in Exodus 25:31 (KJV), where Moses is instructed by God to make the golden candlestick, the language identifying the menorah changes from *it* to *him*. The menorah's chief substance was olive oil, which was renewed daily by the priest in the seven lamps that were like cups holding a half log of oil. The old, burnt wicks were replaced with new ones. In fact, the wicks used to light the flame were prepared from worn-out tunics and turbans of the priests.[4] Notice that the pronoun *his* is used five times:

> And thou shalt make a candlestick of pure gold: of beaten work shall the candlestick be made: his shaft, and his branches, his bowls, his knops, and his flowers, shall be of the same.
> —EXODUS 25:31, KJV

In Exodus God suddenly shifted from calling His furniture "it" to the personal pronoun "His" (Exod. 26:19, KJV; 27:2–3, 11, KJV). This is odd since the menorah is not a person but an object made of gold. *However, all of this furniture was in some manner a type or symbols representing "him," the Messiah or the Holy Spirit.* Also, the entire tabernacle was constructed from living items—such as the skins of animals needed for the coverings and the wood from trees necessary for the beams and the sacred furniture. To the Almighty this was not just a portable tent, but it was constructed as a living and breathing dwelling place where sins were covered and death was exchanged for life through the blood sacrifices and priestly rituals.

It stands to reason that not only did the menorah represent the Holy Spirit Himself, but also in the Book of Revelation the seven candles represent the seven main churches in Asia that Christ addressed through John. The term "him" was not a literal person but was used, I believe, to reveal that behind the natural light was the light from *Him, the Holy Spirit Himself.*

The Menorah and the Church

John experienced a vision while on the island of Patmos in which he saw Christ standing in heaven before seven golden candlesticks. Some suggest these were seven separate and individual candles; however, it appears to be a heavenly menorah, since the earthly menorah was patterned after the heavenly menorah (Exod. 25:40; Heb. 8:5). Each of the seven branches represents one of the seven churches listed in Revelation chapters 2 and 3, as we read, "…and the seven lampstands which you saw are the seven churches" (Rev. 1:20). The seven churches listed in Revelation chapters 2 and 3 are:

- Ephesus
- Smyrna
- Pergamos
- Thyatira
- Sardis
- Philadelphia
- Laodicea

The Holy Spirit is the light of the church, just as the menorah lit the holy place, enabling the priest to have illumination to minister. In Revelation the imagery of Christ's message to the seven churches reflects a specific activity performed by the ancient Jewish priesthood. Every morning the oil and wicks were replaced in the temple menorah, as fresh oil was required to keep the lamps burning. A lamp gone out indicated a lack of oil. The seven branches and lamps represent these seven main churches in John's day. However, five churches were rebuked by Christ for their disobedience or sin, and only two—Philadelphia and Smyrna—were commended. Christ rebuked the church at Ephesus, saying, "Remember therefore from where you have fallen; repent and do the first works, or else I will come to you quickly and remove your lampstand from its place—unless you repent" (Rev. 2:5–6). Christ indicated that without repentance the church would eventually cease to exist, and the city of Ephesus would be in darkness. Thus the oil, a picture of the anointing of the Spirit, brings illumination and light to the church, which, in turn, shines on a dark world, breaking the darkness surrounding people.

From Oil to Wine

Along with oil, another imagery of the Holy Spirit is wine, a product of the grape harvest. As oil represents the anointing, wine represents the joy emanating from a Spirit-filled life. In one of Christ's parables He points out how new wine has an effect on old wineskins.

> Nor do they put new wine into old wineskins, or else the wineskins break, the wine is spilled, and the wineskins are ruined. But they put new wine into new wineskins, and both are preserved.
> —Matthew 9:17

In the KJV the word *bottles* is used. The Greek word is *askos* and refers to a leather wineskin used to store wine, water, or other liquids. This leather bottle was usually made from goatskin, with the four legs being sewed up and the skin of the neck used for the opening where a person could pour or drink from the skin bottle. Once filled, the neck-like opening was tied up to prevent seepage. Wineskin bottles were used in a home, a tent, or when journeying to preserve whatever liquid was needed. In Christ's narrative fresh wine is stored in the bottle.[5]

The difficulty for a wineskin is the effect the outward atmosphere and conditions can have upon the skin itself. This is especially true in a hot, desert setting. If the skin remains continually in sunlight or has been exposed over time to an abundance of smoke from fires where food was being prepared, the heat, light, and smoke actually dry up the skin, eventually making it hard and outwardly brittle. In the parable of Christ He taught that if fresh juice from the grapes was placed in an old, dry wineskin, eventually fermenting, the expansion from the fermentation within the skin would push out the skin, causing cracks to a dry wineskin, which in turn would cause the wine to leak from its container.

There are numerous spiritual lessons to be learned from this parable. First, what is inside of you will eventually be manifest through the heart, and from the heart will precede the issues (actions) of your life. Thus, internal pressure eventually pushes out of you what is concealed on the inside of you. You can wear a mask, fake people out with your smile, and act like everything is smooth as silk until pressure is placed on you and stress builds. Then suddenly tempers flare, and you begin spewing out bitter and hateful words. You may say, "Why did I do that?" Christ taught that, "Out of the abundance of the heart the mouth speaks" (Matt. 12:34).

In this parable the wine represents the Holy Spirit that dwells in a human body made of *skin*. The Bible speaks of the new wine, which at times is a metaphor for the infilling of the Holy Spirit. On the Day of Pentecost the newly filled believers were accused of being drunk on "new wine" (Acts 2:13). The skin is the vessel or container that holds the wine, or is filled with the Holy Spirit. As the Holy Spirit attempts to expand His presence, joy, righteousness, and manifestations within us, we will either submit to His will or resist and rebel against the changes God desires to make in us. Our resistance to the Holy Spirit's flow within us will eventually form cracks in our spiritual life, which causes the joy, peace, and presence of God to leak out of our own spirit.

When God *gets under your skin*, it will stretch your traditions, thinking, attitude, and often your theology and opinions of spiritual manifestations. I have met thousands of individuals during my ministry who found it necessary to change their own self-interpretation or traditional concepts of the Holy Spirit to accommodate the dynamic work the Spirit was doing in their own lives. One rather humorous example occurred in Lamarque, Texas, when more than one hundred individuals from various backgrounds came forward to receive the baptism in the Holy Spirit. Directly in front of me were a woman and her daughter. When the Spirit came upon them, they both began to speak in the prayer language of the Spirit. The older woman began saying, "Oh my, I can't be doing this!" Then she would laugh and speak with new tongues. She said again, "Oh my, I'm not supposed to do this!"

I told her, "Yes, you can, and yes, you are. The Lord has filled you with His Spirit."

She replied, "You don't understand. I have two brothers in the ministry who have taught that tongues ceased, and anyone who does this is either delusional or has an evil spirit possessing them. Now what will I tell them?" Then she began to laugh with her daughter. In her case the wineskin had been stretched to receive the new wine of the Spirit!

The Agitation and the Wineskin

The true presence of God that is felt or seen through manifestations always brings one of three reactions: excitement to the believer, questions for an honest-hearted seeker, and a resistance to anyone with an unbelieving spirit. In Matthew 8, when a demon-possessed man fell at Christ's feet, the chief demon possessing him said to Christ, "Have you come here to torment us before the time?" (Matt. 8:29). The Greek word for "torment" is *basanizo,* which means, "to torture someone or create pain." The overwhelming light and presence of Christ so overpowered the darkness that the evil spirits within the man felt tormented and in pain just to be in Christ's presence. This may be why in several New Testament cases of deliverance the evil spirits would scream out or throw the person to the ground as this glorious light of Christ pierced the darkness. The light exposed the tormentor and paved a path of deliverance to expel those unwelcome intruders from the bodies of those possessed (Mark 9:22; Luke 4:33).

When the clear gospel message is preached on foreign fields outside of the United States among nations with no knowledge of Christ's redemptive covenant, unclean spirits that are being expelled in the name of Christ globally react in the same manner as they did in Christ's day. This indicates the universal influence and power in Christ's name and the fact that all spirits, wherever their stronghold, know His name. All spirits are subject to His name.

The Agitation on Religious People

In the New Testament there were several prominent religious sects that held an iron grip of influence over their followers. These included Pharisees, Sadducees, lawyers, and scribes, all who were "professional believers," often using their religious and social influence to sway public opinion in specific directions. These individuals were all well educated and trained in specialty schools, and some were linked by generations of family members who also clung to the same belief system. Christ's disciples were mostly Galileans—farmers, fishermen, and a tax collector, and to the elite, devout Jerusalem Jews, these fishermen were the uneducated lower class. Once these zealous firebrands began combing the mountains of the Galilee, bringing sinners and commoners to repentance and healing the sick from city to city, the traditional religious sects raised up against them. These simpletons were gaining a massive following among the commoners, who certainly felt more comfortable coming to an outdoor meeting with Jesus than an uptown synagogue in Jerusalem. The disciples of Christ *got under the skin* of the religious stiff-necks.

The Hivite Example

Many stories in the Bible have practical applications for believers today, including one in Joshua chapter 9. Gibeon, a tribe living in the Promised Land, sent representatives to see Joshua. During their journey they encountered heat, poison serpents, scorpions, dry places with no water, and open land without shade trees. The same is true with believers who seek after Christ. We experience fiery trials and verbal "bites" from people being influenced by the enemy, and at times we walk by faith through dry places where our spiritual perception is dull and a refreshing from the Holy Spirit is missing. When the Gibeonites arrived, they informed Joshua, saying:

> This bread of ours we took hot for our provision from our houses on the day we departed to come to you. But now look, it is dry and moldy. And these wineskins which we filled were new, and see, they are torn; and these our garments and our sandals have become old because of the very long journey.
> —JOSHUA 9:12–13

The "trouble in their journey" had affected the life-sustaining elements of bread and water. Their bread had formed mold, their wineskins were battered and ripped, and their shoes and garments had evidence of abuse. Figuratively bread represents the Word (Matt. 4:4), and often the traditions of men will water down the Word, making it of none effect (Matt. 15:6). The skins being torn can be a picture of the abuse and difficult days we experience that cut into our faith and confidence, thus weakening our faith. In the Bible we are instructed to wear special war sandals and be prepared to carry the gospel to distant lands (Eph. 6:15). Yet many believers today are weary in well doing and tired of walking in the dry places.

The bread needs to be fresh manna—or fresh revelation and inspiration every day that feeds your spirit. This is accomplished through personal Bible reading and feeding your spirit from the Word of God through messages, teaching resources, books, and every available tool to keep your spirit strong. The wineskin must be renewed to hold the new wine, and our feet must not be weary in carrying the gospel. The new wine, I believe, that God desires to place in the wineskin is the fresh, end-time outpouring of the Holy Spirit.

Hindrances to the New Wine

However, there are several things that are preventing the new wine from performing its joyful task within believers.

The lessening emphasis on spiritual experiences

Often the North American church becomes so concerned about being active in promoting its denominational interpretation of doctrine that it unwillingly ignores or willfully undermines the importance of having a true experience with Christ. *A man with a true experience is never at the mercy of a man with a theory!* Before there was a doctrine of redemption, there was the experience of Christ's death and resurrection. Long before theologians dissected the operation of spiritual manifestations, there were biblical stories of spiritual manifestations to base the theology upon. Prior to a theological explanation on demonology, numerous individuals in the New Testament were delivered from evil spirits. My point is this: there was first an *experience* before there was a systematic *theology* taught explaining and dissecting those experiences.

With the expansion of knowledge including biblical history, studies on biblical languages (Hebrew, Greek, and Aramaic), and deep discussions and debates, the emphasis has been upon receiving *knowledge* instead of receiving an *experience*. In the Bible there is the letter of the law and the spirit of the law. If we have only the letter, then we will become stiff and only emphasize the intellectual reception of the Word. If we emphasize only the spirit of the law, then we may have manifestations without knowledge. The letter and the spirit should be the power twins of our spiritual growth. Paul wrote:

> Who also made us sufficient as ministers of the new covenant, not of the letter but of the Spirit; for the letter kills, but the Spirit gives life.
> —2 Corinthians 3:6

The exalting of opinions instead of the Word of God

Man's opinions concerning the interpretation of Scripture can at times be based upon certain denominational traditions or their personal upbringing, as were the opinions, customs, and traditions of the Pharisees in Christ's day. Unbiblical personal opinions that stretch or reduce the truth are called *traditions of men*. Christ rebuked the Pharisees for exalting their opinions above the Scripture and told this sect that their traditions had made the Word of God of none effect.

One example is recorded in Matthew 15:1–6. Jesus reminded the Pharisees that God's law required a child to honor his or her father and mother, and if a child cursed his father or mother, a death penalty was meted out to the offender. In ancient Israel it was taught that children provide for their parents once they were unable to work. Money was to be set aside by all the children to care for their parents' needs upon retirement or disability. By Christ's time, however, a change was made in which an adult could take the money reserved for his or her parents and give it to the priests at the temple as a *gift* (called a *korban*). A receipt would be given, and when the time came to provide the money for the parents, the person giving the temple gift was exempt from responsibility. The disgusting aspect was that once the parents died, a person could get the money back by taking the receipt to the temple. Christ said the Pharisees had made the commandment of God of none effect because of their tradition (Matt. 15:6).[6]

Not all traditions are negative actions; some are actually good. Paul wrote, "Therefore, brethren, stand fast and hold the traditions which you were taught, whether by word or our epistle" (2 Thess. 2:15). The Greek word for "traditions" is *paradosis* and means the transmission of a law or precept. Praying every morning at a set time was a tradition of the Jews and is a good tradition to follow. Giving finances every week, or the tithe, is biblical and should be followed. Any tradition based upon Scripture is a good tradition. When, however, ministers or believers begin to exalt their opinions outside of or above the Word of God, then you will hinder the ability of the Word to impact your personal situations. God will confirm His Word, but He is not committed to follow your man-made traditions.

Struggling with the methods of worship versus the *ministry* of worship

Our enjoyment of a specific type of music is usually formed by the music we hear growing up or by the particular style we personally enjoy. If you grew up in the mountains of West Virginia or Kentucky or in southern Ohio, you may enjoy bluegrass gospel music. Tennessee and Alabama are the center of country gospel style music. The most popular music in the southeastern United States is southern gospel music. Even the instruments we either accept or reject in a worship setting are viewed by some as either biblical or not biblical based upon, at times, not the Bible but a person's personal preference. Drums and cymbals are mentioned in Psalm 150. However, some churches refuse to use them in worship. They were great for the tabernacle of David or the ancient temples but too noisy for some local congregations! One man told me he is convinced that, after watching his favorite southern television preacher, the only music in heaven will be southern gospel! I told him, "I guess that makes the four living creatures that are around the throne in Revelation a four-part harmony quartet."

One of the greatest controversies in any local congregation is the *style* of the worship music, including the types of instruments used, the length of the worship, and even the type of the clothing worn by the worship team. Music has split churches, divided members' opinions, and pressured pastors to make changes based up the likes and dislikes of the church's members, especially tithe-paying members.

The challenge is that too many believers have become caught up with the *methods* of worship instead of the *ministry* of worship. True worship is not intended to tickle your senses and bring a smile to you, but to move the divine presence into the worship setting and bring a smile to the face of the Father in heaven. Worship should not replace the Word but should prepare hearts for the Word.

Renewing the Wineskin

When new wine is placed in a dry skin, the skin will not hold the fermentation of the wine. The skin will burst. When the visible operation of God's Spirit is upon the congregation and the style of music and type of worship agitate you, then God is "getting under your (wine) skin!" Your negative attitude is an indicator that your wineskin needs to be renewed. Jesus taught that you must store new wine in new bottles (Matt. 9:17, KJV). The Greek word "new" in "new wine" is *neos* and means, "something brand-new or fresh wine." The Greek word for "new" in "new bottle" (KJV) in *kainos* and can refer to new in the sense of *renewing*, as renewing the quality of the skin. An old wineskin could be renewed by dipping the skin in salty water, which helped to soften it and the salt assisted in killing any bacteria within the skin. Oil is rubbed on the outside of the dry skin to help make it softer. Thus saltwater and oil are necessary to renew the skin.

Scripture speaks of "the washing of regeneration and renewing of the Holy Spirit" (Titus 3:5). The church is to be sanctified and cleansed "with the washing of water by the word" (Eph. 5:26). The renewal of our thoughts is important to allow the expansion of spiritual knowledge to dwell within our minds. The rubbing with oil is the imagery of a fresh anointing, as oil is a picture of the anointing of the Holy Spirit. There have been seasons of extended weariness in my ministry when it was necessary to come apart from the cares of life and ministry and get alone with the Father in prayer and meditating on His Word. My example is that when Christ spent forty days in fasting, isolated in the wilderness, He afterward returned to Galilee "in the power of the Spirit" (Luke 4:14). If the Holy Spirit seems to be getting under your skin, then permit this internal expansion to renew your wineskin and receive the fresh wine of the Spirit.

Chapter Twelve

HOW THE HOLY SPIRIT
BREAKS THE SPIRIT
OF VEXATION

Now godliness with contentment is great gain. For we brought nothing into this world, and it is certain we can carry nothing out. And having food and clothing, with these we shall be content. But those who desire to be rich fall into temptation and a snare, and into many foolish and harmful lusts which drown men in destruction and perdition.

—1 TIMOTHY 6:6–9

A JULY 25, 2012, article by CNN's Jack Cafferty asked the question: "How much money would it take for you to 'feel' wealthy?" The answers in his article were based on the Fidelity Investments Millionaire Outlook Report, a new survey of millionaires that revealed that more than one-quarter of today's millionaires do not feel wealthy but would if they had an extra $5 million!

This report found that the average millionaire is about sixty years old and has at least $3 million in assets. Cafferty concludes, "But for the Donald Trumps of the world, too much money is never enough.

They are driven continually to amass more wealth, buy another company, make another deal. Sometimes not stopping to appreciate what they have. And the accumulation and management of that kind of money involve tremendous stress and energy."[1]

The Fidelity Millionaire Outlook also revealed that 30 percent of today's millionaires are concerned with preserving wealth, and another 20 percent are concerned with generating wealth. Today's millionaires are divided on the current financial environment. Thirty-five percent of millionaires have a negative outlook, 31 percent have a positive outlook, and the remaining 34 percent remain neutral.[2]

The fact is, when it comes to money, enough is never enough for people.

Things Can Bring on Vexation

I once asked individuals what would really make them happy. Some desired a new house fully loaded with the best technology. Others believed that a sudden blessing of huge amounts of money would calm all their fears. Some of the women suggested that if they had a maid, a chef, or a personal cleaning lady, it would be a little "heaven on earth." A few thought it would be exciting to be popular among the community or to travel the world, while a few suggested all they needed to be totally happy would be four paid vacations a year from work.

One of the wealthiest men in biblical history was King Solomon. In 1 Kings 10 Solomon's house was made from cedars of Lebanon. His throne was carved from ivory and covered with gold. When approaching Solomon's throne, a person would see twelve carved lions, six on either side of the throne. In Solomon's day gold and silver were like stones around Jerusalem. Three hundred shields of gold hung on the temple walls—with three pounds of gold in one shield. All the drinking glasses were pure gold. Each year Solomon received gifts of gold, silver, mules, horses, spices, apes, and even peacocks. His abundance led to a building with four thousand stalls for chariots and twelve thousand horsemen. (See also 2 Chronicles 9.) Visitors traveled long distances to hear of his wisdom. The king wrote three thousand proverbs and more than one thousand songs (1 Kings 4:32). Visitors were not just impressed with Solomon's wealth but were overwhelmed at the service of the servants who served:

> And when the queen of Sheba had seen the wisdom of Solomon, the house that he had built, the food on his table, the seating of his servants, the service of his waiters and their apparel, his cupbearers and their apparel, and his entryway by which he went up to the house of the Lord, there was no more spirit in her.
> —2 Chronicles 9:3–4

During his lifetime Solomon wrote three books: the Book of Proverbs, which is addressed to his son, helping the young man to receive knowledge, experience understanding, and walk in wisdom. Solomon penned the Song of Solomon, a love letter to a Shulamite woman he fell in love with. Solomon also gave us the book of Ecclesiastes, a book detailing what he had learned about his experiences in life—both good and bad. In Ecclesiastes Solomon describes life and comments that "all is vanity and vexation of spirit" (Eccles. 1:14, kjv). In this book Solomon used the word "vexation" ten times in the King James Version (Eccles. 1:14, 17; 2:11, 17, 22, 26; 4:4, 6, 16; 6:9). Something that is vain means that it is empty and does not satisfy. *Vexation of spirit* means, "to desire and grope after," or speaks of something that you go for but never reach. In Solomon's case he had seen it all, done it all, and reached a pinnacle of success only to realize that to gain all the fame, wealth, and popularity in the world was vanity.

There are four specific things that Solomon wrote that vexed him. These four will also vex any individual just as they did Solomon.

1. Staying awake worrying about all of your stuff

> For what has man for all his labor, and for the striving of his heart with which he has toiled under the sun? For all his days are sorrowful, and his work burdensome; even in the night his heart takes no rest. This also is vanity.
> —Ecclesiastes 2:22–23

> The sleep of a laborer is sweet,
>   whether he eats little or much,

> but the abundance of a rich man
> permits him no sleep.
>
> —ECCLESIASTES 5:12, NIV

The more possessions you amass, the more "cares of the world" (Mark 4:19) you will become burdened with. The rich may have houses, lands, boats, and even an island, but when floods, hurricanes, and tornadoes strike, they become concerned about protecting their assets and can become consumed with the weight and fear of loss. Solomon worked hard to gain an abundance of things, but a man who owns much has more to lose than a man who owns little. Any type of worry is a vexation.

2. Dealing with jealousy from neighbors and friends

> Again, I saw that for all toil and every skillful work a man is envied by his neighbor. This also is vanity and grasping for the wind.
>
> —ECCLESIASTES 4:4

Solomon realized that his great abundance would make others jealous. A wealthy man can form many false friends who connect with him for ulterior motives, hoping to tap into the wealth or associate with the rich to build their own ego or their own portfolio. Those with less can tend to become jealous of those with more, which causes envy and a spirit of covetousness for the possessions of others. People seek easy money, but we read:

> An inheritance gained hastily at the beginning
> Will not be blessed at the end.
>
> —PROVERBS 20:21

God blesses the works of our hands and does not honor the person who covets from others.

3. Having no sons or family to take over—why work so hard?

> Then I returned, and I saw vanity under the sun:
>
> There is one alone, without companion:
> He has neither son nor brother.
> Yet there is no end to all his labors,

Nor is his eye satisfied with riches.
But he never asks,
"For whom do I toil and deprive myself of good?"
This also is vanity and a grave misfortune.
—ECCLESIASTES 4:7–8

At times I see men and women working hard to gain a huge retirement, and yet some die of heart attacks and stress-related diseases, never making it to their own retirement party. Solomon constructed a temple, built cities, and amassed wealth much of his life, but he arrived at the end of his journey realizing that the most important thing was not how much you collected but the relationships you made, especially the impartation and influence you had over your family. At birth all infants enter the world with their palms clenched as if to hold on to something. At death we exit the world with our palms opened, taking nothing with us. Those with abundance should always remember those among them in need and the work of ministry before they depart.

4. Who would take over in his place after working hard?

Then I hated all my labor in which I had toiled under the sun, because I must leave it to the man who will come after me. And who knows whether he will be wise or a fool? Yet he will rule over all my labor in which I toiled and in which I have shown myself wise under the sun. This also is vanity. Therefore I turned my heart and despaired of all the labor in which I had toiled under the sun. For there is a man whose labor is with wisdom, knowledge, and skill; yet he must leave his heritage to a man who has not labored for it. This also is vanity and a great evil. For what has man for all his labor, and for the striving of his heart with which he has toiled under the sun? For all his days are sorrowful, and his work burdensome; even in the night his heart takes no rest. This also is vanity.
—ECCLESIASTES 2:18–23

Solomon had children and was concerned about who would inherit what he had worked for so long and what condition things would be in after he was gone. Solomon had built a global reputation using his gift of wisdom and wealth, and now he would leave all he worked for to a son who might follow the Word of God or might reject the command-ments of the Lord. After Solomon's death he was replaced by his son Rehoboam, who during his reign made an unwise decision concerning raising taxes, thus dividing Israel and causing the northern ten tribes to separate from the southern kingdom of Judah and Benjamin.

Advice for Dealing With Vexation

Solomon understood the power of vexation and its negative effects. If we move from Solomon's time to the New Testament, Christ and the biblical writers give important insight on dealing with the vexation and cares of life.

1. Be content with who you are.

Being content is to be self-satisfied, which means to be at peace within yourself. A person often speaks of being discontented, which actually means to be disjointed or out of peace with himself. Often a person will become vexed when he or she compares his or her lack with another's increase. Paul wrote about this when he said:

> For we dare not class ourselves or compare ourselves with those who commend themselves. But they, measuring them-selves by themselves, and comparing themselves among them-selves, are not wise.
> —2 Corinthians 10:12

Ministers from smaller churches or infant-level ministry at times compare themselves with ministers of larger congregations or more effective outreaches; according to Paul this should be avoided. If you are successful and compare yourself with someone less successful, it builds a dangerous pride. If you are less successful than others, you can become discouraged. Be content where God has placed you, con-tent with what you have, and plant the seeds of God's Word, expecting increase in your future.

> For we brought nothing into this world, and it is certain we can carry nothing out. And having food and clothing, with these we shall be content. But those who desire to be rich fall into

temptation and a snare, and into many foolish and harmful lusts which drown men in destruction and perdition.

—1 TIMOTHY 6:7–9

Not that I speak in regard to need, for I have learned in whatever state I am, to be content: I know how to be abased, and I know how to abound. Everywhere and in all things I have learned both to be full and to be hungry, both to abound and to suffer need. I can do all things through Christ who strengthens me.

—PHILIPPIANS 4:11–13

Remember that your expensive stuff today is purchased for pennies on the dollar at the auction when you pass away. You can lose a house or a car, and possessions can be repossessed, but no one can take away your precious memories you make with those you love! Your joy must be in your relationships and not with your possessions.

2. Focus on others' needs and not yours.

When Jesus heard it, He departed from there by boat to a deserted place by Himself. But when the multitudes heard it, they followed Him on foot from the cities. And when Jesus went out He saw a great multitude; and He was moved with compassion for them, and healed their sick.

—MATTHEW 14:13–14

Here is the setting. John the Baptizer, the cousin of Christ, had been arrested by Herod and beheaded, and his head had been displayed on a silver charger. Jesus heard of this and was grieved. Desiring to be alone, He went into a desert place for solitude. However, when He saw the people gathering, He was moved with compassion, and instead of concentrating on His own grief and sorrow, He focused upon the needs of the hurting and sick around him. The Greek word for "compassion," *splagchnizomai*, means, "to have pity of sympathy for someone." It literally means to have the bowels yearn for someone. Years ago I heard a minister say that sympathy is more human, but compassion is a Holy Spirit manifestation. Compassion is what you sense when you see a starving child from Haiti and desire to feed him, or when you see handicapped children and desire to help them.

There have been parents whose own child died through a disease or tragic accident who later focused their attention on orphans or supporting orphanages. They realized that they as parents had lost their child, and the orphan as a child had lost his or her parents. The void would be filled from both sides, just as Jesus ministered out of His own pain when John was martyred to relieve the pain in others. When I see my own needs and look around me at the needs of others, I realize mine are usually minimal compared to others.

3. Make an investment of your time to mentor others.

Years ago I met a young Arab boy in Israel and saw he had a brilliant mind and great leadership potential. He was studying to be a lawyer and could already speak several languages. During the first year in college he ran out of money, and I was strongly impressed to assist him in completing his term. He did finish and became a lawyer in Jerusalem and is a fine young leader. I actually saw in him a potential to be a leader among his people in the future in politics.

The Holy Spirit will show you individuals whom His hand is upon and how you can be a blessing to break the spirit of vexation, poverty, or despondency off their minds. Years ago a Christian schoolteacher took under her mentorship a very poor young man and began pouring into him to educate him and even assist him in understanding finances. In later years the young man became a businessman making millions of dollars, never forgetting the schoolteacher who helped him when others ignored him. Helping someone meet their needs will pick them up emotionally, and through spiritual advice and instruction you will plant seeds for their future success.

4. The Holy Spirit is the giver of peace.

Today you can become vexed and oppressed by economic woes, family members in addictive bondages, marital strife, and even by watching the daily news! This vexation and mental oppression can open a door for your spiritual adversary to attack your mind, body, and spirit, as a certain percentage of medical conditions are brought about by stress and are made worse through stressful circumstances. I have always loved the verse in Acts 10:38:

How God anointed Jesus of Nazareth with the Holy Spirit and
with power, who went about doing good and healing all who
were oppressed by the devil, for God was with Him.

The Holy Spirit is a yoke breaker, as indicated in Isaiah 10:27: "...the
yoke will be destroyed because of the anointing." When an animal has
a yoke placed around its neck, a person can control every movement
and impose his will without the creature having any self-control of
its own. The adversary uses the oppression and vexation of spirit to
dominate and manipulate a person, just as a farmer controls the farm
animal by yoking it to a wooden yoke. The power of the Holy Spirit
being released upon or within a person can actually break the oppres-
sive thought patterns and emotional baggage that a person is holding
on to, causing that person to be burdened down. Once this yoke is
broken, then a feeling of peace will settle over the individual.

When the chains or yokes of vexations, depression, and oppression
are broken, these emotional and spiritual chains will be replaced by
peace. We read in Romans 14:17:

> For the kingdom of God is not eating and drinking, but righ-
> teousness and peace and joy in the Holy Spirit.

The basic definition of peace is to be in a state of mind where the
mind and body are quiet or free from mental agitations and frustra-
tions. In the Middle East, when greeting a person it is common for
Jews to say, "Shalom," and for Arabs to say, "Salam." The word *shalom*
not only means peace but is also a greeting that expresses a desire for
the person to be blessed, prosperous, and happy. In the King James
Version the word *peace* is used 429 times and is a very important word.

In the Old Testament there are five different words translated as
peace. In Genesis 15:15 the word for "peace" is *shalom* and is a greeting
for an introduction or when departing from a person. In Genesis 24:21
the Hebrew word for "peace" is *charash* and means to be silent, say
nothing, or to hold your peace. In Exodus 20:24 God established a
peace offering at the temple, and this word for "peace" is *shelem*, which
is a sacrifice of appreciation toward God. The fourth reference to the
word can be found when Aaron "held his peace," which is the Hebrew
word *damam*, meaning to be astonished (Lev. 10:3). Then in Joshua

10:1 Joshua made a peace treaty; the word used for "peace" is *shalam*, meaning to make amends with something or someone.

In the New Testament there are five different Greek words that are translated as "peace." Matthew 10:13 speaks of leaving peace upon a house when departing. This word means to be quiet and to prosper; thus it refers to placing a verbal blessing upon the inhabitants of a house where you were treated well. In Matthew 20:31 two blind men were crying out to Christ and were told to "hold their peace." The Greek phrase for "to hold your peace" means to be still. At times Christ would command demons not to speak, or to "hold their peace"—a word used here referring to muzzling something or preventing someone from speaking (Mark 1:25). Matthew 5:9 uses the word *peacemakers*, referring to someone who can pacify individuals in conflict. The fifth reference is found in Luke 14:4, when the people would not debate Jesus and held their peace—a word here meaning to refrain from meddling. Each definition of peace in the Hebrew and Greek Scriptures is used, and the meaning is determined by the context or setting in the story.[3]

The Possibility of Peace

If you ever visit Israel, one of the first Hebrew words you learn and say quite often is the word *shalom*. This word has a far deeper meaning than what tourists perceive. The common conception is that *shalom* is the word for peace. This is true; however, it can also mean, "to bless, to keep safe, to hedge in, to prosper and to be in health." It is a word encompassing total blessing for someone's life.

Christians often use the word *saved* to describe being converted to Christ and receiving His redemptive covenant. In the English language, the biblical word *saved* has the connotation of being born again and redeemed. However, the word Greek word for "saved" is *sozo* and has a broad meaning of "healed, saved, delivered, protected, and to be made whole and complete." The word *saved* is not just the salvation of the human spirit, but it also covers the *deliverance of the body* and the *freedom of the soul*. When a person is in health and has a clear mind and his spirit is redeemed, that person can be wholly at peace.

Peace is so important with God that in Numbers 25:12, He spoke of giving His people a "covenant of peace."

There are many compound names for God in the Old Testament such as *Jehovah-Jireh*, "God our provider" (Gen. 22:14), and *Jehovah-Rapha'*, meaning, "God our healer" (Exod. 15:26). God also was given a special name in Judges 6:24—*Jehovah-Shalom*, meaning, "God our peace." In the New Testament the apostle Paul penned fourteen letters called *epistles* and opened each with the greeting, "Grace and peace be unto you." The phrase *"grace* unto you" is a Greek greeting, and *"peace* unto you" is a Hebrew greeting. Paul also concluded several of his letters by praying that the peace of God would keep and control the believer (Phil. 4:7; Col. 3:15).

Levels of Peace

The Holy Spirit provides levels of peace. The first level is peace *with* God:

> Therefore, having been justified by faith, we have peace with God through our Lord Jesus Christ.
> —ROMANS 5:1

Living in sin produces discord, but forgiveness of sin produces peace *with* God. Often, when a person is dying, a minister will ask that person if he or she has *made peace with God*, a question that confronts the spiritual condition of that person. Thus peace with God is the initial entry level of peace accompanying the redemptive covenant. You can feel the burden and condemnation of sin leave as a gentle, loving feeling of rest blankets your soul.

Once a person has made peace with God though the forgiveness of sins, that peace is transferred into the mind and spirit of the redeemed soul and releases the peace *of* God within:

> Be anxious for nothing, but in everything by prayer and supplication, with thanksgiving, let your requests be made known to God; and the peace of God, which surpasses all understanding, will guard your hearts and minds through Christ Jesus.
> —PHILIPPIANS 4:6–7

When Paul wrote his epistles, he greeted the saints with peace. In Paul's time believers were living under great persecution, which in turn translated into emotional distress. Grace was God's special favor, and peace was a blessing placed upon believers to bring rest and quietness in the soul. A believer can only be at peace if he is abiding in trust. Isaiah made this clear when he wrote:

> You will keep him in perfect peace,
> Whose mind is stayed on You,
> Because he trusts in You.
>
> —ISAIAH 26:3

The 1611 King James Version says, "perfect peace," when the Hebrew Scripture reads, "*shalom shalom.*" In the English language it would be incorrect grammar to write that God would preserve you in *peace, peace.* Thus the translators used the words *perfect* peace, or complete peace. A person's mind must be "stayed" upon the Lord. This Hebrew word refers to a *stay or a tent pole* that holds up the weight of the tent. The pressure of the tent rests upon the pole, just as the pressures of our minds can rest in peace as we place our mental cares upon Christ. Trusting in the Lord is to take refuge in or have confidence in Him. True peace secures and undergirds the mind. The human brain has two hemispheres—the left and the right hemisphere. Each hemisphere has a specific function that directs the five senses, the functions of the organs, and the ability to reason or think. God gives us peace, peace, or, as I view it, peace for both the left and right hemispheres of the brain!

The central key to freedom from fear and anxiety is to walk in the love of God and understand God's unwavering love for you. John wrote:

> There is no fear in love; but perfect love casts out fear, because fear involves torment. But he who fears has not been made perfect in love. We love Him because He first loved us.
>
> —1 JOHN 4:18–19

The mental oppression and vexation of the human soul grow out of the seeds of fear, insecurity, and stress. Our insecurity is bred from a lack of confidence that God is willing to preserve and provide for us. A fearful believer is not perfected in his or her understanding of God's unconditional love and concern. The only way to understand God's love is to read His love letters to you, the Word of God and understand that He and you are in a covenant through which what you have is His, what He has can be yours, and His eye is ever upon you. One of my favorite promises is found in Matthew 10:29–31:

> Are not two sparrows sold for a copper coin? And not one of them falls to the ground apart from your Father's will. But the very hairs of your head are all numbered. Do not fear therefore; you are of more value than many sparrows.

The sparrow is one of the smallest birds, yet there are more than fifty different species in North and South America alone. In the time of Christ sparrows were sold in the marketplaces. Luke adds that five sparrows were sold for two coins (Luke 12:6). In the time of Christ these birds were very numerous, so when selling the birds, no one paid much attention, and certainly there was no resistance among the people. Jesus spoke of the sparrow falling to the ground, but some commentators (Origen, Clement, Chrysostom) taught that this referred to falling into a snare set by men to capture the birds for sale.[4]

The idea of two sparrows may refer back to Leviticus 14, which reveals that when a leper was cleansed, he was to bring two birds to the priest, one that would be slain and the other released, indicating the cleansing of leprosy (vv. 4–7). The Hebrew word for "birds" in Leviticus 14:4–5 is *tsippowr* and means, a "little bird." It can refer to sparrows. Thus the sparrow may have been the bird used as the offering a leper brought to indicate he was cured. Yet the Father in heaven observed even the smallest bird that was sold and offered as a sacrifice.

Now consider the hairs on your head, something we may not deem as a spiritual lesson, but we pay much attention to our hair, especially when it needs to be cut, styled, or highlighted! The average human has 100,000 hair follicles, each capable of producing 20 individual hairs during a person's lifetime. Blondes average 146,000 follicles, black-haired individuals have 110,000, brown-haired folks have about 100,000, and redheads have the least dense hair with 86,000 hair follicles. Each human hair has a life span of three to seven years, except if a person has experienced a trauma. Hair is so amazing; it cannot be destroyed by hot or cold water or by heat in summer and freezing cold in winter, and it can endure many acids that are placed on it through certain hair styling procedures. The average person loses 60 to 100 stands of hair a day, varying based upon diet, age, and illnesses.[5] God knows the very hairs on your head and can tell you how many you lost this morning and how many still remain intact!

Considering that God's eye is on each sparrow and His detailed knowledge of hair is unmatched, then Christ said we should not be afraid, for the heavenly Father knows what we have need of before we ask. He sent us the Comforter, the Holy Spirit, to give us peace that can surpass our own understanding (Phil. 4:7).

Paul wrote that the "love of money is the root of all evil" (1 Tim. 6:10, kjv). Paul admonished Timothy: "But those who desire to be rich fall into temptation and a snare, and into many foolish and harmful lusts which drown men in destruction and perdition" (v. 9). He warned that greed would pierce a person through with much sorrow (v. 10). James further warned that in the last days the wealth of the rich would be corrupt and useless when God's judgment was poured out against unrighteousness, including the mistreatment of the poor (James 5:1–6). The early church did have certain wealthy individuals who knew how to balance their wealth with their mission to assist in the ministry of Christ and the spreading of the gospel. This is because they never allowed their wealth to create pride or to rule over them. They became the stewards and master of their wealth, distributing it for ministry purposes (Matt. 27:57; Luke 8:2–3; 19:2)

The one way to ensure that greed never grips a prosperous believer is to willingly give away both money and goods to the poor, the widows, and orphans and to support the work of the ministry. Often individuals will amass "stuff" during their lifetime and depart this life with basements, attics, and closets full of *things*. I have learned as the years have passed that it is important to provide a blessing to my family and closest friends by releasing some of the things I have collected or have in my possession, so that they can enjoy them while I am still living! Since you cannot take your "stuff" with you, then release yourself from the worry of losing it by occasionally blessing others with it.

Spiritual vexation can also impact ministers as their churches grow and ministries expand. In the late 1980s our ministry employed five people. I would spend at least fourteen hours a day working in the office and would micromanage every aspect of our seven-point outreach. As we grew to reaching 180 nations of the world each week and expanded from five to almost thirty workers, one of the greatest things I have learned is to hire capable workers who know their assignments and will follow through with them. Distributing responsibilities, sharing workloads, cross training, and releasing the many daily routines to others will also release a minister from the cares of ministry that can lead to spiritual vexation and heaviness. Once again, it is the dynamic work of the Holy Spirit that lifts the burden, releases peace, and brings joy in following Christ.

Chapter Thirteen

CAN A TRUE CHRISTIAN COMMIT THE UNPARDONABLE SIN?

Anyone who speaks a word against the Son of Man, it will be forgiven him; but whoever speaks against the Holy Spirit, it will not be forgiven him, either in this age or in the age to come.

—MATTHEW 12:32

M ANY YEARS AGO in the beginning of my ministry I was preaching in the very small town of Whitmer, West Virginia. That night about twenty-five people were in attendance, and for some reason I preached a message geared toward the unsaved. When I gave the altar invitation, the church, which was mostly believers, came to the altar to pray for lost family members—all except one woman who was sitting on the back bench with a blank stare on her face. I went back to talk to her about her relationship with God. She had no expression, her eyes and countenance looked very empty and lifeless. After asking her if she would receive Christ, she said in a monotone voice, "I cannot because I blasphemed the

Holy Spirit years ago." Nothing I said changed her mind or moved her toward prayer.

After service I asked my grandfather if he knew her, and he said yes. I asked if he know what she had done, and he said, "I know of one incident many years ago when God was dealing with her and she was crying. I invited her to the altar, and she cried out, "Leave me alone, God. I don't want You. Take Your Spirit away from me...leave me alone forever. I don't want to ever feel conviction again!" Granddad said, "Since that time it seems she attends to see if the Holy Spirit conviction will come again to her, but she seems to live a life of no emotion, joy, or happiness."

I stated that perhaps she grieved the Spirit and did not actually blaspheme, but only God knows other things she may have said in her heart or with her words to cause this emptiness and separation; therefore I cannot and will not judge her.

Just what is the sin of *blasphemy*, and can a believer commit this unforgivable sin?

> And anyone who speaks a word against the Son of Man, it will
> be forgiven him; but to him who blasphemes against the Holy
> Spirit, it will not be forgiven.
> —LUKE 12:10

In the context of this verse Jesus was speaking of confessing Him before men and not denying Him when pressure and persecution persisted. Christ warned His disciples in Luke 12:11 that they would be brought before the religious and political leaders in cities. The tendency of some believers during these trials could be to deny the Lord, which would release them from persecution. In some cases they would be asked to blaspheme Christ. Paul even confessed that this was the case when he persecuted the church. He caused many to blaspheme— but he did so in ignorance (Acts 26:11). Paul confessed:

> And I thank Christ Jesus our Lord who has enabled me,
> because He counted me faithful, putting me into the ministry,
> although I was formerly a blasphemer, a persecutor, and an
> insolent man; but I obtained mercy because I did it ignorantly
> in unbelief.
> —1 TIMOTHY 1:12–13

Three of the four Gospel writers make mention of Christ's warning that the sin of blasphemy against the Holy Spirit will not be forgiven (Matt. 12:32; Mark 3:29; Luke 12:10). Mark added that a blasphemer is in danger of "eternal damnation" (Mark 3:29, KJV), and Matthew emphasizes that the blasphemer cannot be forgiven in this life or in the world to come (Matt. 12:32).

The Setting of the Warnings

Christ was anointed by the Holy Spirit to heal all who were oppressed of the devil (Acts 10:38). Part of Christ's deliverance ministry was to expel, or "cast out," evil spirits. In the narrative in Matthew 12 Christ was casting out devils, causing a multitude to follow His ministry, which was a threat to the jealous Pharisees who had controlled the traditional Jewish faith for years. It had been taught by rabbis from previous generations that the Messiah's power over evil spirits was a true sign He was the Messiah. The Pharisees feared a loss of their popularity, position, and domination over the common people through their traditions.

To create fear, the Pharisees publicly announced that Christ's miracles were being assisted by one of the chief demons, called Beelzebub. In reality, the Pharisees knew the Torah and prophets, and they believed in spirits, demons, and the supernatural; yet they accused Christ's miracles for being *from the devil*. This was a terrible insult to the Holy Spirit, who was anointing Christ and giving Him authority over all demonic powers. This is why Christ warned them and others who would follow in their steps of the unforgivable sin of blaspheming the Holy Spirit.

The Greek word "blaspheme" is *blasphemeo*, meaning, "to slander; to accuse; to speak against using derogatory words for the purpose of injuring or harming one's reputation." It can also allude to profane, foul, and unclean language.[1] Before detailing the possibility of blaspheming the Spirit, there are several sins against the Spirit referred to in Scripture, yet they are not classified as blasphemy.

The first is *resisting* the Holy Spirit. The deacon Stephen was preaching a message to a total Jewish audience, revealing the prophetic trail in Scripture concerning Christ being the Messiah. Instead of believing the prophets, they resisted the preaching and later stoned Stephen to death, after he rebuked them, saying:

> You stiffnecked and uncircumcised in heart and ears! You always resist the Holy Spirit; as your fathers did, so do you.
> —ACTS 7:51

To resist is to strongly oppose in the mind or emotions or to physically resist, such as resisting temptation and Satan (James 4:7). When truth is preached, and you willfully choose not to believe it or fight against it, then you are resisting the Holy Spirit. To "repent" means to turn, but when the neck is stiff, it is impossible to turn it, as the person is stuck in his own traditions and ideas. Saul of Tarsus heard Stephen's message, resisted, and consented to have him stoned to death. Yet later this resister and hater of Christians was himself converted, and his name changed to Paul (Acts 7:58; Acts 9:1–19).

The second sin is to *grieve* the Holy Spirit, as penned in Ephesians 4:30:

> And do not grieve the Holy Spirit of God, by whom you were sealed for the day of redemption.

The word *grieve* here is a word meaning, "to make someone sad or sorrowful, especially by your words or actions." The very next verse reveals actions you commit that cause the Holy Spirit to be grieved:

> Let all bitterness, wrath, anger, clamor, and evil speaking be put away from you, with all malice. And be kind to one another, tenderhearted, forgiving one another, even as God in Christ forgave you.
> —EPHESIANS 4:31–32

The above fleshly sins and attitudes are manifested with your actions but also with your spoken words. When you lose your temper, become angry, and speak evil of others, not only does your spirit become heavy, but also the Holy Spirit will be grieved and saddened. As an example, my wife and I will not watch any movie using God's name in vain. Even though we are not speaking it, the Holy Spirit within us is saddened and grieved. The Holy Spirit Himself is in the Godhead—and thus it is as though He is being *damned and cursed* just as the Father is. When the Spirit is grieved, you will lose your joy and peace. This type of profanity is "corrupt communication," which is not to come from your mouth (Eph. 4:29, KJV) or, for that matter, is not to be listened to.

The third sin is to *vex* the Spirit. This was the sin of Israel, as written in Isaiah 63:10 (KJV):

> But they rebelled, and vexed his holy Spirit: therefore he was turned to be their enemy, and he fought against them.

The Hebrew root word for "vex" in this passage means, "to carve out" in the sense of worry, pain, and anger. The word seems to imply that sinning and disobeying God cut deep into the heart of the Holy Spirit and bring Him great pain. I recall that years ago someone sent me a video of a major march in San Francisco that was so sickening that I told the person, "I am too grieved to see the rest, and I have no desire to see what these with reprobate minds are doing, including blaspheming God with perverted words painted on signs they were holding up." Israel sinned in the wilderness, rebelling with their words and actions, and grieved the Holy Spirit.

These three—resisting, grieving, and vexing the Holy Spirit—will offend Him; however, these are not considered to be the level of blasphemy, as they can be repented of and forgiven.

The fourth and most serious sin is to blaspheme the Holy Spirit. Christ gave a warning to the Pharisees, a religious sect that knew the Law and prophets and prided themselves in being God's chosen ones to carry His Word. Yet they willfully sinned by using hateful, negative words to ascribe the power of Christ to an evil spirit.

Can a Believer Blaspheme?

Throughout my ministry I have met people, and our ministry has been contacted over the years by men and women, questioning if they had committed the unpardonable sin of blaspheming the Holy Spirit. After many years of observing this tormenting thought attacking individuals who, at the same time, confessed they loved the Lord, I have four observations to share as to what may be buried under the root of these feelings.

First, the thought of blasphemy often arises after a believer has fallen into a very serious sin, especially a sin of the flesh that has cost his or her integrity, reputation, or even family. The darkness of their disobedience was so deep that they lost peace of mind in the fog of darkness and are being mentally tormented by their actions, often unable to forgive themselves. The enemy took advantage of their condition and shot darts into their mind saying that God's love had run out and they had crossed a line of no return. This, of course, is a lie. Certain sins may result in a high price to pay, but fleshly sins can be forgiven when repented of. The sense of guilt and remorse must be replaced eventually with the voice of mercy, grace, and forgiveness to lift the fallen one from the pit of despair. The low feeling of despair and the fact the Spirit is grieved can create an emotion of loss, interpreted as evidence that the unforgivable sin was committed.

The second observation is that when a believer who is used to experiencing the presence of God suddenly journeys through a long, unexplained dry spell in which the person cannot sense the presence of the Lord in church, in his or her spirit, or when attempting to pray. This total drought of emotional joy can come as a result of a severe trial, the death of a loved one, a sickness that requires medication that dulls the inner feelings, or numerous other circumstances that can strip a person of the emotional peace that comes with the presence of the Holy Spirit. At times when someone has said, "I've done nothing wrong, and yet I have lost the sense of God's presence," I often discover he or she is on a strong medication that suppresses all feelings, making it a challenge to be sensitive to the Holy Spirit. They have not blasphemed, but the medication suppresses their ability to be sharp and sensitive to the person of the Spirit. They must understand this and continue to believe by faith that the Lord has not, and will not, depart from them in their time of crisis, as we walk by faith and not by sight (2 Cor. 5:7).

The last year of my father's life was quite difficult as he was on dialysis several days a week and was also on several forms of medication. I remember seeing him weak, and his countenance had dropped. He said, "Son, I am having a hard time praying. I feel like I'm not getting through." He later confessed that his body was weary, his mind was tired, and his spirit was weak from a lack of quality time in God's presence. He was the same mighty man of faith that he had always been, but his mind and body were tired from the sickness that attacked him.

Thus, this is my third observation: believers can encounter emotional and mental depression because of the physical and chemical changes in their bodies. The once strong warriors of prayer and teachers of the Word eventually age, and with age comes physical weakness, memory loss, or the inability to drive to church. Mental oppression and depression, whether it is a spiritual attack or a physical, chemical, or biological change, can make even a seasoned believer question, "Where did the Lord's presence go?"

There is one more observation that I personally have experienced in the past. At times believers can say something with their mouths that grieves the Spirit, and they will think the Lord has departed from them—and it is possible the Spirit's presence can depart for a season because He is grieved.

Many years ago I came under an attack from the enemy, who used the mouths of others to assault me and tell stories that were totally false. In my attempt to defend myself, I began to make statements to friends about two ministers whom I blamed for this confusion and distortion. My defense went on for weeks, telling everyone I knew my own side of the account, until one Sunday morning in Alabama I preached an entire message without *one ounce* of the anointing of the Spirit. I felt dead on the inside and sensed no unction, which had never happened to me before. This went on for twenty-one days, until in my misery I cried out to the Lord and asked Him to reveal what was wrong. He rebuked me and informed me that I have grieved His Spirit with my conversation about the two ministers and that I needed to repent, including repenting to the men I was angry with. I was obedient, the anointing was restored, and the revivals continued for many weeks, blessing thousands!

When a believer seemingly loses God's presence, there can be *practical* reasons for the lack of unction due to varied physical and emotional circumstances. I can assure you that if you truly love God and His Word and desire His presence, you have not blasphemed the Spirit; you need to simply evaluate your present situation, making any corrections needed to bring back your confidence in God's love for you. If *before* you were converted to Christ, you said negative things in ignorance, then pray to the heavenly Father, telling Him you spoke in ignorance and are repenting for your words. If you were raised in a denomination that denounced the work of the Spirit, denying the power, Paul said you should turn away from them. Never be associated with those who deny or resist the power of the Holy Spirit. (See 2 Timothy 3:1–5, especially verse 5.)

Can a true believer blaspheme the Holy Spirit? I would suggest anyone who blasphemes the Holy Spirit is not a true believer, as no true believer would ever have the desire to speak evil or hateful of the Holy Spirit, or, may I add, any minister of any denominational background who is encouraging others to draw closer to God through the Holy Spirit.

Willing and Ignorant Blasphemy

In the realm of blasphemy there is a blasphemy by *willingness* and one by *ignorance*. Paul confessed he caused some to blaspheme (the name of Christ) but did so in ignorance and in unbelief (1 Tim. 1:13). The Pharisees boasted of their level of understanding the Scriptures, yet as they saw the miracles of Christ and observed His power over demons time and time again, they said evil words in jealousy. They sinned against knowledge. There are times when a sinner is possessed by evil spirits, and the demons will speak through that person's voice and say terrible and blasphemous things against Christ and the Holy Spirit. In such cases the person possessed is not responsible for his or her comments, as this is the voice of an unclean spirit speaking through the person's mouth. Thus, anything said by a totally demon-possessed person is far different from a person with a sound, reasoning mind who chooses to slander the Holy One.

I have always been fearful for men in ministry who stand in pulpits and declare that speaking in tongues is "of the devil" or accuse any miracle of healing through Christ's name of being "Satanic." There is one particular religious sect in America that continually teaches that any alleged spiritual manifestation in any church is demonic in nature. This is exhibiting the same spirit as those *Word-centered* Pharisees in Christ's day. Ministers should refrain from reckless and careless remarks just because your theology differs from others. This Holy Spirit–fighting organization would never allow music in their church, the lifting of hands, the clapping of hands, public prayer, or any emotional expression. I am uncertain what they would do if the Holy Spirit actually invaded their routine, but there is nothing to fear because He will never visit the house where He is not welcomed, and He does not always strive with men (Gen. 6:3).

Always Respect the Holy Spirit

Some time back I was in California preparing to minister, and a few hours before service I joined three other men at a restaurant near the hotel. As we were standing in line, suddenly in walked a well-known NBA basketball player, showboating and making his presence quite known. We were seated and ordered our food. A few moments later the ball player pulled up a chair to our booth and began talking to us. He was somewhat intoxicated and rather obnoxious as I spoke of spiritual things and confronted him on his own spiritual condition. He eventually confessed that his mother raised him in church and played the piano in the same church for sixty years, and she had recently died. She was Spirit filled. He said, "Look, man, I don't know about all your Jesus freak stuff and don't really care. But I know one thing, the Holy Ghost stuff is real, and I ain't never gonna say nothing bad about that…I ain't touching that!" I have no doubt his mother put the *fear of the Lord* in him as he grew and strayed from his upbringing. Despite his terrible spiritual condition, he had respect for the Holy Spirit.

I suggest if you know nothing about the Holy Spirit, and perhaps this is your first exposure in writing, be cautious in speaking negative words about Him. Second and very important, please do not judge the power or gifting of the Holy Spirit upon the failure of His vessels. Human failure among alleged spiritual men and women has brought a reproach and blasphemy against Christ's name. Often when a noted minister falls into a public sin, he is from a Pentecostal-charismatic background, and the body of Christ enters into damage control to prevent converts and seekers from being turned off by someone who was preaching victory over sin and defeating fleshly lusts, yet fell into forbidden war zones and came out wounded. The Holy Spirit does not work through perfect vessels but through willing vessels, and He must continually help our infirmities or weaknesses.

Nothing Christ did—including the miracles, raising Lazarus after four days, and coming out of the grave Himself—changed the opinions of the hard-hearted, ultra-traditional Pharisees. For some, all of the amazing signs and wonders, healing, miracles, and other spiritual gifts have no impact upon them, as their traditions and unbelief have made the Word of God of none effect! There are religious blasphemers and nonreligious blasphemers. Years ago on the West Coast I saw pictures of a public march of men with men, with the most blasphemous signs alleging that Mary, Jesus, and even God were all perverts. One sign—which accused the Holy Spirit of being a pervert who needed sexual relations—indicated a blasphemer. A blasphemer is turned over to a reprobate mind and has no chance of ever repenting or turning, as the sin crosses the mercy line and walks into the eternal punishment zone.

If you are a Christian and are concerned about this sin, yet you pray, love God, read the Word, and attend church, it is a mental attack and a tormenting thought that you should cast down and rebuke. No blasphemer would be concerned about God's presence or their own relationship with Him, as their calloused heart has sealed their destiny.

Varied circumstances can alter your sense of emotional well-being. This is why believers must walk by faith and not by sight, and may I also add, walk by faith and not by circumstances! However, positive or negative circumstances tend to either increase or decrease our sense of spirituality, which in turn deceives us into thinking we have erred and have offended God to the point of His rejection of us. The only sin that cannot be forgiven is blasphemy against the Holy Spirit, which has committed by some who are given over to uncleanness and a reprobate mind. When believers humble themselves, pray, and turn from their carnal ways, God will hear and restore them to Himself.

Chapter Fourteen

MY NEVER-BEFORE-
REVEALED CONFESSIONS

By You I have been upheld from birth;
You are He who took me out of my mother's womb.
My praise shall be continually of You.

—PSALM 71:6

I T IS TIME for a series of personal confessions. Never before when ministering in public or in any previous article or book have I written the personal confessions that I am about to share. Some will seem humorous, some rather ludicrous, and others quite serious. However, the purpose of this chapter is to reveal how the Holy Spirit's influence and power works within in the spirit and mind of those whom He touches, even from an early age, gently removing emotional scars, strengthening our weaknesses, and revealing God's will for our lives.

Let's journey back to the mountains of southwestern Virginia, where from the ages of six to ten I was attending elementary school in Big Stone Gap, Virginia. I had loving parents but was continually harassed in school for my two front teeth, which stood out in such a way that I was called a rabbit and nicknamed "Bugs Bunny." I got my skin tone from my dad's side of the family instead of my mom's olive-skinned Italian side. There on my face were big brown freckles, giving me my second nickname in public school, "Freckle Face." For some reason I was slightly bowlegged, very noticeable when running or playing sports. Then there was the nose. Mom's family had the large Italian nose with a slight hook at the top of the bridge, but I inherited my dad's long, straight nose—one that to me looked like a miniature ski slope for a mosquito. I am sure it was exaggerated in my own mind, but there wasn't much I liked about myself, and other kids reminded me of those things. When I looked in the mirror, I could only hear the haunting echoes of kids at school reminding me of my face, the freckles, big teeth, and how ugly I was. In retrospect it seems silly now, but remember that when your own child is being verbally abused, there is nothing funny about it to them, and as a parent, pay attention, because verbal abuse causes wounds.

Things did not get better from ages twelve to fourteen. Although I was gifted in certain sports (I ran track and played football in junior high), I was quite skinny and unable to physically defend myself from numerous school bullies and other harassers, whose highlight of the day included pushing and shoving smaller fellows into the lockers as though it were a contest to see how many bruises they could make and how many verbal threats of intimidation they could initiate. At that time in the public schools of Northern Virginia, I found very few teens who were Christians or even cared to be one. My father was the pastor of a local church, and I was reluctant to tell anyone what my father's job was. Once it was discovered, the verbal harassment began, as I was called a "Holy Roller," "Jesus freak," and other names not mentionable in this book.

On one occasion when it was discovered in art class that I was a preacher's kid, a group of boys tied my shoes together and demanded me to hop like a rabbit while others laughed. Then they poured paint on paper and warned that if did not lick it up, they would fight me after school and bloody me up. I was terrified, and the entire class was heaving in laughter. I had to sit in that same class and be harassed for one year. I told my parents, but it didn't seem serious to them. In our present time there have been youths who take their own lives because of harassment and being bullied. It is very serious and emotionally damaging, and again, parents should pay attention when their child comes home speaking about it.

From ages fifteen to seventeen we moved from Northern Virginia to Salem, Virginia. I can recall the guys in high school talking about all the girls that they were dating and speaking as though they were modern, irresistible playboys. At that time I had little interest in dating any schoolgirl. Actually, they would have not been interested in me because of my commitment to Christ—I didn't smoke, drink alcohol, or go to movies—thus I was certainly a very *odd* person in the eyes of the majority of my senior class. It was at this time, age sixteen (in eleventh grade), that I received a call to preach during an all-night Sunday prayer meeting at my dad's church. When word spread, I was marked with the nickname "preacher," and of course it opened the door to more verbal harassment from certain students. For two years of high school I carried a large Dake's Bible each day to school, witnessed about Christ during every opportunity, and would pray over my food in the cafeteria. This was not for a show but was because of my commitment to Christ and my desire to win others. In that time (1976–77) I knew of no Christian school in our area, as these private schools were being organized in cities with larger churches. I believe I would have aced school with straight As in a private setting, but the continual harassment made each day an unpleasant seven hours. I never knew in which class the verbal abuse would begin, and often sitting in the cafeteria, walking the halls, or just changing classes could be an unpleasant experience. Once it was discovered I was planning on being a minister, I was tested by vile profanity and shoved around to get me to fight, so they could say, "Some Christian you are."

I can remember my high school graduation. The majority of the girls in my senior class were hugging everyone and crying. I was so happy and was not about to shed a tear. I was now free to travel and take the gospel to the many churches where I would later be invited. Traveling, however, brought on a different type of stress. During the earliest days of traveling to small churches, many offerings were so small that at times what I received for several nights of ministry barely covered the gas expense to and from the meetings, especially to places requiring eight hours or more of driving. I had to borrow my mom's car on several occasions and ask her for a small loan to put gas into the car. This was a normal procedure for about a year or so.

God had certainly touched my heart to enter the ministry as a traveling evangelist. This may sound exciting to some, but there are many aspects of evangelism people may not consider. I traveled by car, by myself, as a teenager until I was married at age twenty-two to such major cities as New York, Chicago, and others (with no cell phones, GPS, or emergency OnStar). For many years I stayed during the entire days of meetings in the minister's home or the home of one of the members, where I was required to adjust to their schedules and adjust to new surroundings week after week. Most of the time I remained in my room with Bibles, books, notepads, and other study helps for the entire day and only came out of "hiding" for dinner and to head over to the church for the service.

I have shared this part throughout my years of ministry—from the age of about sixteen to twenty-one I fought severe depression, and the depression was made worse when I was invited to a new church, with all new people, and to a home I had never stayed in. I dreaded the trip and had terrible anxiety for years. It would be more than *thirty-three years later* that I would discover I actually had a form of autism (Asperger's syndrome), a social autism, making it challenging for me to be around people I don't know, and also making it difficult to carry on conversations for long periods with strangers. This caused me to be a recluse. Over the years I have thought of all of these circumstances and thought, "And God called me to preach?"

My confession is: I had no self-confidence, no self-esteem, and was obsessed with a mentality of failure. At age eighteen I was even told by a pastor in Virginia that if I did not attend the denominational school, I would fail at ministry, and if I did not follow the denominational system, I would never amount to anything. One minister stood in my face and said, "You will never make it; you will fall on your face." How's that for encouragement!

This was my life, without embellishing the facts, which to this day causes me to say, "What did God see in me to lead me into ministry, when I was a recluse, depressed, and carried a failure spirit?"

Two Events Changed My Life

After traveling alone for five years (from the age of eighteen to twenty-two), two events changed my thinking and outlook: one was spiritual, and the other was natural. Both were life changing in their own respect.

On April 2, 1982, I walked a lovely Southern belle who had overwhelmed my heart with her beauty and charm down the aisle of her home church in Northport, Alabama, and entered into a marriage covenant with her. Finding Pam, my perfect helper, met more than the emotional and physical needs of this reclusive, twenty-two-year-old evangelist—her peaceful presence brought a calm settling to my own spirit. After marrying Pam, it didn't concern me about being as skinny as a skeleton, as white as a ghost, with a mop of black hair and that unwanted nose, because someone loved me for who I was and not for what I was (a minister). I discovered that *two are better than one*, and where I was weak, she was strong. When I became discouraged, she was my encourager. All of those *no self-confidence, low self-esteem thoughts* vanished like a fog in the morning sunrise when she held me in her arms and told me she loved me.

The second and very important change maker was when I began spending hours each day praying in the Holy Spirit during my private prayer time. I received this sacred gift at age eleven during a youth camp, but for many years I had not released the prayer language in my life during my younger days. The Holy Spirit is the revealer of mysteries, and my time with Him in prayer began fine-tuning my spiritual ears to hear the still small voice that would speak words, instruction, and messages of inspiration. I began studying six to eight hours at a time, and I prayed as long as one to three hours every day before ministering. From ages nineteen to twenty-five I was suddenly preparing and preaching messages that some began calling "classics" that are still talked about thirty-five years after they were preached! Two noted ones were "Heaven—Location Destination" and "How Big Is God." My English grammar and spelling were so bad that I almost failed school due to low grades. However, in my weakest ability, which was writing, the Holy Spirit began to sharpen an unknown skill and taught me how to paint pictures with words, which today has led to me becoming a best-selling and award-winning author of Christian books.

The Holy Spirit also brought forth from the well of my spirit a gift that was in our family DNA, which I had never tapped into until age thirty-three—the gift of songwriting. As of today I have written forty songs that have been recorded, some by nationally noted soloists and Southern Gospel groups. I credit the expansion of these gifts to the gift giver, the Holy Spirit. The confidence I now have is not in my flesh but in the ability of the Spirit to work in and through me. Through allowing the Holy Spirit to direct my path every day, we now have a global ministry reaching 180 nations, from our headquarters in Cleveland consisting of three major buildings (totaling 140,000 square feet), supported by twenty-five workers. At age sixteen I never thought of, dreamed, or considered the possibility of such a global outreach.

What Is Your Excuse?

What is your excuse for not following the complete direction of the Holy Spirit for your life or for being fearful to follow spiritual principles? Perhaps you are like Moses. After slaying an Egyptian and running for his life, Moses spent forty years living in a rocky wilderness watching sheep. When God visited him through a burning bush, calling him as a pastor to liberate His people, Moses said three things that reveal how he felt about himself. He said to God, "Who am I?" (Exod. 3:11). After forty years of feeding, shearing, and watching sheep, Moses had low self-esteem. God gave Moses specific instructions to demand the king of Egypt to let His people go. Moses replied, "They will not believe me" (Exod. 4:1). Moses apparently felt God was wasting His time even talking with him. The third excuse was, "I can't speak well" (v. 10). Hebrew scholars believe Moses was indicating that he had forgotten how to speak the Egyptian language and would not confront Pharaoh as he was now unable to speak in the eloquent words required when standing before Pharaoh. God had it all planned out, and He gave Moses specific supernatural signs to grip the attention of Egypt's king and permitted Aaron to be Moses's voice.

Moses's weakness was that his focus was upon himself instead of God's ability. Years later this weakness manifested when the Israelites craved water, and Moses yelled back, "Must we [he and Aaron] fetch you water out of this rock?" (Num. 20:10, KJV). Moses placed the responsibility to provide water upon himself and Aaron, and not upon God's power. For this act he was not permitted to enter the Promised Land.

Once Israel entered the wilderness, Moses was overwhelmed with the continual bickering and counseling sessions from this mixed multitude of ex-slaves. Finally the Lord instructed him to invite seventy elders to the door of the tabernacle, and He transferred the same spirit and anointing that was upon Moses to the seventy men. To lead such a massive multitude required more than one man full of the Holy Spirit; it required a group of wise leaders under the inspiration of the Holy Spirit (Num. 11:25). My own life and this biblical narrative indicate that you can move from *excuses* to a spiritual *experience* to a spirit of *excellence* in ministry and walk in God's favor.

Gideon—a Parallel for Believers Today

There is an important lesson for believers today to be found in the pattern of Gideon. In Gideon's day tribal raiders were continually invading Israel at harvesttime, stealing the grain harvested by farmers. Gideon lived during an invasion of the Midianites, and no leader in Israel was willing to organize an army to defend the land and resist these unwanted attackers. Gideon was visited by an angel and instructed to organize a small army, and God would supernaturally defeat the spoilers.

The name *Gideon* in Hebrew comes from the verb *gada,* meaning, "to hew down or cut down." His name implies that he was a warrior, as the verb *gada* is used when two people are slugging it out and one wins. The word figuratively means to cut someone down to size. His name implies that his destiny was to hew down and cut down his enemies. However, just as Moses, Gideon was an excuse maker who was not fulfilling the destiny *concealed in his name.* Gideon's excuses parallel Moses's statements, also falling into three groups, slightly different from Moses's statements.

When the angel called Gideon a mighty man of valor and gave him instructions, Gideon replied to the angel:

> And he said unto him, Oh my Lord, wherewith shall I save Israel? behold, my family is poor in Manasseh, and I am the least in my father's house.
>
> —JUDGES 6:15, KJV

Gideon said, "My family is poor!" I would ask, "What does being poor have to do with organizing an army?" The answer is speculation, but perhaps Gideon felt because he was from a very low-income family, he had no respect among the other tribes of Israel, as common people tend to follow those with higher positions or wealth, believing their success can make a difference in the situation. Like Gideon, many believers today offer excuses to the Lord of their inability to enter the assignment stage of God's work because they do not have financial provisions for ministry possible. However, what's in your heart can motivate your desire. Years ago one woman, a stay-at-home mother of three, desired to tour Israel, and she sold doughnuts for months door to door, telling people her dream was to go on an Israel tour. It took five months, but she raised all the money. I had no money to print my first book (only five hundred copies). However, I traded my drum set to the printer, and he printed the five hundred books I desired. Where there is a *desire*, there will emerge a *direction*, and that direction usually leads to a *destination*.

Gideon's second excuse was that he was from Manasseh, indicating he felt he was from the wrong tribe of Israel to organize this army. Manasseh, the firstborn son of Joseph, was born, along with his brother, Ephraim, when Joseph was in Egypt. The name *Ephraim* means "fruitful," but the name *Manasseh* means "God made me to forget" (Gen. 41:51–52). When the patriarch Jacob blessed the two sons of Joseph, Manasseh was the eldest and traditionally would have received the patriarch's firstborn blessing. However, Jacob switched his hands and placed the right hand of blessing upon Manasseh's brother, Ephraim (Gen. 48:17–20). When your name means "God has made me to forget," and your brother receives your blessing, it is easy to feel less loved and appreciated by your peers. Jacob predicted Manasseh would do well, but Ephraim would do better, and many nations would come from his seed. Both Ephraim and Manasseh were adopted into the Hebrew tribal clan; however, Manasseh was given the small towns (Num. 32:41).

Gideon's second excuse sounds like many believers today who say, "If I were just born in the right family with the right connections in the right place at the right time, I could have really accomplished something for the kingdom of God." God enjoys taking what is small and insignificant and raising it up for His glory. I remind people that Jesus was raised in Nazareth, a town so insignificant that Nathanael said, "Can anything good come out of Nazareth?" (John 1:46). Prior to Christ's arrival no one cared about Nazareth, but something good did come from Nazareth—Jesus Christ! Today the entire Christian world desires to visit Nazareth on a Holy Land tour to visit Christ's hometown.

Gideon expressed a third excuse when he said, "I am the least in my father's house" (Judg. 6:15). The idea of being "least" can have numerous interpretations. It can refer to being the youngest member of the family, the smallest in stature, or the least favorable among the other children. Being the least has never been a hindrance to God using a person for a great assignment. Israel was the smallest among the nations, but it will become the world's Messianic headquarters during the millennial reign of Messiah. Israel's first king, Saul, was from the smallest tribe, Benjamin (1 Sam. 9:21). David was a teenager, the youngest among his brothers, and was anointed as the future king (1 Sam. 16).

What was the one moment in Gideon's life that changed his attitude and opinions of himself? After all, he was a master excuse maker even before this angel of the Lord. The following verse was the key to Gideon's motivation and defeat of the enemy:

> But the Spirit of the LORD came upon Gideon; then he blew the trumpet, and the Abiezrites gathered behind him.
> —JUDGES 6:34

The Holy Spirit suddenly energized the mind and spirit of this early judge of Israel, enabling him with faith to defeat the adversary. God used this man who had little self-confidence, and God will use you, despite how you feel about yourself. You are not your *appearance,* but you are your *personality,* and God taps your personality, making it like a magnet to attract others. Your *word* is more important than your *work,* as your work must be backed up by your integrity, which is sealed with your promises and verbal commitments. You are not the promises you *make* but the promises you *keep.* The real you is not the *public* you but the *private* you. You are not what *critics* say you are but what *God* says you are. Gideon saw himself differently than God did, and when the Holy Spirit came upon Gideon, all his insecurities melted like snowballs in a fire.

I could have used excuses, believing the critics and never fulfilling God's purpose or walking out His will. However, permitting the Holy Spirit to inwardly empower you will transform your weakness into strength, your defeats into victory, your fear into faith, and your lack into increase. I have shared this section in this book with you to illustrate that just as there is a natural DNA within your blood that gives you certain characteristics and a special design, there is a what I term *God DNA* encoded in the Holy Spirit, which can transform you from how you see yourself to how God sees you and exchange weaknesses for abilities. There are untapped gifts locked within your mind and spirit that require a key to open the door of possibilities. The Holy Spirit knows the code to your doors, and when you walk into His will and purpose, the impossible will become possible. If God can call me into a global ministry, then nothing is impossible to them who believe.

Chapter Fifteen

THE NINE GREATEST LESSONS THE HOLY SPIRIT HAS TAUGHT ME

However, when He, the Spirit of truth, has come, He will guide you into all truth; for He will not speak on His own authority, but whatever He hears He will speak; and He will tell you things to come.

—JOHN 16:13

I FEEL GREATLY HONORED to be fourth in a line of ministers. On my mother's side of the family, the man who raised her mother was R. L. Rexrode. His background was in the Church of the Brethren, and in his early days he worked for the Secret Service. RL accepted the call into the ministry and traveled during the difficult times of the Great Depression, often not having making enough income to care for the family. However, his faith in God sustained him. My great-grandfather, Pete Bava, came from Italy. This Italian Catholic experienced a miraculous healing and received Christ as Savior, afterward experiencing the Holy Spirit baptism. Even in his eighties he burned with zeal for the Lord. His son, John Bava, was converted to Christ and received the infilling of the Spirit at age seventeen, during a revival where R. L.

Rexrode was ministering. John had two daughters, one who became my mother, Juanita. She too received the Holy Spirit baptism at an early age.

My father, Fred Stone, was converted in the late 1940s during the great Coalfield Revival, which erupted in the heart of McDowell County, Virginia. Church services continued nightly for forty-two months, bearing the fruit of three hundred souls won to Christ. Seventy young men emerged from the fires of that revival and were called into the ministry. Dad was converted at age seventeen, and shortly thereafter he hungered to experience the baptism in the Holy Spirit, receiving the gift shortly after his conversion. For me, it was during a youth camp at a church campground in Roanoke, Virginia, at age eleven that I encountered the Holy Spirit and received the baptism of the Spirit.

I preached my first message at my father's church in Salem, Virginia, at age sixteen, and two years later at age eighteen I began traveling full-time, ministering in three states. From small half-filled churches to overflow crowds and from rural congregations to megachurches, the Holy Spirit has been my chief teacher.

Holy Spirit Insights

During my ministry the Holy Spirit has taught me nine significant insights.

1. The anointing of your mentor will rub off on you.

Every minister needs a mentor, a respected, older, seasoned soldier whose life is soaked with the anointing. What you rub up against can rub off on you. Sitting under a spiritual spout that is pouring out the unction of God will eventually splash onto the soul of the mentee, for the anointing is tangible and transferable. This was clear with Elijah, the mentor, and Elisha, the mentee. The former was a giver, and the other was a receiver; one was the teacher (Elijah), and the other (Elisha) was the student. At the time of Elijah's departure to heaven Elisha demanded a *double portion* of the Spirit that was upon Elijah. The double measure is evident when counting the miracles:

Elijah performed sixteen recorded miracles, and Elisha performed thirty-two—double the number of his teacher.[1]

Christ poured knowledge, understanding, and wisdom into twelve men for forty-two months, and following His ascension in Acts 1, the chosen apostles tarried in Jerusalem until the Holy Spirit endued (clothed) them with power from on high (Luke 24:49).

When the divine presence was transferred from Moses and Aaron to the seventy elders, the elders began prophesying in the camp. The Spirit blanketed the area to the extent that two men, Eldad and Medad, who were not a part of the seventy, began prophesying in the congregation (Num. 11:26). Others wanted Moses to sit these two men down, but Moses said, "Oh, that all the LORD's people were prophets and that the LORD would put His Spirit upon them!" (v. 29). Eldad and Medad found themselves near the anointing on the seventy men, and a residue of God's presence descended upon both. When you hang around with others, their negative or positive attitude, their faith or unbelief, and their anointing of the Spirit or lack thereof will eventually be imparted to you.

I was blessed with three mentors at age eighteen: my father, a minister named Floyd Lawhon, and Dr. T. L. Lowery. By example my father taught me how to pray and operate in the nine spiritual gifts. Floyd Lawhon taught me the need of spending more time with God than with people in order to bring more spiritual results in altar services. T. L. Lowery demonstrated the power of God through the gifts of healing and miracles. When I was near Dr. Lowery, his anointing caused my faith to rise to new heights. As years passed, I began to see the same types of anointing and prayer times that were upon these three men manifested in my services. Thus the anointing that is upon your mentor can and will be transferred into your life. Be cautious as to who becomes your teacher, because your life will mirror what you are taught by word and example.

2. You must pray continually in the Spirit.

Some who are unfamiliar with praying in the Spirit may not totally comprehend the significance of this statement. Before my father passed, he gave me this word, "Son, the last days are going to be very trying for people, and it is important that believers pray excessively in the Spirit to have strength and wisdom to survive the attacks of the enemy." I believe we can pray *with* the Spirit and also pray *in* the Spirit. According to 1 John 2:20, praying with the Spirit is to pray with the *unction* and direction of the Spirit, or as some would say, to pray with the *inspiration* of the Spirit. This type of prayer is prayed with your understanding and can be felt deep within the soul and spirit while the words are being expressed to God.

The second pattern of prayer is to pray or intercede *in* the Spirit. Jude said we build our faith when we pray in the Holy Spirit (Jude 20). Praying in the Spirit is to pray in the prayer language of the Spirit, which in return causes our inner spirit to be recharged and renewed. Thus we can pray with our understanding and pray in the Spirit—both biblical and both effective prayer methods.

For those who think the concept of praying excessively or praying much in the Spirit is extreme, read Paul's letter to the church at Corinth, a church that was heavily focused upon the spiritual gifts—especially vocal gifts (tongues, prophecy, and interpretation). Paul gave the believers instructions on the operation of these vocal gifts in chapter 14 and later confessed, "I thank my God I speak with tongues more than you all" (v. 18). The Amplified says it this way: "I thank God I speak in [strange] tongues (languages) more than any of you or all of you put together." Imagine Paul saying that he spoke in tongues more than the entire church combined. However, he spoke using the language of his understanding in the local congregation so that they could all understand his message, and he spoke in tongues more in his private devotions when he was in intercession (vv. 18–19).

Prayer should not be just a Sunday morning ritual bringing relief to believers who for six days are too busy to spend time with God. Prayer should be daily and continual. Paul wrote, "Pray without ceasing" (1 Thess. 5:17). He also told the church at Ephesus, "I…do not cease to give thanks for you, making mention of you in my prayers" (Eph. 1:15–16). Notice Paul's words to Timothy: "I thank God, whom I serve with a pure conscience, as my forefathers did, as without ceasing I remember you in my prayers night and day" (2 Tim. 1:3). We read in Ephesians 6:18, "Praying always with all prayer and supplication in the Spirit, being watchful to this end with all perseverance and supplica-tion for all the saints." The NIV says it this way: "And pray in the Spirit on all occasions with all kinds of prayers and requests. With this in mind, be alert and always keep on praying for all the saints."

It is very difficult to pray for long periods of time using our mental understanding or in our native language, as the human mind can be easily distracted and diverted from our focus, unless of course a person is praying with a strong unction from the Holy Spirit. However, praying in the Spirit (the prayer language) bypasses your understanding, making it easier to intercede longer, as the human mind cannot interfere with the words being said. Paul said that a person's understanding is unfruitful when that person is speaking with tongues (1 Cor. 14:14). This verse implies to some that tongues have no real purpose, until you understand that in prayer, darts of unbelief and doubt are often shot into the mind by the adversary to block your faith. However, when I pray in the Spirit, my human intellect is bypassed, and my spirit is praying to God. This praying in the Spirit enables me to always pray the will of God.

3. Your inner spirit is alert even when you are sleeping.

Every human is a body, soul, and spirit (1 Thess. 5:23). When we are asleep, our body is at rest, but our soul (deep in our mind) is still active, causing dreams. The human spirit is eternal and therefore never requires any rest or sleep (Ps. 121:4). I have discovered that even if my body is asleep, my soul, and especially my spirit, can still be alert to my surroundings and to the presence of negative spiritual forces that may be in the area. Some of the greatest revelations I have received from the Lord, and the times I have heard His voice, were right at the moment I was in a deep sleep, just on the verge of waking up—that in-between state.

On one occasion I recall coming out of a deep sleep and hearing the words, "We got him! We got bin Laden! Verify with DNA…we need DNA evidence!" I awoke my wife and told her what I had heard. I went to my office and said, "I think we are going to kill bin Laden, and they will want DNA evidence." Exactly one week later Osama bin Laden was killed, and I later discovered that DNA evidence was required to confirm it was him. This was a revelation of the future from the Holy Spirit, who the Bible says "will tell you things to come" (John 16:13).

The Book of Job describes how God speaks through a dream at night:

For God may speak in one way, or in another,
Yet man does not perceive it.
In a dream, in a vision of the night,
When deep sleep falls upon men,
While slumbering on their beds,
Then He opens the ears of men,
And seals their instruction.
In order to turn man from his deed,
And conceal pride from man,
He keeps back his soul from the Pit,
And his life from perishing by the sword.

—Job 33:14–18

A dream often manifests in the mind or the realm of the soul, and a vision is a manifestation from the inner spirit of the individual. God uses both dreams and visions to give instruction, warning, and revelations of the future. This is why your spirit must remain pure from spiritual defilement. The Holy Spirit uses your spirit as the microphone to relay His voice to your intellect and bring instruction.

4. The intimacy of the Holy Spirit helps you with intimacy with your companion.

This may seem rather odd to suggest, but even as the Holy Spirit guides us into a more intimate relationship with God, believers who are filled with the Holy Spirit tend to express compassion, affection, and love in a more personal and intimate manner than others.

One of our close ministry couples has a testimony proving this point. Prior to being in ministry, the husband left his wife because of a serious and dangerous drug addiction. Over time he was converted to Christ and accepted a call into ministry. His wife did not believe his conversion was genuine, but she chose one night to attend a revival meeting where he was preaching. Near the conclusion of his message the Holy Spirit moved, releasing an utterance in tongues, and the interpretation was given to the church. At that moment, supernaturally, God removed all hurt and pain from the woman, released forgiveness for her ex-husband, and they were remarried and have ministered together for many years.

Paul taught that men are to love their wives as Christ loved the church (Eph. 5:25). A husband and wife are not to deprive themselves of physical relationships, for if they do, Satan can tempt them for being inconsistent (1 Cor. 7:5). When we ignore the Holy Spirit's call, instruction, and direction, we too can open an opportunity for Satan to misguide, building pressure within that leads to actions of disobedience. The attributes of love, compassion, and affection are all imparted by the Holy Spirit and have a positive effect on those who receive Him. The Pharisees proved you could be *clean* but *mean*, outwardly religious but inwardly rude (Matt. 23:27). They rejected the work of the Spirit through Christ and His disciples. However, those who received found righteousness, peace, and joy in the Holy Spirit (Rom. 14:17).

The Word of God and the Holy Spirit are an unbeatable team. God's Word is powerful; it impacts the rational and reasoning part of the human psyche. We are not living on blind faith, but we have a foundation of truth, which can be reasoned and expounded upon in an intellectual conversation. The Holy Spirit, however, touches the emotional part of the human psyche. When spiritual conviction strikes the soul of a sinner, he or she may begin to weep tears of repentance. When powerful worship and praise are released in a gathering of believers, the Spirit can be felt, and often hands are raised. Some may even leap for joy in the more charismatic congregations.

It is not good for churches to downgrade the *emotional connection* of the Holy Spirit among the followers of Christ. The word *emotion* is a French word, but it is derived from the Latin, which means, "without and move." We derive the word *motivation* from the same words. Emotions are a part of the body, soul, and spirit makeup of each human, and without emotions there is no motivation. Thus when a local congregation rejects any form of emotion in their worship setting, the people will look as though they are attending a lecture, as there is no movement or response from the pew sitters.

Christ loves the church, and husbands are to love their wives as Christ loves the church. Part of our love is *intimacy*, a word that by definition has the connection of love and affection. The love of God overflows and gives us the desire to love others. Our personal relationship with our companions will be enhanced and affection increased through the impartation of the intimacy created by a close relationship with the Holy Spirit.

5. The Holy Spirit signals danger by using burdens.

The word *burden* is recorded sixty-nine times in the King James Version of Scripture. The word means, "to go down under; a weighty load, to inflict heaviness in the mind and spirit of a person." Often Old Testaments prophets spoke warnings under great burdens, as their words were often rejected by God's own people. Zechariah used the phrase "The burden of the word of the LORD" when prophesying warnings to Judah and Israel (Zech 9:1; 12:1). Experiencing burdens are a part of our spiritual walk.

> Who are kept by the power of God through faith unto salvation ready to be revealed in the last time. Wherein ye greatly rejoice, though now for a season, if need be, ye are in heaviness through manifold temptations.
>
> —1 PETER 1:5–6, KJV

This heaviness, or weight in your spirit can build up through battles with temptation, severe trials of the faith, and personal trouble with the family or the job. God, however, uses the inner feeling of a burden as a spiritual *signal* that there may be some form of danger or trouble in your path. At times a believer will be burdened to pray for a specific situation or person.

I recall one Saturday morning when I was so greatly burdened and heavy in my spirit that a feeling of foreboding danger was covering my mind like a dark cloud. I knew from experience this was an indicator to pray. I went to our ministry prayer barn and began travailing in heavy intercession for more than one hour. I sensed a spirit of premature death on someone, and I knew I was praying for that person's life to be spared, although I had no revelation as to whom I was praying for. I prayed until the burden lifted.

Three days later my office manager met me outside my office and said, "I must go to Alabama to see my mother. She just died, but they brought her back to life." I told him I had prayed for someone to live that was on the verge of a premature death. He later found out she died five times that day and was revived by people who knew a procedure to bring her back. She had a 3 percent chance of living, and my office manager was told that if she lived, she would be a vegetable and have no quality of life, or it would be low. I believe the prayer stripped the hold of the power of death, and she was not only raised up but went back to work with no complications whatsoever! Following the prayer burden led to a path of life on her behalf.

The same type of prayer burden occurred days before an unexpected series of tornadoes, including an F-4, struck our city of Cleveland, Tennessee. Much intercession was being made as believers sensed coming danger and began praying for protection, unaware of what their burden involved. Days later I was hosting a conference in a building on a hill when the F-4 hit our town, exploding buildings, uprooting trees, and even bringing death to several people. We remained in the building praying the entire time, and no car, home, or life was lost by those in the facility that night. Someone had already prayed in advance before the trouble came. The Holy Spirit knows both the good and bad laid in your path, and burdens are often red lights to stop what you're doing and find a prayer closet for deeper intercession.

6. Singing in the Spirit releases you from heaviness (Acts 16:25).

If you have never heard a person or a group of individuals *sing in the spirit*, or sing in unison in the prayer language of the Spirit, then you have missed what I believe is a little heaven on earth. Singing in the Spirit is mentioned by Paul in 1 Corinthians 14:15:

> What is the conclusion then? I will pray with the spirit, and
> I will also pray with the understanding. I will sing with the
> spirit, and I will also sing with the understanding.

It was Paul who spoke of the three forms of singing for believers in Ephesians 5:19, where he mentioned "psalms and hymns and spiritual songs," and he adds that we should sing and make melody in our hearts. Singing psalms was common among the Jews, as the Book of Psalms in the Bible was set to music. The Greek word here is *psalmos,* which by definition is a sacred ode set to music and often accompanied by a harp or another form of instrument. The Greek word for "hymns" is *humnos,* and again is a sacred song that was perhaps linked to the Book of Psalms or some other form of religious and spiritual music. In the traditional Christian church, the hymns are the old songs written in the earlier days, usually during the eighteenth and nineteenth century, and were used by choirs in Europe and North America. The hymn "Amazing Grace" is considered a classic hymn, along with "It Is Well With My Soul" and numerous others. The phrase "spiritual songs" can be interpreted as a song that is birthed by the Holy Spirit Himself, or a divinely inspired song. As an example, in the early 1990s I was ministering in Florida when I began singing a spiritual song with the words "Let the veil down, and let the praise go up." This was a spiritually inspired song, and later verses were added. Years have passed, and this song has been sung by tens of thousands since then in churches and meetings around the world. This would be considered a "spiritual song."

It is difficult to remain sad and despondent when singing a spiritual song. This is why singing and worship music are significant parts of a worship experience. Notice that a minister does not preach first and afterward call the choir to minister, but we worship first through music, and ministering the Word follows. This is because the music and singing often break the hardened soil of the human heart, enabling the seed of the Word to enter and be implanted in the spirit of the listener. An example is when David played his harp, the tormenting spirit controlling Saul departed from him, and he "would become refreshed and well" (1 Sam. 16:23). Prior to giving a prophetic word, Elisha called for a musician to begin playing music. As the tones of the instrument filled the air, we read, "Then it happened, when the musician played, that the hand of the LORD came upon him" (2 Kings 3:15). In the Apocalypse, prior to the release of the tribulation judgments, the twenty-four elders are seen holding harps and singing a new song exalting Christ as the Lamb of God (Rev. 5:8–9). These examples should illustrate the importance of releasing the spiritual songs in your heart by singing and worship.

In the context of Ephesians, when Paul wrote of "making melody in your heart," he then instructed believers not to be "drunk with wine" but to be "filled with the Spirit" (Eph. 5:18). Greek scholars note that the phrase "be filled" is in the Greek tense of *continually being filled*— not just a one-time experience but a continual flow and refilling. It appears Paul is saying that when we sing from *our spirit* and sing *in the Spirit*, the song ministers both to God and to our own spirit, building up and edifying ourselves.

When Paul and Silas were arrested, beaten, and placed in wooden stocks, they chose to sing a song at midnight, *worshipping in their captivity.* God sent an earthquake that split the foundation of the prison, breaking the iron bars holding other prisoners in captivity. It makes little sense to break out in singing after you have been arrested, beaten, and locked up for preaching. Yet, praise *rattled their cage,* and their freedom from chains also led to the freedom of others around them (Acts 16:24–26). Singing broke the heaviness of spirit and led to a "jailhouse rock" revival. I have learned that it is virtually impossible to remain heavy in spirit when releasing a song from your spirit. At times, instead of *saying* your praise, try *singing* your praise. There is one book in the Bible with 150 chapters of songs—the Book of Psalms. From a youth David understood the breakthrough power of the song.

7. My mind can interpret what the Spirit is saying (1 Cor. 14:13).

Some believers, even Spirit-filled believers, are unaware that when they speak with other tongues there is also an gift of "interpretation" in which the Holy Spirit will interpret the prayer back to their minds, and the person speaking can have a perception of the general theme of what is being spoken (1 Cor. 12:30; 14:5, 13, 27). This gift is not a *translation* but an *interpretation,* and there is a difference. A translation is viewed as a word-for-word exchange of what is being said from one language to another. English translations of the Bible are from Hebrew, Aramaic, and Greek to the English language. Other languages may have slightly different words used in their culture that translate differently than our English translations. Biblical translators examine each original word and find the best word to translate for that specific language version. An *interpretation,* however, can be a word-for-word exchange, but it can also be a comparison of what is being said.

When preaching overseas in a foreign nation, a minister uses an interpreter to interpret the message to the audience. A humorous example was when one of our missionaries was ministering in a very remote village in India. He was attempting to compare the power of the Holy Spirit, but these villagers didn't even have televisions or radios. The interpreter could not find any word to describe what the speaker was saying. There was, however, one vacuum cleaner in the village, which was used in a lower-class hotel. The Indian interpreter began describing the force of the vacuum cleaner to remove dirt from the floor as the air picks it up. There is no biblical word for a vacuum cleaner, but the analogy was effective, and the people understood the *concept* of the power of the Spirit to remove unclean things from your life.

To interpret a tongue from the Spirit, the person often gives a general meaning of what is being said. One person may interpret the opening phrase as, "Thus says the Lord..." Another may say, "The Spirit of the Lord says..." Still another may say, "The Lord desires to speak to you..." This was a common gift in the early church when the Spirit released a vocal revelation. Some examples include Acts 13:2, which states: "As they ministered to the Lord and fasted, the Holy Spirit said, 'Now separate to Me Barnabas and Saul for the work to which I have called them.'" In another reference the Holy Spirit spoke to the church at Jerusalem, and they sent a letter to Antioch with Paul and Barnabas, saying, "For it seemed good to the Holy Spirit, and to us..." (Acts 15:28). When Paul said that the Holy Spirit "testifies in every city" that chains awaited him in Jerusalem, he was referencing prophetic warnings given to him by men who were prophets in the church (Acts 20:23). Paul warned Timothy concerning the last days by writing, "The Spirit expressly says..." (1 Tim. 4:1), which means the Holy Spirit was speaking verbally through someone in the church and indicating events that would transpire in the last days.

This gift of interpretation operates not only in a charismatic worship service but also in your private prayer devotions. He (or she) who prays in a tongue should pray that he interprets (1 Cor. 14:13). Here is how the gift of interpretation can operate. If you have ever been deep in intercessory prayer, praying in the prayer language of the Spirit, your mind may suddenly began to focus on a person or a serious situation while you are praying. I have learned that at times as you are praying in the Spirit, your intellect is alert to the mind and will of God, and the Spirit is revealing to you the situation(s) that He is interceding for on your behalf. At other times, when you shift from praying in the Spirit to praying in your native language (English in my case), you may begin to call out names of people or declare special decrees and confession. This is actually a clue that reveals the general theme or situations the Holy Spirit was presenting to the Father.

In full gospel churches, after a public utterance in tongues a person will stand to give the interpretation for the congregation. However, you can also receive the interpretation in your own spirit, as the Spirit will inspire your soul with an inspiration of what or whom you are praying for.

8. The anointing works in weak vessels.

I have learned that God does not work through many perfect vessels, as not many believers have reached the heights of spiritual perfection and struggle with weaknesses, but He has always flowed through obedient vessels. Perfection, from a New Testament sense, is not being faultless, but it is better rendered as complete and whole in one's thinking, actions, words, and character. When I speak of being *weak*, the common Greek word is *astheneo* and can mean being feeble in any sense of the word—physical, emotional, or mental. Paul was physically abused and beaten for the gospel and was at times weak in his body. However, he wrote that when he was weak, through Christ he was made strong (2 Cor. 12:10). The internal energy that emerged out of Paul through the Holy Spirit not only sustained him in his infirmities but also motivated him to rise above his physical pain. The word *strong* in 2 Corinthians 12:10 means, "to be given power and made capable to accomplish something."

Believers struggle with lack of self-esteem, fear of failure, doubt, guilt from their past, lack of confidence in their own prayers being answered, and other weaknesses. The fact that Christ chose common men to turn the world upside down (Acts 17:6) with the gospel reminds me of Paul's words:

> But God has chosen the foolish things of the world to put to shame the wise, and God has chosen the weak things of the world to put to shame the things which are mighty.
>
> —1 Corinthians 1:27

At times a weakness expresses itself in a moral weakness. During my lifetime I have known of men and women greatly used of God who fell into satanic traps or self-invited snares. Afterward believers would question, "How can they be anointed and do such things?" The precious anointing did not prevent them from being exposed to the world system and the influence of temptation, as temptation is common to all men (1 Cor. 10:13). The failure came, not because the Holy Spirit was not indwelling them, but because the person yielded to the voice of the tempter. Christ was anointed at the Jordan River, and within forty days He met the tempter head-on in the wilderness. He heard the enemy's voice, but He refused to follow the suggestions of Satan (Matt. 4:1–10).

Other weaknesses are physical. To illustrate how the anointing works through physically weak vessels, my own father in his late fifties became a diabetic, and in the last two years of his life (he passed at age seventy-eight) he took dialysis three days a week. Yet when Dad was suffering with high sugar levels in his seventies, he continued to minister to the sick with healing prayers and saw amazing results, including several individuals who were miraculously healed of cancer. His situation reminded me of when the prophet Elisha received a "double portion" of the spirit of Elijah, and yet he died on a deathbed from an unknown sickness. (See 2 Kings 13:14, 20.) The spirit is always willing, but the flesh is weak (Matt. 26:41). Take a look at the leaders in the early church—a fisherman named Peter who lost his temper to the point of cursing, Thomas who doubted the resurrection of Christ, and James and John who wanted to be listed at the top as the Messiah's favorite disciples, sitting on His right hand in Christ's kingdom. Obviously if God only anointed perfect people, then most churches would lack anointed believers.

I have struggled with my own weaknesses. When I was in high school, I detested the subject of English. My boredom of the subject was so intense that I made no effort to study or advance my knowledge. My mother saw my failing grades and said, "Son, you must do better because one day you may need to write or speak to people."

I told Mom, "I am never going to write a book and never going to speak publicly, so why do I need to learn all these rules of grammar and writing?"

At age eighteen I wrote my first thirty-two-page book, followed by three more the following year. I can recall numerous misspelled words, and my sentence structure and grammar had to be continually corrected—but isn't that what a proofreader is paid to do? I began to depend upon the inspiration and gifting of the Holy Spirit to help me with the *content* and *subject matter*, letting others correct my poor grammar. Today our books appear on national best sellers' lists, and some have received national awards. The Holy Spirit, despite my weakness, imparted wisdom and knowledge. The Bible says, "The Spirit also helpeth our infirmities" (Rom. 8:26, KJV). The word *infirmities* can also mean a feebleness or weakness of the mind, body, or the spirit. He helps us in our weakness—not to *dwell* on the weakness, but to rise *above* the weakness. If we could mature to *perfection* without the Holy Spirit, then we would not need Him to indwell us. He is given to help our weakness.

9. The Holy Spirit brings peace to difficult situations.
In Isaiah 28:11–12 we read:

> For with stammering lips and another tongue
> He will speak to this people,
> To whom He said, "This is the rest with which
> You may cause the weary to rest,"
> And, "This is the refreshing";
> Yet they would not hear.

The apostle Paul quotes the above passage in 1 Corinthians 14:21 when presenting his discourse concerning the purpose and orderly operation of the vocal gifts of tongues and prophecy. Isaiah mentioned that this manifestation would initiate a "rest," causing the weary to rest. There are several Hebrew words for *rest* in the Old Testament. God rested on the seventh day (Gen. 2:2). The singular word *rest* is first used in Genesis 8:9, where the dove of Noah returned to the ark, having no place to rest the soles of its feet. This word *rest* in Isaiah 28:12 figuratively means, "to console and give consolation to." The word holds the image of a mother who consoles her children.

I cannot count the number of times that I was very weary in body, soul, or spirit and with little energy to function, causing the desire to pray and study to depart from me. In these times I would find a place of solitude and simply begin to flow in the prayer language of the Spirit. During the process of the prayer I could sense strength being renewed within me. The Holy Spirit brings rest to the *whole person*—body, soul, and spirit. One of the nine fruit of the Spirit is peace (Gal. 5:22).

There are other lessons I have learned through years of ministry. The Holy Spirit is the ultimate teacher, and you as the student will be ever learning the many mysteries He unlocks for you in your lifetime.

Chapter Sixteen

THE HIDDEN MESSAGE IN THE FEAST OF TABERNACLES

Speak to the children of Israel, saying: "The fifteenth day of this seventh month shall be the Feast of Tabernacles for seven days to the LORD. On the first day there shall be a holy convocation. You shall do no customary work on it. For seven days you shall offer an offering made by fire to the LORD. On the eighth day you shall have a holy convocation, and you shall offer an offering made by fire to the LORD. It is a sacred assembly, and you shall do no customary work on it.

—LEVITICUS 23:34–36

THE LAST OF Israel's seven feasts is called *Sukkot*, or in the English, *Tabernacles*. This feast begins on the fifteenth day of the seventh month and continues for seven days. Each day was accompanied by burnt offerings on the brass altar of sacrifice. Each feast has a specific designation commemorating a major event with Israel, and the Feast of Tabernacles, also called Feast of Booths, commemorates Israel living in the wilderness during their forty-year journey. This feast also coincides with the conclusion of the harvest season and the beginning of the rain and new planting season in the winter, chiefly the barley and wheat. During Tabernacles seventy bullocks are offered that represent the seventy souls that came out of Jacob (Exod. 1:5).

On the last day of the feast the priest on duty performed the water libation ceremony. The high priest, dressed in his eight garments of beauty, descended from the temple platform to the Pool of Siloam on the southern slopes outside of the city walls, leading a group of joyful priests through the Water Gate to the pool below. The high priest would fill a golden vessel with the *living water* from the pool, returning to the temple through the Eastern Gate. Fellow priests had cut willow branches twenty-five feet in length, each priest standing shoulder to shoulder at thirty feet apart, moving their feet in unison and swishing the branches from left to right in unison. This swishing action produced the sound of a *rushing wind* and was a visible illustration of the Holy Spirit's breath that would come to the temple. When the Holy Spirit descended on the Day of Pentecost, the believers gathered in the temple area heard the sound of a "rushing mighty wind" (Acts 2:2).

During this unique ritual a flute player, also termed "the pierced one," called for both the wind and water to enter the temple. Near the brass altar were two containers, one of silver holding wine, and one of gold containing the living water. At a predetermined moment in the ceremony, the high priest mixes the wine and water into one vessel. Other priests then circle the brass altar seven times, forming a willow canopy over the altar. These traditions have specific implications for the Messiah. Christ would be pierced in His hands, feet, and side, with blood dripping from the sharp thorns piercing His head. The prophet Zechariah predicted that the Jews would one day look upon Him whom they had pierced (Zech. 12:10). Christ is certainly the "pierced one." The wine and water is also significant, as wine in the Eucharist is symbolic of the blood of Christ (John 6:54–55; 1 Cor. 11:25). The temple in Jerusalem was a community of priests who were ceremonially cleansed by the water at the laver and daily offered blood from sacrifices on the altar. At the moment of Christ's death the centurion thrust a spear into Christ's heart, sending forth blood and water (John 19:34). The mixing and eventual pouring out of the water and wine on the altar on the last day of the feast was a picture of Christ, who would bring forth the water and blood from His body, providing Himself as our redemption at the altar of redemption!

The rejoicing is demonstrated with an object called the *lulav*, made from four tree branches. These four branches are from four different species and represent the four experiences in life. The first is the palm branch, which is a Jewish picture of joy. Then a myrtle branch is tied with it, representing rest. The willow branch has been a symbol of sorrow and weeping and can be confirmed as such when the Jewish captives in Babylon hung their harps upon willow trees and refused to sing the Lord's song in a strange land (Ps. 137:1–9). The fourth branch is the citron, or a branch from a citrus tree, which is slightly bitter and sour, representing the times of bitterness that are experienced throughout seasons in our life.

Jesus Attended This Feast

According to John's Gospel, Christ attended this feast during His earthly ministry:

> On the last day, that great day of the feast, Jesus stood and cried out, saying, "If anyone thirsts, let him come to Me and drink. He who believes in Me, as the Scripture has said, out of his heart will flow rivers of living water." But this He spoke concerning the Spirit, whom those believing in Him would receive; for the Holy Spirit was not yet given, because Jesus was not yet glorified.
>
> —JOHN 7:37–39

This feast in John 7 was the Feast of Tabernacles, and the "great day" and "last day" is the ceremony of the water libation. In John's narrative Christ is standing at the temple near the brass altar where the high priest is pouring out the wine and oil from the golden vessel and praying prayers for the Holy Spirit to be poured out. Suddenly there is a loud voice (Jesus "cried out," verse 37), saying to come to Him and drink, for out of your belly will flow rivers of living water.

Somewhere in this same location would be where the Holy Spirit would blow like a wind and the Spirit would baptize the first believers in His power (Acts 1:8; 2:1–4). Observe the amazing setting. The Feast of Tabernacles and the libation service was for petitioning God for both natural rain for the coming harvests and for spiritual rain in the form of the Holy Spirit being poured out. Water is poured out upon the four corners of the altar, and the Holy Spirit would be poured out globally, on all four directions of the earth. Thus Jesus connects the last day of the Feast of Tabernacles with the upcoming outpouring of the Spirit.

The Eighth Day of the Feast

The Torah says this feast is to continue for seven days (Lev. 23:39). However, later an additional eighth day was added, called *Shemini Atzeret*, or the *rejoicing in the Torah*. Jesus remained in Jerusalem at this time, as it was here that the religious leaders brought a woman to Him who was caught in the act of adultery (John 8:3).

Jesus had remained in Jerusalem during the conclusion of the eighth day, spending the night on the Mount of Olives (v. 1). In the morning He returned to the temple for the eighth day, which would have been the rejoicing in the Torah. That morning the Pharisees threw a woman at His feet who had been caught in the act of adultery. She may have actually been a prostitute, as there were huge crowds of men over twenty years of age from across Israel present for the feasts. Notice that the adulterous man is not present to be stoned along with her. The Law of Moses required her to be stoned. The Pharisees tempted Christ by demanding Him what should happen to the woman. Instead of giving a verbal response, Christ gave an illustrated message by writing on the ground.

This is significant, considering the "trial of bitter waters" referred to in Numbers 5. The law stated that if a husband was suspicious that his wife had secretly committed adultery and he could not prove it, he brought her to the priest, who performed a rather bizarre ritual. The priest wrote the curses of the law on parchment, mixed water with dirt from the floor in a vessel, then poured the water over the curses, causing the words from the ink that were diluted with water to enter a cup. The woman was then required to drink from this mixture. If she was not guilty, she would have no ill effect. If, however, she was guilty, her thigh would begin to swell, revealing her secret sin to the priest and to her husband.

It is possible that the very dirt Christ wrote in was the same dirt used for the trial of bitter waters! Or perhaps His actions were a part of what Jeremiah the prophet wrote in Jeremiah 17:13:

> O LORD, the hope of Israel,
> All who forsake You shall be ashamed.
> "Those who depart from Me
> Shall be written in the earth,
> Because they have forsaken the LORD,
> The fountain of living waters."

This act on the eighth day of the Feast identified Christ as the living Torah or the living Word of God. Whatever He wrote in the dust scattered the accusers, releasing her from her punishment and bringing redemption from Christ to her life.

Tabernacles in the Millennium

Moving forward in prophetic time, the thousand-year rule of Christ on earth from Jerusalem with His saints is called *the millennial reign* because it lasts for a thousand years, which, in Latin, is a millennium. According to the prophet Ezekiel, all believers and all earthly inhabitants will observe the Sabbath, the new moons, and special feasts during this time. According to Zechariah, one of the yearly feasts that all nations must attend is the Feast of Tabernacles:

> And it shall come to pass that everyone who is left of all the nations which came against Jerusalem shall go up from year to year to worship the King, the LORD of hosts, and to keep the Feast of Tabernacles. And it shall be that whichever of the families of the earth do not come up to Jerusalem to worship the King, the LORD of hosts, on them there will be no rain.
> —ZECHARIAH 14:16–17

The priestly rituals preformed during the Feast of Tabernacles are connected to asking God for rain in the coming months as the seed is planted. In the millennium, if nations refuse to attend the ceremonies and joyful celebrations of Tabernacles, then God will withhold the blessing of rain from their land:

> If the family of Egypt will not come up and enter in, they shall have no rain; they shall receive the plague with which the LORD strikes the nations who do not come up to keep the Feast of Tabernacles. This shall be the punishment of Egypt and the punishment of all the nations that do not come up to keep the Feast of Tabernacles.
>   —ZECHARIAH 14:18–19

The Feast of Tabernacles is the climax of a time known as *the seasons of our joy.* The Jewish concept of the days between the Feasts of Trumpets (the seventh month and first day) and the end of Tabernacles (the seventh month and the twenty-first day—a seven-day festival) is that the Feasts of Trumpets prepares a warning for the people that the Day of Atonement is approaching when God judges His people. However, great joy always follows repentance and the removal of guilt. The Feast of Tabernacles is truly a season of great rejoicing.

Jews and Gentiles Together

In the future, Tabernacles will be an assigned season in which the Messiah will call all of Israel and the Gentile nations to Jerusalem for a celebration. Today this is the only feast of the seven biblical feasts where both Jews and Gentiles participate in the rejoicing. Modern Israel is filled with tens of thousands of tourists from around the world, arriving by plane to spend seven days in the Holy Land with devout Jews and Messianic believers.

While Tabernacles brings Jews and Gentiles together, there is a ritual performed by the priest on Pentecost symbolizing the link of Jews and Gentiles. The priest prepares two identical loaves of bread and waves them before the Lord at Pentecost. These loaves represent the Jews and Gentiles coming together, which was the most important aspect of the coming of the Holy Spirit. In Christ's time the devout Jews had little contact with Gentiles and considered them uncircumcised and unclean. However, the Holy Spirit brought Jews into the covenant at Pentecost, later introducing the Holy Spirit at the home of Cornelius, where the Holy Spirit baptized the entire family of this Italian centurion, initiating the first family of Gentiles into the new covenant. These are the two loaves at Pentecost that are in the hands of the priest, just as the true church consists of both Jews and Gentiles who are one new man in Christ (Eph. 2:15).

Christ spoke during the water libation ritual of the Spirit infilling believers and rivers of living water flowing out of their bellies (innermost being). The Holy Spirit dwells within the spirit of the baptized believers and flows from their spirit to bring forth a river of salvation, a river of sanctification, a river of healing, and times of refreshing. These truths indicate how the Holy Spirit code is concealed in certain rituals and customs of the feasts.

The water can be a picture of water baptism, and the wine can be a symbol of the blood of Christ. We enter our new covenant of redemption through the blood of Christ and seal our public testimony of faith in the water of baptism. The Holy Spirit is the present witness to these spiritual truths.

Chapter Seventeen

THE FIRSTFRUITS
OF THE SPIRIT

Not only that, but we also who have the firstfruits of
the Spirit, even we ourselves groan within ourselves,
eagerly waiting for the adoption, the redemption of our
body.

—ROMANS 8:23

JUST WHAT IS the meaning of the "firstfruits of the Spirit"? The
term *firstfruits* is mentioned thirty-two times in the King James
Version of the Bible, seven times in the New Testament. Among the
seven feasts of Israel, the third feast is called the Feast of Firstfruits. It
was the third of the spring feasts and was a time to mark the first of
the ripened barley.

The process was as follows. When the fruit began to ripen on the
trees, the owners would mark the first ripened fruit by tying a reed
around it. This would include figs, grapes, and pomegranates, the three
main fruits of the seven foods of Israel. As the harvest arrived, the
owners would identify the firstfruits by the reed used to mark them.
When the time came to present the firstfruits to God, the worshippers would arrive walking, riding horses, or carrying families in carts,

carrying their baskets with firstfruits to the temple in Jerusalem. Those closer to the city brought fresh fruit; those coming long distances presented dried fruit to prevent their offering from spoiling during their journey, which could take days.[1] It was common to present to God all seven foods of the land—barley, wheat, grapes, olives, pomegranates, figs, and honey (Deut. 8:8).

The law governing the firstfruits is recorded in Leviticus 23:10–13:

> Speak to the children of Israel, and say to them: "When you come into the land which I give to you, and reap its harvest, then you shall bring a sheaf of the firstfruits of your harvest to the priest. He shall wave the sheaf before the LORD, to be accepted on your behalf; on the day after the Sabbath the priest shall wave it. And you shall offer on that day, when you wave the sheaf, a male lamb of the first year, without blemish, as a burnt offering to the LORD. Its grain offering shall be two-tenths of an ephah of fine flour mixed with oil, an offering made by fire to the LORD, for a sweet aroma; and its drink offering shall be of wine, one-fourth of a hin."

The Feast of Firstfruits was a prophetic preview of Christ's resurrection and how He presented Himself before the Father in the heavenly temple as the final sacrifice for sins. Firstfruits began the day after the Sabbath of Passover, the Sabbath being a Saturday, thus on Sunday morning. Early on Sunday morning—the first day of the week, Matthew 28:1 reveals that several women were standing at the tomb of Jesus, not knowing He was already raised from the grave. When Mary saw Him, she did not recognize Him until He spoke, saying, "Do not cling to Me, for I have not yet ascended to My Father" (John 20:17). In Christ's time, on this same morning of His resurrection, there was a presentation of firstfruits occurring at the temple in Jerusalem. The high priest had arisen early Sunday morning, marking and cutting a sheaf of ripened barley from a field just outside the Eastern Gate, carrying it back to the temple and offering the barley sheaf to God along with the burnt offering of a lamb. He did this for forty-nine days (called *counting the omer*, Deut. 16:9–10), until the Day of Pentecost arrived.

As the priest was offering the lamb on the brass altar at the temple in Jerusalem on the first day of Firstfruits, Christ was presenting

Himself in the heavenly temple as the Lamb that was slain for the redemption of mankind. The high priest also offered the sheaf on the altar as the firstfruits offering. When Christ arose, there was a group of saints who also arose with Him and were seen for a short period walking in Jerusalem (Matt. 27:52–53).

Christ was the firstfruits of the resurrection, and these risen saints in Jerusalem were classified as the firstfruits that rose with Him.

> But now Christ is risen from the dead, and has become the firstfruits of those who have fallen asleep.
> —1 CORINTHIANS 15:20

In the law of firstfruits, by the high priest offering the first of the ripened fruit or grains to God at the temple, the Lord would ensure that the remaining harvest fields would be blessed. Christ being the first to raise Himself from the dead indicates that all those who died in Christ and are buried in fields and cemeteries around the world are *set apart* for a great resurrection in the future! A remnant of saints were raised with Christ, and since Christ is the firstfruits, this remnant is a picture of the firstfruits of the resurrection that will occur when the "dead in Christ will rise first" at the ingathering of the saints (1 Thess. 4:16).

Christ instructed Mary to not touch Him (or delay Him), as He was on an assignment to ascend to the Father for a specific purpose. The sacred furniture in the heavenly temple required Christ's atonement, as sin had first manifested in the universe with the rebellion of Satan and a third of the angels in ages past (Luke 10:18; Rev. 12:4, 9). The writer of Hebrews reveals what Christ did when He entered the heavenly temple:

> But Christ came as High Priest of the good things to come, with the greater and more perfect tabernacle not made with hands, that is, not of this creation. Not with the blood of goats and calves, but with His own blood He entered the Most Holy Place once for all, having obtained eternal redemption.
> —HEBREWS 9:11–12

Christ purified the sacred heavenly vessels, as He would forty days later ascend to His permanent position as the High Priest of our confession of faith, ever living to make intercession for us.

The Firstfruits Lump

Romans 11:16 records:

> For if the firstfruit is holy, the lump is also holy; and if the root is holy, so are the branches.

In this verse the "lump" refers to the dough that the priest formed to bake the bread each week for the twelve loaves laid on the table of showbread. The priest would pinch off a portion of the dough and present it to the Lord, making the remaining dough holy or set apart for the table. As a note, the principle of the first being set apart and the remaining being blessed is the same principle used concerning the tithe and the increase. By presenting the tithe (the tenth) of your field, harvest, or money to God at His house, the remaining 90 percent of the harvest, fruits, and money are blessed, and God sets the increase blessing for the rest.

With such an important concept as firstfruits, what was the meaning of Paul's words the "firstfruits of the Spirit"? He wrote that we who have the firstfruits of the Spirit "groan within ourselves" (Rom. 8:23). After writing of the firstfruits of the Spirit, Paul then gives an explanation three verses later in verse 26 of how the Holy Spirit helps us when we don't know what to pray for:

> Likewise the Spirit also helps in our weaknesses. For we do not know what we should pray for as we ought, but the Spirit Himself makes intercession for us with groanings which cannot be uttered.

The Holy Spirit makes available nine spiritual gifts, listed in 1 Corinthians 12:8–10.

- Word of wisdom
- Word of knowledge

- Faith

- Gifts of healing

- Working of miracles

- Prophecy

- Discerning of spirits

- Divers (different) kinds of tongues

- Interpretation of tongues

One of these gifts is called *"divers* kinds of tongues" (1 Cor. 12:10, KJV, emphasis added). Many believers are unaware that there is a difference between the *prayer language* given to believers upon receiving the baptism of the Holy Spirit and the *gift of different kinds of tongues.* Both are given by the Holy Spirit, and both are a prayer language; however, one is given as an initial evidence of the infilling of the Holy Spirit, and the other is a special gift that follows the initial infilling of the Holy Spirit.

To further understand this, look at the word *gift* in Scripture. The Day of Pentecost was the initial outpouring of the Spirit, and all believers "began to speak with tongues, as the Spirit gave them utterance" (Acts 2:4). These languages were not some odd *gibberish,* but uneducated Galileans and common people were speaking in languages they had never learned, and they were understood by the Jews out of every nation who were attending the feast at Pentecost. The worshippers were amazed (v. 7). Peter spoke, saying:

> Repent, and let every one of you be baptized in the name of Jesus Christ for the remission of sins; and you shall receive the gift of the Holy Spirit. For the promise is to you and to your children, and to all who are afar off, as many as the Lord our God will call.
>
> —ACTS 2:38–39

The Greek word here for "gift" is *doreah,* which means, "a gratuity, such as someone receiving a tip." This particular gift of the Spirit is accompanied by an initial prayer language imparted by the Holy Spirit. Believers in three different narratives recognized they had received the Holy Spirit as He spoke through them in other tongues (Acts 2:4; 10:45–46; 19:1–7). This gift of the initial evidence of the Spirit, however, was different from the gift of different (divers) kinds of tongues referred to in 1 Corinthians 12. After Paul mentioned the nine gifts of the Holy Spirit, he then posed a series of questions to believers:

> Now you are the body of Christ, and members individually. And God has appointed these in the church: first apostles, second prophets, third teachers, after that miracles, then gifts of healings, helps, administrations, varieties of tongues. Are all apostles? Are all prophets? Are all teachers? Are all workers of miracles? Do all have gifts of healings? Do all speak with tongues? Do all interpret? But earnestly desire the best gifts. And yet I show you a more excellent way.
>
> —1 CORINTHIANS 12:27–31

Paul is speaking about the operation of the nine gifts of the Spirit working within the body of Christ. He uses the Greek word *charismata*, not *doreah*, when identifying these as "gifts." There is the gift of the Holy Spirit (*doreah*), which is the baptism in the Holy Spirit accompanied by speaking with other tongues. There is also a gift of "kinds of tongues" (*charismata*), which gives the speaker the ability to speak in various languages unknown to the speaker, which are a sign to the unbeliever. Everyone can receive the initial gift of the Holy Spirit and seek a prayer language, as it is "to you and to your children, and to all who are afar off, as many as the Lord our God will call," meaning call to repentance (Acts 2:39). However, not everyone has the gift (*charismata*) of divers tongues.

In any given congregation, only a small remnant of believers have a gift to teach or the patience to assist in the ministry of helps. James wrote that a sick person in the church should call the elders and be anointed in the name of the Lord for healing (James 5:14). This was an instruction for all churches, because not everyone had a gift of laying on of hands for healing; thus God made a provision for personal ministry for those in need. Notice that Paul wrote in 1 Corinthians 12:30, "Do all speak with tongues? Do all interpret?" In 1 Corinthians 14 Paul spent ample time instructing the church at Corinth of the need to interpret the tongues in a worship service. According to Paul, a person in the church who has the *doreah,* or baptismal level of the Spirit, can "speak to himself and to God" in a worship setting (v. 28). However, if someone gives what is termed a message in tongues to the entire congregation (the *charismata* tongues), then it must be interpreted to edify the church (vv. 26–33).

Many reading this book may have never witnessed the operation of tongues and interpretation in their churches; however, when I was growing up it was not uncommon to witness this manifestation. To understand the difference between the baptism of the Holy Spirit, the gift of the Holy Spirit, and the gift of tongues, in church settings I have asked, "How many have received the prayer language of the Spirit?" Often 95 percent of the people in attendance have. I then ask, "How many have ever given forth a public message in tongues that was inter-preted?" Perhaps only 2 percent have. Thus, not all speak with "(divers) tongues," but all can receive the individual prayer language.

How does this link with the firstfruits of the Spirit?

The Firstfruits of the Spirit

Just as the fruits, grains, and dough were set apart and marked as the first of many, there is a firstfruits of the Holy Spirit, which is linked to groaning and praying in the prayer language, revealed when viewing the context of Paul's writing in Romans 8:22–28. I believe that the initial prayer language of the Spirit is the beginning, or the firstfruits blessings, that then opens the door to all other nine gifts of the Spirit. We often speak of the word *tithe,* which is the tenth. If you have ten dollars, the tenth would be one dollar, leaving nine dollars remaining. In this example, the initial baptism of the Holy Spirit is the *tithe,* so to speak, on the rest of the blessings that will follow!

Paul lists nine charismata or spiritual gifts (1 Cor. 12:7–10). However, a person can only receive these nine after they have received the initial gift of the Holy Spirit Himself. Thus, the firstfruits would be the ini-tial baptism of the Holy Spirit, which then opens the door to the other nine spiritual gifts being available and freely imparted to edify and comfort the members in the body of Christ,and to be used as tools of evangelism to reach the unreached.

Honoring the Firstfruits

The third spring feast of Israel is Firstfruits, indicating that God is serious about each person presenting the first from the field to Him so that the remaining harvest would be blessed. On the first day of Creation God separated the light from the darkness (Gen. 1:5). The "law of the first" is a law of "separation." The firstborn of the animals were to be separated from the flock and set aside for God (Exod. 13:2). The firstfruits of the harvest were marked in the fields and on the trees and were cut from their stems, vines, and trees to be presented to the Lord as a firstfruits offering (Deut. 26:2). God went as far as to say that every firstborn son who opened the womb is marked and separated unto him as holy (Exod. 22:29). The nation of Israel was called God's firstborn (Exod. 4:22). Pharaoh plotted to kill all male sons (including the firstborns) among the Hebrews, throwing them into the Nile after their births. God heard and saw his strategy and later slew all of Egypt's firstborn (v. 23), concluding Pharaoh's *dynasty* by Pharaoh *dying nasty* with his armies by drowning in the Red Sea. The point is...you cannot mistreat the firstborn, and you must honor the firstfruits.

If believers will honor the firstfruits of the Spirit—the very first manifestation of the initial baptism of the Spirit—then the other charismata will flow into their lives. Those who resist the firstfruits manifestation never experience any of the other nine gifts in their lives or ministry.

Chapter Eighteen

THE KEY
TO HIGHLY BLESSED
AND HAPPY CHRISTIANS

He who follows righteousness and mercy
Finds life, righteousness, and honor.

—PROVERBS 21:21

IN MY MANY years of ministry I have observed that too many people are unhappy with their present circumstances, yet they tend to accept things as they are without attempting to change their situation—sort of whatever is just is. This fact can be seen in what is called by some the "law of 5 percent." As few as 1 percent of the people make it to what is called "the top"—a level of business success and financial independence where they are in total charge of their destiny. These people view an obstacle or opposition and *immediately* attempt to solve the problem and overcome it.

Additionally, it appears that only about 4 percent reach the leadership level and oversee a ministry, small business, or supervise the overseeing of people. This 4 percent can encounter the same obstacles or opposition but will *eventually*, over time, work to overcome it.

Some suggest the remaining 95 percent reach a plateau and remain content in whatever they are doing, with little or no desire to become a leader or advance to an executive level position. This group *may or may not work* to overcome, and many will simply blame someone else or look for someone else to step in and solve the problems they see. This group is often heard saying, "That's not my job," or "Work's over; I'm headed home," and they pass the buck of responsibility to others.

Many biblical narratives also reveal similar patterns of leadership—perhaps revealing why some people are selected to be a part of the *inner circle* and others remain with the *main* team. In Luke 6:13–16 Christ selected twelve disciples to join His traveling evangelistic caravan. However, among the twelve, three were selected as special *inner circle* partners with Christ: Peter, James, and John. These three men stuck close to Christ on the Mount of Transfiguration, as the other nine remained in the valley below (Matt. 17:1–2). Christ took eleven disciples into the Garden of Gethsemane, yet invited Peter, James, and John to go a little further with Him, nearer to His prayer rock where He initiated three hours of agonizing intercession (Matt. 26:36–39). Why were Peter, James, and John in the upper percentage among the others?

After the Day of Pentecost Peter became the head apostle to the Jews (called the "apostleship to the circumcised" in Galatians 2:8). James was appointed the leading apostle over the Jerusalem church, and John rose to the position of the presiding bishop of the church after the deaths of the original apostles and later was banished to Patmos, where he received the vision of the Apocalypse (Rev. 1–22). What about the other apostles who were a part of the original twelve (omitting Judas and including Matthias)? All were commissioned to teach, cast out evil spirits, and heal the sick. Then why is there little biblical information listed about the following men?

- Andrew
- Philip
- Bartholomew
- Simon the Zealot
- Thomas
- Justus (Matthias)

After their mention in the four Gospels, these six men seldom appear, from the Book of Acts throughout the entire New Testament epistles. Why were three men selected above the others, and why were the others seemingly less mentioned? Why are only a few Christians truly effective in what they set their minds and spirits to do, and others simply just *get by*?

Lessons From a War

During the Korean War many Americans were taken captive as prisoners of war (POWs). After entering the terrible conditions of the prison camp, where they were confined behind fences, concrete walls, and barbed wire, the POWs were watched closely by their enemies for several weeks. Eventually the group was separated. The Korean captors had secretly observed the actions of the group to find the men who seemed to be the leaders among the group. After a few weeks these suspected leaders were taken to one area and the regulars to another. The Koreans had discovered that if the regulars were placed near a strong personality with leadership skills, the POWs could follow the plans of that stronger personality, eventually making an attempt to escape. Without strong leadership the others lost their willpower to plan an escape and simply settled in their minds that they were in this condition and could do nothing about it.

When America fought the Germans, and Americans were taken as prisoners, the German captors too noticed how certain prisoners were looked upon with more respect than others within the group, and marked them as possible leaders. These men were placed in an escape-proof prison, thus discouraging others from making any attempt to escape. The Germans knew it was possible these leaders could plan and unite the group. In both cases about 5 percent of the men in the camps turned out to be stronger personalities. A leader is a person who takes charge when others are still thinking about a solution. A leader is a person whom others will follow because they trust that leader's judgment or have confidence in his or her dream, vision, or ability. In both cases, Korea and Germany, the men marked as leaders included about 5 percent of the group.

The 5 Percent Barrier

Notice how this percentage begins to manifest in narratives throughout the Bible. After David was anointed king, he later had to flee from Saul's palace and was surrounded by six hundred men who aligned themselves as David's wilderness army, protecting David and fighting on his behalf (1 Sam. 23:13, 23). Out of these six hundred men we are told there were thirty men who were mightier than the others (2 Sam. 23:13). Out of these thirty, David observed three men who were mightier than them all. The first of these three was Adino, who slew eight hundred men at once with a spear (v. 8). The next in line was Eleazar, who fought enemies until his hand stuck to his sword (v. 10). The third was named Shammah, who rose up and ran the Philistine army from his bean patch (vv. 11–12). Out of six hundred men, thirty men equates to about 5 percent! Thus in David's army there were thirty men (5 percent) who stood out among the six hundred!

For some reason the 5 percent becomes a common average in many areas of life. Five percent of businesses grow and become very successful. In a city about 5 percent of the churches will actually make an impact on the community. Among college athletes only about 5 percent can move on to make their sport their career—as a player, a coach, or organizing a sports-related business. I have been raised in church all of my life and have observed that in any church of any size there are about 5 percent of the people who do all of the giving, the work, the teaching, and carry the burden. Others may give, attend, and participate, but there is a core of people without whom the ministry outreach and effectiveness would slowly fade.

How the Holy Spirit Changes the Averages

Look back upon the names of those disciples I previously mentioned that seemingly had lesser impact than Peter, James, and John—the inner three.

- ◆ Andrew
- ◆ Philip

- Bartholomew

- Simon the Zealot

- Thomas

- Justus (Matthias)

Notice the following three facts. First, none of the above ever penned an epistle or wrote a book that was placed in the New Testament. Second, they are seldom mentioned outside of the four Gospels, and third, there is no biblical record of any of them doing great feats or traveling in ministry. But if we look beyond the biblical record into the historical writings and traditions of the early church, then fresh insight is revealed.

According to the book *Foxe's Book of Martyrs*, which traces the history of what happened to the apostles in their lives and ministry, Philip carried the gospel message to Upper Asia, where he was scourged and crucified. Matthias was eventually stoned in Jerusalem and afterward beheaded. Andrew eventually journeyed to Adesa as a missionary and experienced martyrdom by being crucified. The apostle Bartholomew translated Matthew's Gospel in India and later in his ministry was beaten and crucified. Perhaps the most amazing story is that of Thomas, who had been nicknamed by Christians "doubting Thomas" for not believing that Christ had risen from the dead (John 20). Thomas was said to have traveled to India, where God used him to perform astonishing miracles, convincing the heathens that Christ was the true God. However, this apostle was thrust through with a spear and met his death on foreign soil.[1]

These men are part of the same ten who fled and forsook Christ after He was arrested. These chosen ones were hiding behind shut doors when Christ appeared in their room, proving to them He was alive after His resurrection (John 20:19). One disciple, Thomas, even declared his unbelief when he said he would not believe unless he could feel the prints made from the nails (vv. 24–25). What changed these men—the men who were not in the inner circle? Please note Acts 1:13–14, which reveals a special meeting occurring after the ascension of Christ to heaven:

> And when they had entered, they went up into the upper room where they were staying: Peter, James, John, and Andrew; Philip and Thomas; Bartholomew and Matthew; James the son of Alphaeus and Simon the Zealot; and Judas the son of James. These all continued with one accord in prayer and supplication, with the women and Mary the mother of Jesus, and with His brothers.

The names listed above are the names of the eleven apostles (Judas was dead) after Christ's ascension as they were preparing to appoint a replacement for Judas. These same men in this Upper Room would also be present on the Day of Pentecost when the mighty outpouring of the Holy Spirit occurred! Peter, who previously had denied he knew Christ, was the uncompromising voice among the apostles at Pentecost, preaching to an entire Jewish audience without backing down from the facts. The power of the Holy Spirit clothed these men in a boldness unknown to them before.

Jesus said men would receive power after the Holy Spirit comes upon them, and they would be "witnesses" for Him (Acts 1:8). The Greek word for "witnesses" is *martus* and can refer to a judicial witness in a court, as one who is called to the stand to testify, presenting evidence as a witness. This Greek word, however, by analogy is a martyr, and is the same Greek word used when Stephen was stoned to death and called a martyr (Acts 22:20) and Antipas was marked as a faithful martyr in Revelation 2:13. Thus, out of the twelve apostles (including Matthias in the number), eleven of the twelve died as martyrs for the cause of the gospel. They used their voices to testify as a witness and willingly gave up their bodies to receive the martyr's crown.

What gave these man such boldness to come out of a locked room, walk into an upper room, then preach from room to room, house to house, and city to city until their death? The answer is a boldness imparted through the Holy Spirit. Most people are unaware that I am quite backward and a rather shy individual. I spend most of my day in a private office behind closed doors, reading, studying, or praying. I am not a social butterfly by any means, keeping only a small group of close friends near me. When carrying on a conversation with individuals I do not know, I am very limited in my interest and subject matter and therefore am not an interesting person to speak with, unless it is a discussion on the Scriptures, which can go on for hours. However, something very unusual occurs the moment I stand before people to speak the Word of God and teach from Scripture. There is an unction that begins flowing like a river, making the words easy to comprehend and easy to speak.

When I was a young teenaged minister, some called this "a gift to communicate," and it was considered almost a novelty among some church attendees who, in the early days, packed out small churches to hear this "kid preacher" who preached like a man who was forty and not eighteen. However, this was not just some unique *gift*; it was the anointing of the Holy Spirit that I experienced at age eleven, which matured me into a preaching minister by age eighteen. Shyness turns to boldness when the unction of the Spirit begins stirring your spirit.

The apostles were called ignorant and unlearned men, but religious leaders took note that these men "had been with Jesus" (Acts 4:13). It was not their enticing words or debating skills that impressed the more educated elite among the Jewish sects in Jerusalem. The most impressive aspect of the apostles is revealed in these words:

> Now when they saw the boldness of Peter and John, and perceived that they were uneducated and untrained men, they marveled. And they realized that they had been with Jesus.
> —ACTS 4:13

The Greek word for "boldness" comes from two Greek words, *pas,* "all" and *rhesis,* "speech," meaning, "freedom of speech or unrestrained utterance." It means, "to speak out with liberty, plainly and having an absence of fear or intimidation; having confidence."[2] Paul spoke of being in chains in prison and how his circumstances made him "bold to speak the word without fear" (Phil. 1:14). It was the boldness of Peter and John that impressed the high priest and his relatives who heard Peter proclaim the gospel (Acts 4:6–13).

The first encounter with the Holy Spirit is when you are drawn by Him to receive Christ as your Savior (John 14:5). This drawing leads to repentance and is when you are "born of the Spirit" (John 3:6–8). The second encounter is when the Holy Spirit begins to work within you to initiate the grace of sanctification, or the changing of your desires from carnal to spiritual, from the flesh thoughts to the spiritual thoughts (Rom. 15:16). The third encounter will be the baptism in the Holy Spirit, accompanied by the prayer language of the Spirit. After receiving the infilling of the Spirit, there is the opportunity to receive certain gifts of the Spirit. From this point on we must grow in the grace and knowledge of God and exercise the gift of praying in the Spirit.

The 95 percent often complain of their situation, tend to believe they are stuck in their circumstances, and simply go with the flow. If you are in the 95 percent who tend to accept things as they are, continuing in the mundane of life and have little motivation for change, the Holy Spirit can inspire and motive you just as He did the apostles of Christ. The Holy Spirit will expand your vision, enlarge your tents, and increase your possibilities as the Helper from heaven is now within you and directing your steps.

Chapter Nineteen

FREQUENTLY ASKED QUESTIONS ABOUT THE HOLY SPIRIT

But the Helper, the Holy Spirit, whom the Father will send in My name, He will teach you all things, and bring to your remembrance all things that I said to you.
—John 14:26

Question: Why do so many people say "Holy Spirit" and not "Holy Ghost"? Is there a difference between the two terms and if so what is the difference?

Answer: The term "Holy Ghost" is found in the 1611 King James Version of the Bible. Most other translations translate the word "Ghost" as "Spirit." Thus, the difference in the use of the two words is often linked more to the biblical translation a person reads while growing up or the translation they are using today. In the actual Greek New Testament, the word for "Ghost" and "Spirit," as it relates to the *Holy Spirit*, is always the same Greek word, *pneuma*, and refers to breath, spirit beings, the soul of men, and to the Holy Spirit Himself. Thus, to use the term "Holy Ghost" or "Holy Spirit" is actually the same term and often depends upon the personal choice of the individual.

The older believers have been taught from the popular 1611 King James Version of the Scriptures, in which the term "Holy Ghost" is found ninety times in the New Testament. When I was growing up in the church, all teachers and ministers used the words "Holy Ghost" when speaking of the Spirit of the Lord. One of the reasons other version use the words "Holy Spirit" is that tens of thousands of new believers who came to the knowledge of the spiritual charismata in the 1960s and onward had difficulty trying to imagine a "Holy Ghost," because the word *ghost* had come to be linked with haunted houses, ghosts, and negative spirits. The biblical imagery is simply the Spirit of God, and so the term "Holy Spirit" began to be used.

In my opinion, because the Greek word is the same in both interpretations and both meanings are acceptable, it should be up to the individual preference as to which term one chooses to use, "Holy Spirit" or "Holy Ghost," and no one should oppose another person for the choice made. We certainly do not need more division in the body of Christ on this issue; the Holy Spirit is not the author of confusion but of peace (1 Cor. 14:33). He is present among His people, which should illustrate that He is fully aware of your intent and your heart when inviting Him into your life and His presence into your worship setting.

Question: Is there a difference between being "filled" with the Spirit and being "baptized" with the Spirit?

Answer: First, the Holy Spirit was active in both Testaments. In the old covenant He came upon the individual, giving the person the ability or strength to fulfill His assignment. (See Judges 3:10; 6:34; 11:29; 14:6; 15:14.) Under the new covenant the Holy Spirit abides and remains within the believer and is not just a temporary presence that comes upon and then lifts from a person.

When we think of the word *filled*, we see an object that was empty, such as a glass, that is now filled with water to the brim—thus the glass is filled. The Greek word used for "filled" is *pletho*, which translates as, "accomplish, full (to come) and furnish." The infilling of the Spirit is more than the Spirit filling a person's spirit with the power of God. The purpose is to furnish the believer with what he or she is lacking in spiritual fruit, gifts, and abilities.

It was John the Baptist who first used the term *baptize* when he said that Christ would "baptize you with the Holy Spirit and fire" (Matt. 3:11). John "baptized" in water, but predicted the future "baptism" in the Spirit. The same Greek word is used when speaking of *water* and *Spirit* baptism: *baptizo*, meaning, "to immerse or to submerge." John was baptizing men in water unto repentance by submerging them in the waters of the Jordan River. John, however, was also aware that a new baptism was coming, initiated by Christ Himself, and this would be a baptism in the Spirit accompanied with a purging-type fire that would remove the unclean elements from a person's life (Matt. 3:11–12). The idea of Spirit baptism is linked with the idea of the process of water baptism. In water baptism a human is submerged totally under the water, and in the Spirit baptism the inner spirit is completely "filled" or submerged in the Holy Spirit's power (Acts 1:8). The newly baptized believer comes out of the water with his or her past washed away and is given a new beginning. The newly Spirit-baptized believer experiences a circumcision of the heart and a new beginning in Christ following his or her conversion and baptism.

Christ predicted the Spirit baptism for His followers in Acts 1:4–5:

> And being assembled together with them, He commanded them not to depart from Jerusalem, but to wait for the Promise of the Father, "which," He said, "you have heard from Me; for John truly baptized with water, but you shall be baptized with the Holy Spirit not many days from now."

There have been debates and disagreements for years over the difference between being "filled" with the Spirit and being "baptized" in the Spirit. Some have suggested that all believers are already filled with the Spirit, but the baptism is a separate act that empowers believers with a special enduing of power (Luke 24:29). It is true that when a believer receives the redemptive covenant through Christ, he or she is "born of the Spirit" (John 3:6–8), meaning the Holy Spirit has brought that person into the new birth and created a new redeemed spirit within. No one can come to God without being drawn by the Spirit.

The baptism of the Spirit, however, provides a different *measure* of the Spirit than the born-again measure. This is seen in that when the apostles were converted to Christ, their names were written in heaven, and they were provided spiritual authority in Christ's name (Luke 10:19–20). However, after Christ's ascension, these *saved* men were commanded to wait in Jerusalem for the promise of the Father and to receive "power from on high" (Luke 24:49). Jesus taught that demons were cast out by the power of the Spirit of God, thus these apostles operated in an anointing prior to Pentecost (Matt. 12:28). Yet there was a need for a total infilling, a baptism of power and anointing to bring them into fellowship with the new Comforter Christ sent, who would assist them in their ministry. Some Christians fail to understand that the Holy Spirit is the "other Comforter," sent to earth since the physical presence of the man Christ was taken to heaven as our High Priest (John 16:7). He is more than a "Ghost" or a "Spirit" or an invisible phantom force, but He is an actual person who performs His own work of baptism on each believer who will receive His gifts.

I have explained that the difference between being "baptized in the Holy Spirit" and being "filled with the Holy Spirit" is that the baptism is the initial act of the infilling of the Spirit. The moment He enters the human spirit and the believer speaks with tongues, that is the act of baptism. However, the moment He totally covers you in His power, you have been filled, and this infilling is a word to describe the completion of the act of baptism. This is why a person is baptized and filled with the Spirit at the same time. In the New Testament, especially from Acts through the epistles of Paul, in order to avoid a confusion between water and Spirit baptism, the term "baptized" is often used for water baptism (Acts 8:12; 16:15; 19:5; 22:16; 1 Cor. 1:16), and the phrase "filled with the Spirit" indicates the baptism of the Holy Spirit (Acts 2:4; 9:17; 13:52).

In my major meetings I will ask any who desire to receive the baptism in the Holy Spirit with the prayer language to come forward. As they receive the gift, I will say, "Many are being filled with the Spirit." Thus "baptism" is the term for *promise* of the gift and when receiving the initial gift, whereas "filling" is the result of receiving the gift.

Question: I know of Christians who are very critical and say negative things about other Christians who believe in praying for the sick or speaking in tongues. Are their words bordering on blasphemy of the Holy Spirit, or are they in danger spiritually?

Answer: All Christians I have met who do this are people who either grew up in a local church, or were converted to Christ later in life and now attend a local church, or claim to be Christians yet possess no fruit of spiritual growth in their lives. The biblical doctrines and interpretation of Scriptures among the raised-in-church group are based upon the teachings they heard during their upbringing. The second group may have more of a mix of ideas, as they came to Christ later in life, perhaps with their own opinions and traditions. The third group, to be honest, doesn't have a clue about what the Bible teaches or how to live and walk out your faith.

Criticism against the beliefs of others can be based upon preconceived ideas, the traditions linked with denominational doctrinal teachings, biased opinions because of fear of another teaching contrary to what has been taught creeping in, and, at times, plain spiritual ignorance. I have seen people critical of anyone praying for the sick, yet these church members could not quote any verse either in favor of or against what they were criticizing. The same is true with the Holy Spirit. Depending upon your faith tradition, there are numerous beliefs concerning the credibility of the modern-day charismatic gifts in the church.

Paul is an example of a man raised to know the Law of Moses as a Pharisee, and in his own mind he believed Christians were a new cult that threatened Judaism and the observance of the Law. He persecuted believers from city to city, arrested some, and forced some to blaspheme Christ. After his own conversion he confessed that he acted in ignorance. Paul's confession is revealing:

> Although I was formerly a blasphemer, a persecutor, and an insolent man; but I obtained mercy because I did it ignorantly in unbelief.
>
> —1 TIMOTHY 1:13–14

Criticism of the Holy Spirit seems to be divided among three groups. The first believes they are doing God a favor by defending the *true* faith; however, they are totally in ignorance concerning spiritual charismata. Those believers they fellowship with are of like belief with them, and they never attend another group's evangelistic meeting where the actual Holy Spirit is moving. They judge all things from their own denominational eyeglasses and use blinders to refuse to see anything outside of their own field or sheepfold. They don't understand that Jesus has other sheep that are not of their fold (John 10:16). These are usually the most outspoken and critical.

The second group is aware of the scriptural promises and have friends who have received the Holy Spirit, but themselves choose not to believe in the charismata for themselves and often do not see a need for these gift or manifestations. They have the Bible, and the emotional expressions linked to worship or other charismatic demonstrations are considered unneeded and undesirable.

The third group is often totally blank, dull of understanding and hearing, and about as informed as a deer is when a hunter is standing around the corner. They make outlandish statements, and when you quote Scripture, their one-line response is, "Ah, that's just your opinion!" When you explain details, you get the same response: "That's just your opinion." This mental laziness is a verbal cop-out for their lack of understanding or comprehension of the facts.

It is important to be able to assess the intent in which the words are spoken—were they stated willfully or ignorantly? The Pharisees were rebuked for their unbelief, as they willfully chose to ignore the visible evidence that Christ was the Messiah. Thomas also experienced his season of unbelief, but his words were based upon what he saw when Christ died. The difference: the Pharisees were hypocritical unbelievers, and Thomas was an honest-hearted doubter who simply wanted evidence to restore his faith and trust. If a person questions the Holy Spirit because of ignorance, then where little is known, little is required.

If a person has true knowledge and has ever tasted of the heavenly gift and been made a partaker of the Holy Spirit, and falls away from the faith, the writer of Hebrews warned that the person is in serious danger, as he is crucifying Christ anew with his actions (Heb. 6:4–6).

Unbelief is a sin that Christians can commit, just as unforgiveness is also a sin that is often attached to the disobedient. If a person sins against *knowledge*, the sin is a greater sin than a sin of *ignorance*. This is clear when Peter wrote:

> For if, after they have escaped the pollutions of the world through the knowledge of the Lord and Savior Jesus Christ, they are again entangled in them and overcome, the latter end is worse for them than the beginning. For it would have been better for them not to have known the way of righteousness, than having known it, to turn from the holy commandment delivered to them.
>
> —2 PETER 2:20–21

Yes, there is a danger for a Christian who willfully ignores Scripture and instead makes negative remarks against the Holy Spirit and His manifestations. To believe that for four thousand years the Spirit was active on earth but now has ceased His miraculous operation is nothing short of unbelief, and unbelief will be the one force that prevents many people from entering the kingdom.

Question: Why do some full gospel groups teach that speaking in other tongues is the *initial* evidence of the Holy Spirit? I believe that the fruit of the Spirit are the actual evidence of a Spirit-filled life.

Answer: First, look at the meaning of the word *initial*. The word does not mean or imply *only*, as though tongues are the only evidence of the Holy Spirit. The word *initial* can mean, "first in an order of a list or first of many." Many full gospel groups allude to speaking in tongues as the initial evidence for the following reasons.

First, Christ promised the Holy Spirit to His disciples and told them to wait in Jerusalem until the Spirit came. How did Peter and the others know when the Spirit had arrived? They did not see another person or the image of a man enter the room where they were sitting. They heard the wind, saw tongues of fire, and began to speak in other tongues. This combination was enough for Peter to announce that Joel's prediction of the outpouring of the Spirit had come. As we read further in Acts, when the apostles preached on the Holy Spirit, they always knew when He had arrived on the scene and baptized believers, for the believers began to speak with other tongues.

After the Samaritans were converted to Christ, Peter and John traveled to the city of Samaria to lay hands upon them to receive the Holy Ghost. (See Acts 8.) When the first Gentile, Cornelius, heard the gospel preached by Peter, the Holy Spirit fell upon the group, and they all began to speak in other tongues. (See Acts 10.) When Peter later stood before the apostolic committee in Jerusalem, who questioned how Gentiles could have received Christ, Peter revealed that they were all baptized in the Holy Spirit in the same manner as the apostles were on the Day of Pentecost. This fact settled the controversy in the minds of the Jerusalem council as to whether God had accepted the Gentiles into the covenant.

When Paul traveled to Ephesus, he found twelve disciples of John who had been baptized in water but knew nothing of the baptism in the Holy Spirit. When Paul laid hands upon them, they all began to speak with other tongues and prophesy. (See Acts 19.) The fact is, the Book of Acts reveals the actions of the Holy Spirit in the infant church, and in these references and others where it is implied, the first manifestation of the Spirit when He filled believers was that He spoke through them as a witness to both the speaker and the hearer that He had entered the physical body of the believer and taken up residence within the believer's temple! Thus, by the patterns in Acts, the full gospel people have taught that upon receiving the baptism in the Holy Spirit, the first evidence will be that He will speak through the person, giving a witness that He is dwelling within. This action is for the benefit of both the seeker and the hearer. The seeker knows when he speaks, and the hearer knows when he hears. Thus there are three witnesses: the Spirit Himself, the speaker who is ministering, and the hearer who is in attendance when the Spirit comes.

Once the Spirit has arrived and indwelt a believer, the believer should certainly seek to grow and mature in the nine fruit of the Spirit mentioned in Galatians 6. Fruit can only grow on a living tree that has been properly planted and cared for. The tree must have good roots, sunshine, and water. Figuratively, a believer is like a tree planted by the rivers of water that brings forth fruit in seasons (Ps. 1:1–3). Salvation plants us and roots us in the covenant, the water is the baptism of the Holy Spirit, the light is the Word of God, and the fruit is a normal by-product of maturing and growth. Fruit grows on healthy trees, and the fruit of the Spirit will be seen as believers mature in the Spirit.

Question: Paul mentioned men speaking in the tongues of men and of angels. Is it possible that one of the prayer languages is heavenly? What language would it be?

Answer: The reference to speaking in the tongues of men and of angels is 1 Corinthians 13:1. This verse certainly implies that men can speak in both earthly and heavenly languages. There are literally thousands of languages on the planet, which are spoken in nations and in remote tribal regions. If a language is globally recognized, such as Spanish, French, or English, it can be noted when spoken what language it is. If a believer received a prayer language of a remote tribe, it may sound very odd to the listener in the West—perhaps like broken sounds or odd words—but actually be a tongue spoken in a remote Amazon village, for example.

The tongue of angels would be the language of heaven itself. The devout Jews believe that the heavenly language is a form of the Hebrew language. In my book *Breaking the Jewish Code* I give the following example:[1]

> In 1768, the Rev. John Parkhurst produced the first Hebrew-English lexicon. In the introduction he stated that he believed that six thousand years ago, Hebrew was the first language spoken on Earth between Adam and God.[2] If this is correct, you might speak Hebrew when you get to heaven! There is a Jewish tradition that the first man, Adam, spoke an ancient form of the Hebrew language in the Garden of Eden. We know Adam had knowledge of a language, as he named the animals (Gen. 2:19–20). Both Adam and his wife, Eve, *heard* the voice of God in the garden (Gen. 3:8). God entered Eden in the "cool of the day" (Gen. 3:8). The Hebrew word for cool is *ruach*, and it alludes to the "wind, breath, or the air." We would say that God rode into the garden on the wind. This agrees with the scripture that says, "He [God] rode upon a cherub, and flew; and He was seen upon the wings of the wind" (2 Sam. 22:11).

The language Adam spoke was passed on from Adam to Noah, the first ten generations of men (Gen. 5:3–32)....

At approximately 2344–2342 BC, the floodwaters swept over the earth, bringing global destruction. There were eight survivors: Noah and his wife, their three sons, and their wives (1 Pet. 3:20). It is likely Noah would have continued to speak the original language of Adam. Three generations later, Nimrod, Noah's great-grandson, constructed the first mega-structure called the Tower of Babel in the plains of Shinar (Gen. 11). Nimrod's goal was to escape any future flood:

> He also said he would be revenged on God, if he should have a mind to drown the world again; for that he would build a tower too high for the waters to be able to reach! and that he would avenge himself on God for destroying their forefathers![3]

During the tower's construction, all the earth's inhabitants spoke one language.

> And the LORD said, "Indeed the people are one and they all have one language, and this is what they begin to do; now nothing that they propose to do will be withheld from them. Come, let Us go down and there confuse their language, that they may not understand one another's speech."
> —GENESIS 11:6–7

God saw that man's unbridled knowledge could again cause evil inclinations to spread. In a sudden moment, He struck the tower to the ground and scattered the people by confusing their languages. Nimrod's kingdom was called Babel, whose Akkadian meaning is "gate of God," but the Hebrew meaning is from the verb *balal*, meaning, "confuse or confound." It was at Babel that various world languages were birthed (vv. 7–9).

Hundreds of years later, in the Torah Moses wrote of God dividing the nations at the tower:

> When the Most High divided their inheritance to
>   the nations,
> When He separated the sons of Adam,
> He set the boundaries of the peoples

According to the number of the children of Israel.
For the Lord's portion is His people;
Jacob is the place of His inheritance.
                                    —DEUTERONOMY 32:8–9

Even the early church father Origen reflected on the early language of mankind when he wrote:

> All the people upon the earth are to be regarded as having used one divine language, and so long as they lived harmoniously together were preserved in the use of this divine language, and they remained from moving from the east so long as they were imbued with the sentiments of the "light," and the "reflection" of the eternal light.[4]

The original language was a *divine language*, originating with Adam in the garden. According to Origen, there was one group that did not travel to the plains of Shinar with Nimrod, and they alone retained the pure language, spoken from the beginning of time:

> Those who preserved their original language continued, by reason of their not having migrated from the east, in possession of the east, and of their eastern language. And let him notice, that these alone became the portion of the Lord, and His people who were called Jacob, and Israel the cord of his inheritance.[5]

Since the Hebrew tongue became the language of God's chosen people, it is assumed that Adam spoke some early form of the Hebrew dialect. Jewish writings such as the *Mishna* (Genesis Rabbah 38) teaches that Adam spoke in the Hebrew language. The *Mishna* comments that Adam called Eve "woman" (*'ishah*), the Hebrew term for a woman or a female (Gen. 2:23). He later named her Eve (Gen. 3:20), or *Chavah* (meaning "life giver") in the Hebrew language. Of course, the word *Hebrew* was unknown in the time of Adam, and his language would simply be the language of Adam. However, he was speaking the language God gave him. Being created a full-grown man without systematic training from infancy to adulthood, his teaching came directly from God. The name *Hebrew* originated out of Shem's great-grandson's name *Eber* (Gen. 10:21). It comes from the verb '*abar*, meaning to "pass through, or region beyond." Abraham was the first Hebrew (Gen. 14:13), because he passed over from his native land to the Promised Land. The Abrahamic covenant was sealed when God *passed through* the sacrifices, and in Egypt God passed over the Israelite homes that were protected by the lamb's blood (Exod. 12:13). Joshua and Israel passed over Jordan, possessing their inheritance (Josh. 1:2). The sojourning, or wandering, of the Jewish people has fulfilled the meaning of the name Hebrew.

The apostle Paul was a former Jewish rabbi, trained as a Pharisee under noted rabbi Gamaliel. Paul was educated in numerous languages of his time. Paul mentions God speaking to him in Hebrew when he was converted:

> And when we all had fallen to the ground, I heard a voice speaking to me and saying in the Hebrew language, "Saul, Saul, why are you persecuting Me? It is hard for you to kick against the goads." So I said, "Who are You, Lord?" And He said, "I am Jesus, whom you are persecuting. But rise and stand on your feet; for I have appeared to you for this purpose, to make you a minister and a witness both of the things which you have seen and of the things which I will yet reveal to you."
>
> —ACTS 26:14–16

God could have addressed Paul in Greek, Latin, Aramaic, or Hebrew, since all four languages were spoken in Israel. God, however, used the *sacred tongue* from which the Torah and Prophets are written—the Hebrew language.[6] America's early founders were keenly aware of the significance of the Hebrew language. William Bradford (1590–1657), governor of the Plymouth Colony, stated that he studied Hebrew so when he died he might be able to speak in the "most ancient language, the Holy Tongue in which God and the angels spoke."[7] In 1777, Ezra Stiles, president of Yale, stated that studying Hebrew was essential to a gentleman's education. He said, "Isn't it [Hebrew] the language I am sure to hear in heaven?"[8] Even Martin Luther, not known for his kind remarks toward the Jews, commented about the Hebrew language, "The Hebrew language is the best language of all, with the richest vocabulary."[9]

It is possible that a form of what is called Hebrew is spoken in heaven. However, whatever the language of the angels is, it is possible for the Holy Spirit to impart earthly and heavenly tongues to a believer. While Scripture is unclear, the earthly languages can be understood by earthly men, and the heavenly may be a direct language of angelic messengers. Paul emphasized that whatever tongue is spoken, all spiritual charismata must be operated in love. (See 1 Corinthians 13.)

Question: I have always heard that Satan can counterfeit the gifts, including speaking with tongues. How can a person know he or she is not being deceived and does not have a counterfeit gift?

Answer: First consider the idea of something that in counterfeited. A counterfeit is a copy of something that is original and already in existence. We have no counterfeit three-dollar bills as there are no actual three-dollar bills in circulation. Have you ever seen a single seventy-five-cent coin? Of course not, because an original seventy-five-cent coin does not exist in US currency. If you create something, such as a painting, that has never existed, it is an original and not a copy. The Holy Spirit is the original!

In life something is counterfeited only if there is a value in the original. In Israel some unscrupulous individuals make a living by taking silver and making counterfeit coins from the Roman period. The true coins are sold from $150 to as high as $500,000 each, depending upon rarity. A keen and experienced eye can spot the flaws in the fake because of the way the metal was heated and the strike method used in the Roman period. Each day in America, thousands of counterfeit dollars are removed from circulation by banks. Bank tellers have told me they are skilled at finding counterfeit paper currency because it does not have the same *feel* of real money. The ability to expose the counterfeit is found in the fact they handle real money all day long. You do not study counterfeits to expose counterfeits; you handle real money so much that it takes little or no effort to spot the phony.

Jesus provided clear promises for believers fearful of receiving a wrong spirit when asking for the Holy Spirit. We read:

> So I say to you, ask, and it will be given to you; seek, and you will find; knock, and it will be opened to you. For everyone who asks receives, and he who seeks finds, and to him who knocks it will be opened. If a son asks for bread from any father among you, will he give him a stone? Or if he asks for a fish, will he give him a serpent instead of a fish? Or if he asks for an egg, will he offer him a scorpion? If you then, being evil, know how to give good gifts to your children, how much more will your heavenly Father give the Holy Spirit to those who ask Him!
>
> —LUKE 11:9–13

Christ uses the analogy of the willingness of carnal men to give good gifts to their children and the fact that if the child asks for food (bread, fish, or an egg), the father would not tease the child or frighten the little one by replacing what he needs and desires with something that would be harmful to him. Christ was aware of the future and knew that the mystery and mystique of the Holy Spirit could cause some to become fearful of asking the Father for the Holy Spirit. Christ operated through the power of the Spirit and was accused of being aligned with the prince of devils. The Pharisees used this statement as a scare tactic to drive a wedge of confusion and fear between Christ and the multitudes seeking His touch. No one in the crowd wished to connect with anyone tapping into wrong spirits—thus the Pharisees' strategy was to make them think what they were seeing was demonically inspired and not of God.

This same type of religious strategy has, in the past, affected Christians, especially in North America, and prevented them from reaching out to their full gospel brethren who teach the importance of the baptism in the Holy Spirit. It should be clear to any believer who reads Luke 11:9–13, that a sincere child of God should never be hesitant in asking the heavenly Father for the gift of the Holy Spirit. The believer must remember that he or she is asking God, and not man, for the gift of the Holy Spirit, and Christ gave clear promises for receiving the gift.

Since there is a manifestation of speaking in tongues accompanying the Holy Spirit, there is a concern among some that the person speaking may be operating in a *counterfeit tongue* and not the actual gift. Since tongues can be both earthly and heavenly languages (1 Cor. 13:1), it is difficult for a person to determine if the sound of the language spoken is of men (a known tongue) or heavenly, unless the hearer is familiar with the tongue being spoken. This is why Paul emphasized that spiritual gifts and spiritual actions must be performed and operate in love and with love. He wrote:

> Though I speak with the tongues of men and of angels, but have not love, I have become sounding brass or a clanging cymbal. And though I have the gift of prophecy, and understand all mysteries and all knowledge, and though I have all faith, so that I could remove mountains, but have not love, I am nothing. And though I bestow all my goods to feed the poor, and though I give my body to be burned, but have not love, it profits me nothing.
> —1 CORINTHIANS 13:1–3

In reality, the issue is not can a gift be counterfeited, but does the receiver of the true spiritual gift demonstrate the love of God in his or her words and deeds? If not, then Paul said the act of speaking in tongues was useless noise (sounding brass), and all of a person's good deeds are for naught if the motivation for ministry is not love. When a person has the wrong attitude or wrong spirit, then his words and gifting will be sour and bitter, which allows other believers to discern that the spirit of the person is wrong, and thus the gifts are void of influence.

Question: What did Paul mean when he said that if you speak in an unknown tongue, you are speaking "mysteries"?

Answer: The verse reads, "For he who speaks in a tongue does not speak to men but to God, for no one understands him; however, in the spirit he speaks mysteries" (1 Cor. 14:2). The idea is that the person speaking is unaware of the language he is speaking, thus what he speaks is to him a mystery. However, the Holy Spirit is the one giving the words (speaking in the Spirit), and the Father understands what is spoken. The *mystery* here is the high level of spiritual truth, or the mind of

God, that is at that moment unknown to the speaker. When praying in the Spirit, amazing insight, knowledge, and wisdom can be released.

There are also plots and plans being designed for a person's spiritual destruction that can be exposed by the Holy Spirit through intercessory prayer. The unknown strategy is exposed, and the Spirit provides ways of escape from the setups of the adversary. Also, these mysteries can be interpreted back to you through prayer.

Question: If ministers claim to be filled with the power of the Holy Spirit, then why is it that many of those same ministers who emphasize the anointing find themselves in moral trouble? My pastor used this argument to tell the church that what these ministers claim is not real or it would keep them from sinning!

Answer: This is a very good question and does pose a quagmire when comparing the power of the *message* with the weakness of the *minister*. The first fact is that *temptation* is a part of life for all men (and women), regardless of age, race, or denominational beliefs (1 Cor. 10:13). Temptation manifests through three categories: lust of the flesh, lust of the eyes, and the pride of life (1 John 2:16). Ministers from both camps—those who believe in the spiritual gifts and those who resist or do not accept the gifts—have yielded to temptation and fallen into sin. Thus one cannot judge the failure on the fact that they were or were not men who believed in the anointing or the work of the Spirit. Temptation comes to all men and women at times.

It is important to understand that the *anointing* of the Spirit does not prevent temptation. Jesus was anointed at the Jordan River and was immediately led into the wilderness to be tempted of the devil (Matt. 3:16–17; 4:1). The Holy Spirit did not *prevent* the test, but He gave Christ strength to *overcome* the test. The Holy Spirit "reproves" (a word meaning "to convict, rebuke or strongly admonish") a believer if that person sins (John 16:9). However, the Holy Spirit will not stop a believer who chooses to be disobedient or do wrong. Defeating sin only comes when we walk in the Spirit, as it is written, "I say then: Walk in the Spirit, and you shall not fulfill the lust of the flesh" (Gal. 5:16). To "walk in the Spirit" is not to zone out in a trance and fall on the floor like a log and not get up for five hours to avoid being in contact with humans. Walking in the Spirit refers to maintaining a mentally alert, spiritually sensitive attitude throughout the day so that anything that rises before you contrary to the Word and will of God will be struck down by the knowledge of spiritual truth you have received.

Also, consider that those who have received the gift of the Spirit and are leading others into this experience are more likely to be targets of the enemy than others who teach without power and have a weak influence in the community or the nation. Peter was an apostle to the Jews and Paul to the Gentiles. Paul was Jewish, a former Pharisee and a convert to Christ, and experienced severe physical abuse, beatings, and jail time, which Peter never encountered. Paul's troubles were instigated by a messenger (Greek, *aggelos*, or "angel") of Satan that struck him with one blow after another and one hindrance after another (2 Cor. 12:7). Paul's threat level against the satanic kingdom was greater than that of others, as his influence was far more widespread in Asia Minor, Israel, and Jerusalem.

When a minister falls, another minister's comment that the fallen minister's spiritual experience was not *real* would be like saying Peter was never really converted because he denied the Lord! Or that Samson's gift was not real because he allowed a woman to steal the secret of his covenant. David was anointed with the sacred oil and the Spirit of God came upon him (1 Sam. 16:13). However, later in his life he committed adultery and had the husband of the woman set up to be killed (2 Sam. 11). Was David's original anointing a fraud, because certainly if what he experienced was *real*, then he would have never fallen into this trap. In these cases it was not the fault of the Holy Spirit but the failure of the men to resist sin. Never judge the ability of God upon the success or failure of His followers. The Holy Spirit *guides* you into all truth (John 16:13)—however, you must follow.

Question: Today it is evident that people from all denominations are receiving the gift of the Holy Spirit. However, there are still Christians who read and know the Bible who teach against the nine spiritual gifts operating today and warn people to avoid the charismatics, Pentecostals, or even the "Spirit-filled Baptists." Why is this so?

Answer: I will answer from my own observation. First, there is a negative effect for placing *name tags* on biblical doctrine. The worship psalms admonish us to clap our hands (Ps. 47:1), lift our hands (Ps. 141:2; see also 1 Tim. 2:8), and sing aloud (Ps. 59:16), and Paul instructed believers, "Do not forbid to speak with tongues" (1 Cor. 14:39). Yet these four actions are labeled as *charismatic-Pentecostal* practices. Because they are labeled as such, the more nominal denominations refuse to worship in any method that would also tag them as a more charismatic congregation. These are not charismatic actions; they are biblical instructions, and if you believe the whole Bible, then you must apply these admonitions to your own life.

Then there is the element of *emotion* involved in worship. To some, mixing emotion in worship is as *unnatural* as laughing and joking at your companion's funeral. Emotions like weeping and laughter are normal reactions to sadness, joy, and life in general. We scream at ball games, laugh at jokes, cry at funerals, smile at friends, and express our feelings through emotions. For years full gospel believers have been accused of being emotional in their worship and accused of basing their religion on experience. The fact is that many mainline churches have no desire to see hand clapping, hand raising, and shouts of "Praise the Lord" or "Hallelujah" piercing the quiet setting of their Sunday routines. The resistance to emotion is a major hindrance to the flow of the Holy Spirit. He can be felt when His presence is near, and it is virtually impossible not to respond to His presence in some manner. For those who say, "I am quiet and praising God from my heart," I would remind you that, "Out of the abundance of the heart the mouth speaks" (Matt. 12:34). If praise is in your heart, then it will emit out of your mouth. Your emotions cease within your body when you're dead and your spirit has departed. Until you are dead, you are an emotional creature.

The third element is fear. I have met believers whose family members were raised under the teaching that the spiritual manifestations of the Spirit are not valid today but are either man-made, emotionalism, the flesh, or, in some cases, demonic deception. One family member may encounter the Holy Spirit but fear the verbal retaliation, rejection, or confusion caused among the more staunch unbelievers in the family. Fear of the reaction of others (including those he or she works with daily) and the possible persecution to follow causes the person to back away from accepting certain manifestations of the Holy Spirit and simply say, "I don't believe it that way." Fear of rejection builds walls of resistance.

The fourth reason for resistance is that since speaking in tongues and spiritual gifts flow through human vessels, outside observers point out the character flaws, moral weaknesses, and abuse of these gifts among other church members, concluding that the gifts are not real or are counterfeit because the Lord would never work through someone with the flaws of those claiming they have received these gifts. These watchdogs of *true spirituality* often fail to point out that Noah built an ark but later lay around drunk and naked in his tent. Samson was God's anointed champion who could break chains, but he could not shake off his own fetters of lust, which cost him his anointing. David was a man after God's own heart, yet he became a middle-aged voyeur, a "peeping Tom," which led him into an affair with the wife of one of his soldiers. Peter cursed, Thomas doubted, and Paul and Peter had a hotheaded argument over circumcision. Were these men fakes because of failure? No, because Noah, Samson, and David are listed as heroes of faith in Hebrews 11!

Fear is the main factor for resistance: fear of emotion or of rejection by family or your denomination. The sad fact is that the Holy Spirit is the agent of imparting faith, and by receiving His *fullness*, faith will replace fear, joy will sustain you in times of rejection, and He will comfort you in times of persecution.

Chapter Twenty

HOW TO RECEIVE
THE BAPTISM OF
THE HOLY SPIRIT

And when He had said this, He breathed on them, and said to them, "Receive the Holy Spirit."

—JOHN 20:22

As I STATED earlier, I received the baptism in the Holy Spirit at age eleven during a church youth camp in Roanoke, Virginia. As I grew in God's grace and biblical knowledge, I also grew stronger in my spiritual maturity and in understanding the workings of the Holy Spirit in my life. After I entered the evangelistic ministry, soon our revivals were extended from one week to five, to seven, and once to eleven weeks in length. These extended revivals became a magnet attracting to the services countless mainline denominational members with a spiritual hunger and interest in receiving the baptism of the Holy Spirit with the evidence of speaking with other tongues. From age eighteen to this present time I have personally witnessed more than seventy-four thousand believers receive the baptism in the Holy Spirit. Let me share with you the simple process I have used for many years to lead believers into the experience of receiving the Holy Spirit.

First, this gift is for believers only. It cannot be received if you have not repented of your sins and entered into a redemptive covenant with Christ. Even if you are a believer, you should confess to Christ and repent of any sins in your life and ask God to remove them and cleanse and renew your heart and Spirit through the precious blood of Christ.

Second, to receive the gift, you, as a believer, must ask the Father. Christ said, "Ask, and it will be given to you; seek, and you will find; knock, and it will be opened to you" (Matt. 7:7). There is a spiritual principle throughout the Scriptures that receiving comes only after asking. When you ask, you must also ask in faith, nothing wavering, understanding that God's will is to give good gifts to His children (James 1:6–7). Pray in faith:

> *Father, You promised that You would pour out Your Spirit in the last days, and I am hungry for the gift of the Holy Spirit. In Christ's name, baptize me in the Holy Spirit. I receive the gift now! Impart to me the prayer language of the Holy Spirit for Your glory.*

Third, once you have repented to clear your spirit and soul, asked for the gift, and believed, then begin to worship the Lord with your mouth and your words. Praise is not praise unless it is spoken. Keep your mind on Christ and His marvelous blessings. Expect to receive!

On the Day of Pentecost, when the Holy Spirit baptized the believers, they all began to speak with tongues, "as the Spirit gave them utterance" (Acts 2:4). What does "gave them utterance" mean? One other translation says, "...and began to speak in other tongues as the Spirit enabled them" (NIV). Another states, "...as the Spirit kept giving them clear and loud expression [in each tongue in appropriate words]" (AMP). You must do the speaking, and the Holy Spirit imparts the words. The Lord is not coming down and pulling your mouth open with His hands, then taking over your five senses while you become the puppet and lose self-control. Paul wrote that the "spirits of the prophets are subject to the prophets" (1 Cor. 14:32). The Amplified expresses the idea clearly, "For the spirits of the prophets (the speakers in tongues) are under the speaker's control." This statement is important to understand when receiving the prayer language of the Spirit.

How does a person receive a language he or she has never known or spoken, and when does that person know what to say or how to speak? The tens of thousands who have received the Holy Spirit in our ministry all have the same experience in this area. After asking the Holy Spirit to fill them, the seekers sense deep within their spirit words they have never heard and that were unfamiliar with their understanding. As they began to speak what they heard, the anointing was suddenly released, and they began flowing in the words of the prayer language. This is what occurred to me when I was eleven.

Some may suggest that believers are simply making up words or sounds in their mind, and the utterance they speak is not an actual language or anything supernatural. However, Paul taught that when a believer speaks in tongues, his spirit is praying to God (1 Cor. 14:14). My inner spirit has ears to hear just as my body has physical ears. My inner spirit has a voice that can communicate just as my physical body has a voice, vocal cords, and a voice box through which I can speak. The reason a believer can hear the words of the Spirit before he actually speaks is because the Holy Spirit dwells within the spirit of that person, imparting indwelling power and a language. However, the believer must speak as the Spirit inspires him with the words.

On about nine occasions during my ministry I spoke in tongues in a fluent language during church services, on several occasions in Israel, or in a setting with foreign individuals. To me it was an unknown tongue, meaning unknown to my natural understanding. Yet the language was the language spoken by the foreign person who was in my presence, and in each case it was a message from the Lord directly for that individual or in some instances a sign to the unbeliever (1 Cor. 14:22). In Cartersville, Georgia, I was praying for a woman at the altar and began to speak in tongues, but I was speaking in her native tongue. The Lord called her by her birth name and told her she would be returning home to visit her family. There were three things she had been praying for, and the Lord gave her answers to those three things in her native tongue.

When I received the baptism of the Spirit at age eleven, I received a prayer language. However, as I grew in my prayer life, the Lord imparted the gift of "divers tongues," which is the supernatural gift of speaking languages. This gift was present also in Rufus Dunford's life and in my father's, Fred Stone's, ministry.

When you are praying and you begin to hear the *words* forming deep in your spirit, then speak them out with your mouth. In altar services across the nation I so much enjoy watching believers the moment they speak as the Spirit gives them utterance. Immediately there is a change in their countenance, as joy sweeps over their soul. Many begin weeping, smiling, and rejoicing as they feel the anointing of the Spirit surging up in their spirit!

It is important that once you have received the Spirit, you must *exercise the gift*. By this I mean, do not neglect the gift, but when you are in your private devotions or in your time of prayer, allow the Holy Spirit to make intercession in the prayer language of the Spirit. Remember, your spirit is praying to God, and the Lord understands the words of your intercession (Rom. 8:26–28).

Conclusion

CLOSING COMMENTS

Perhaps you have read certain sections of this book that are different from the traditions or theological interpretations you have been taught or raised to believe. Maybe you have even presently been taught that certain charismata have ceased or are no longer necessary in our time. There are some who may read some of the amazing Hebraic insights and will tend to accept some and ignore others. I suggest that you study this subject in greater detail, and instead of consulting doubters who reject the Holy Spirit's work today, begin seeking out believers who have received the Spirit. Listen to their testimonies of God's grace and recognize the giftings they are enjoying.

Personally, the credit for the many spiritual blessings and growth of our global ministry, which now reaches 180 nations in the world, along with the inspiration to preach, teach, write, and minister, can only be credited directly to the strength and wisdom that accompany my own baptism of the Holy Spirit and my willingness to learn to follow His voice in my life and ministry. I trust you too will discover this wonderful gift.

Restoring the Language of God

Communication between God and man began the moment Adam arose from the dust, saw the face of God, and began a daily walk with his Father in Eden. We read, "Now the whole earth had one language and one speech" (Gen 11:1). The original language of Adam was passed from generation to generation until the time of the tower of Babel. God said, "Let Us go down and there confuse their language, that they may not understand one another's speech" (v. 7). After the collapse of the tower men joined their own language group and were scattered throughout the earth.

For about twenty-three hundred years each nation was identified by its own ethnic group and language. The numerous earthly tongues served each nation and tribe, while lack of intercommunication with others built barriers, as each group remained linked with its own language group. However, when the Spirit brought forth languages to the believers on the Day of Pentecost, the unlearned Galileans were speaking in the languages of sixteen nations, represented by the tens of thousands of Jews assembled at the temple (Acts 2:7–11). Notice the reaction that day among the devout Jews.

- "They were all amazed and marveled" (Acts 2:7).
- They called it the "wonderful works of God" (Acts 2:11).
- They were "all amazed and perplexed" (Acts 2:12).
- They questioned, "Whatever could this mean?" (Acts 2:12).
- Some were mocking (Acts 2:13).

There were the mockers, the doubters, the questioners, the amazers, and the praisers! The same reactions are evident when the Spirit is poured out today. In the beginning the unity of mankind was splintered at Babel with the division of tongues. On Pentecost that division was healed when the believers, as a sign, began to speak in the languages of the Jewish worshippers. Before Babel, the original language given to Adam was directly inspired from God Himself. Adam spoke the God tongue in the garden, and the "one language" in early history would have been the same words and tongue spoken in the garden. The divisions of languages at the tower broke the single language that united the world.

Pentecost restored the language of God. It was not the fact that sixteen nations heard men speak in their native tongue, but the concept that the Holy Spirit Himself—a member of the Godhead—imparts a supernatural language to the spirit of believers, enabling them to speak directly to the Almighty in the same manner that Adam stood face-to-face in Eden, fellowshipping with his Creator and Father. When you speak in prayer tongues, either earthly or heavenly, you have restored the "language of God" to your own spirit.

Some doubters and skeptics view tongue speaking as gibberish, baby talk or verbal bunk, to name a few phrases. However, as I reported at the beginning of this book, a Jewish rabbi in Jerusalem recognized this gift and identified it as the "language of God." God used this blessing to provide each believer a special path of communication to reach directly into His presence, assisting us when we are uncertain of what to pray for or when we need our faith built or we desire spiritual edification. Spiritual mysteries (I call them the *codes of the Holy Spirit*) are unlocked through the master key opened through the door of Spirit baptism.

I encourage you to reread this book and receive the insight into your spirit as seed that will produce a spiritual harvest. If you have receievd the gift of the Holy Spirit, then tap into the fresh insight for spiritual growth. If you have not received, then take the instruction coupled with spiritual hunger and seek God for the gift of the Holy Spirit. Once you have received, exercise the gift and allow the Holy spirit to lead you throughout your life.

Notes

Chapter 2
Is God Three—or Is God One?

1. Zohar II 43b, as quoted in Rabbi Tzvi Nass, *Plurality in the Godhead, or How Can Three Be One?* (1863), http://juchre.org/plurality/plurality.htm (accessed October 29, 2012).

2. Zohar, vol. 3, Amsterdam edition, 288.

3. Comment by Rabbi Moses ben Nachman on Exodus 3, "Ancient Jewish Writings About the Trinity," http://www.layevangelism.com/qreference/chapter10e.htm (accessed October 29, 2012).

Chapter 3
The Mystery of the *Ruach ha-Kodesh*

1. E. W. Bullinger, *The Companion Bible* (Grand Rapids, MI: Kregel Publications, 1999), Appendix 9.

2. *Encyclopedia Judaica*, vol. 11 (Philadelphia, PA: Coronet Book, 1994), 367.

3. Joseph Shulam with Hilary Le Cornu, *A Commentary on the Jewish Roots of Acts* (n.p.: Netivyah Bible Instruction Ministry, 2012).

4. *Encyclopedia Judaica*, 366.

5. W. E. Vine, *W. E. Vine's Complete Expository Dictionary of Old and New Testament Words* (Nashville: Thomas Nelson Publishers, 1996), s.v. "comfort."

6. Ibid.

7. *Encyclopedia Judaica*, 366.

8. The author knew Vendal Jones, a rather controversial figure in the Christian and Jewish community, but a researcher of Judaism who lived in Texas and has since passed away. He shared this information in the early 1980s.

9. Rick Renner, *Sparkling Gems From the Greek* (Tulsa, OK: Teach All Nations, 2003), 298–299.

10. Perry Fred Stone, *Fire on the Altar* (Cleveland, TN: VOE Ministries, 2003), 73–75.

Chapter 4
The Holy Spirit's Favorite Word

1. Renner, *Sparkling Gems From the Greek*, 732.

2. YouTube.com, "Testimony Colonel Sanders KFC 1979_Full," http://www.youtube.com/watch?v=mLfFfZ_a8Pw&feature=related (accessed November 7, 2012).

Chapter 5
The Code of the Dove and the Holy Spirit

1. The information on the dove was preached many years ago by C. M. Ward, the national radio speaker for the Assemblies of God, and was shared with me by Pastor Aaron Cooper in 1981.

2. Biblesoft's *New Exhaustive Strong's Numbers and Concordance with Expanded Greek-Hebrew Dictionary.* Copyright © 1994, Biblesoft and International Bible Translators, Inc., s.v. *"yownah,"* OT:3123.

3. James Freeman, *Manner and Customs of the Bible* (Plainfield, NJ: Logos International, 1972), 688.

Chapter 6
The Chemistry of the Anointing

1. Perry Stone Jr., *Breath of the Holies* (Cleveland, TN: Voice of Evangelism, n.d.).

2. William K. Dankenbring, "Mystery of the Olive Tree," http://www.triumphpro.com/olive-tree-mystery.htm (accessed November 7, 2012).

3. JewishEncyclopedia.com, "Anointing," http://www.jewish encyclopedia.com/articles/1559-anointing (accessed November 7, 2012).

4. R. S. Sreejith, A. K. Reddy, S. S. Ganeshpuri, and P. Garg, *"Oestrus Ovis* Opthalmomyiasis With Keratitis," *Indian Journal of Medical Microbiology* 28, no. 4 (October–December 2010): 399–402; http://www.bioline.org.br/request?mb10118 (accessed November 7, 2012).

5. JewishEncyclopedia.com, "Baal-Zebub," http://www.jewish encyclopedia.com/articles/2255-baal-zebub (accessed November 7, 2012).

6. This information about the olive tree was compiled during a 2010 Israel Tour and was given to me by Jewish guides living in Jerusalem.

Chapter 7
Getting Soaked on the Joel 2 Road

1. This quote from *Look* magazine was cited in Perry Stone, *Acts 29* (out of print).

2. *Gill's Exposition of the Entire Bible*, s.v. "Acts 1:13," as viewed at Bible.cc, "Acts 1:13," http://bible.cc/acts/1-13.htm (accessed November 8, 2012).

3. Perry Stone, *Opening the Gates of Heaven* (Lake Mary, FL: Charisma House, 2012), 125–126.

4. Vine, *W. E. Vine's Expository Dictionary of New Testament Words*, s.v. "restitution."

Chapter 9
The Importance of Testing Spirits

1. HealingandRevival.com, "Leaves of Healing," http://www.healingandrevival.com/BioJADowie.htm (accessed November 9, 2012). Also, Gordon P. Gardiner, *The Apostle of Divine Healing: The Story of John Alexander Dowie*, https://sites.google.com/site/leavesofhealing/leavesofhealingthelifegardiner (accessed November 9, 2012).

2. Biblesoft's *New Exhaustive Strong's Numbers and Concordance with Expanded Greek-Hebrew Dictionary*, s.v. "airo."

Chapter 10
What Does God Think About Women Preachers?

1. Boyce Blackwater, *Light From the Greek New Testament* (Anderson, IN: Warner Press, 1956), 56–57.

2. Ibid.

3. Clement of Alexandria, *Stromata* 3.6.53; Jacques-Paul Migne, *Patrologia Graeca*, vol 14, col. 1278 A-C, as referenced in Wikipedia.com, s.v. "Deaconess," http://en.wikipedia.org/wiki/Deaconess (accessed November 9, 2012).

4. Charles K. True, *A Concise History of the Christian Church* (New York: Nelson and Phillips, 1834), 26.

5. *Didascalia Apostolorum* III.12.1–4, http://www.womenpriests.org/minwest/didascalia.asp (accessed November 9, 2012).

6. F. X. Funk, *Apostolic Constitutions* VII, 19–20; *Didascalia et Constitutiones Apostolorum*, Paderborn 1906, 1:530.

Chapter 11
The Code Concealed in the Menorah

1. Philip Birnbaum, *A Book of Jewish Concepts* (New York: Hebrew Publishing Company, 1975), 366–367.

2. Rachel Hachlili, *The Menorah, the Ancient 7-Armed Candelabrum: Origin, Form and Significance* (Leiden, The Netherlands: Brill Academic Pub, 2002), 188–189.

3. Flavius Josephus, *Antiquities* 3; *Wars of the Jews* 5.217, 144–145, 182.

4. *Babylonian Talmud: Tractate Shabbath*, Folio 21a, http://www.halakhah.com/shabbath/shabbath_21.html#21a_24 (accessed November 12, 2012).

5. The Talmudic Village in northern Israel has reconstructed an entire town from the Roman period and has on display an old, dry wineskin. The explanation is given by tour guides, and the author has seen and heard this display and taught himself for many years.

6. *Dake's Annotated Bible* I (Lawrenceville, GA: Dake's Bible Sales), 16, note k.

Chapter 12
How the Holy Spirit Breaks the Spirit of Vexation

1. Jack Cafferty, "How Much Money Would It Take for You to 'Feel' Wealthy?", *Cafferty File* (blog), July 25, 2012, http://caffertyfile.blogs.cnn.com/2012/07/25/how-much-money-would-it-take-for-you-to-feel-wealthy/ (accessed November 12, 2012).

2. Fidelity Investments, "Fidelity Survey Finds 86 Percent of Millionaires Are Self-Made," July 19, 2012, press release, http://fiiscontent.fidelity.com/944345.PDF (accessed November 12, 2012).

3. The words listed come from word studies in the Scriptures found in PC Study Bible version 4.

4. *Adam Clarke's Commentary*, electronic database, copyright © 1996 by Biblesoft, s.v. "Matthew 10:29."

5. "Amazing Facts About Your Hairs and Nails," http://har103.hubpages.com/hub/Amazing-facts-about-your-Hairs-and-Nails (accessed November 12, 2012).

Chapter 13
Can a True Christian Commit the Unpardonable Sin?

1. Renner, *Sparkling Gems From the Greek*, 239.

Chapter 15
The Nine Greatest Lessons the Holy Spirit Has Taught Me

1. For a comparison, see the notes in the *Dake's Annotated Bible* under 2 Kings 2.

Chapter 17
The Firstfruits of the Spirit

1. Temple Institute, "Shavuot," https://www.templeinstitute.org/shavuot.htm (accessed November 13, 2012).

Chapter 18
The Key to Highly Blessed and Happy Christians

1. John Foxe, *Foxe's Book of Martyrs* (North Brunswick, NJ: Bridge-Logos, 2001).
2. Vine, *W. E. Vine's Expository Dictionary of Old and New Testament Words*, s. v. "boldness."

Chapter 19
Frequently Asked Questions About the Holy Spirit

1. Perry Stone, *Breaking the Jewish Code* (Lake Mary, FL: Charisma House, 2009), 35–39.
2. John Parkhurst, *A Hebrew Lexicon* (London: William Baynes & Paternoster Row, 1728 [Julian Calendar]), vii, Preface, third paragraph.
3. Flavius Josephus, *Antiquities of the Jews*, book 1, chapter 4, section 2, http://www.biblestudytools.com/history/flavius-josephus/antiquities-jews/book-1/chapter-4.html (accessed November 13, 2012).
4. Origen, *Against Celsus*, book 5, chapter 30, http://www.ccel.org/ccel/schaff/anf04.vi.ix.v.xxx.html (accessed November 13, 2012).
5. Ibid., chapter 31, http://www.ccel.org/ccel/schaff/anf04.vi.ix.v.xxxi.html (accessed November 13, 2012).
6. The entire Old Testament was written in the Hebrew language, with the exception of portions of Daniel and Ezra, which were written in Aramaic (Dan. 2:4–7:28).
7. Marvin R. Wilson, *Our Father Abraham: Jewish Roots of the Christian Faith* (Grand Rapids, MI: Wm. B. Eerdmans Publishing, 1998), 128.
8. Ibid., 130–131.
9. Ibid., 136.

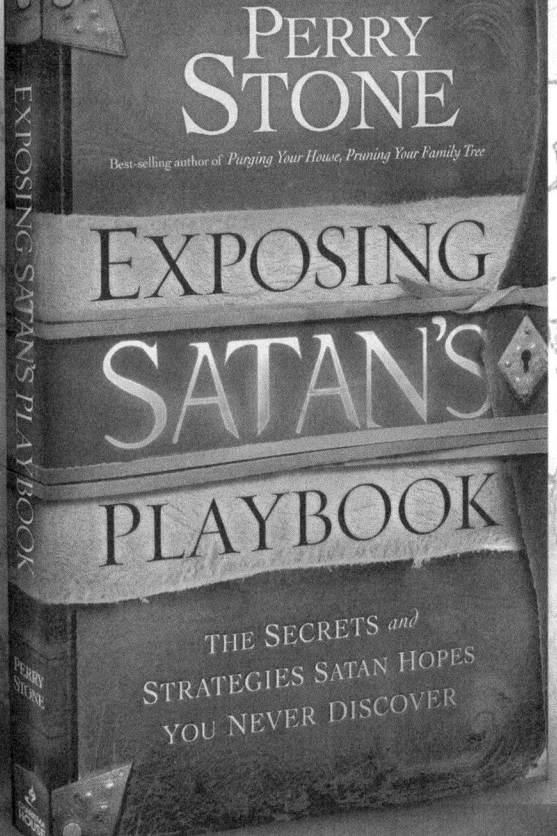

MORE FROM BEST-SELLING AUTHOR PERRY STONE

PERRY STONE BRINGS HIS UNIQUE BLEND OF BIBLE KNOWLEDGE AND SPIRITUAL INSIGHT TO EVERY TOPIC HE COVERS.

978-1-61638-157-8 / US $15.99

978-1-61638-186-8 / US $15.99

978-1-61638-350-3 / US $15.99

978-1-61638-622-1 / US $15.99

978-1-61638-653-5 / US $15.99

FREE NEWSLETTERS
TO HELP EMPOWER YOUR LIFE

Why subscribe today?

☐ **DELIVERED DIRECTLY TO YOU.** All you have to do is open your inbox and read.

☐ **EXCLUSIVE CONTENT.** We cover the news overlooked by the mainstream press.

☐ **STAY CURRENT.** Find the latest court rulings, revivals, and cultural trends.

☐ **UPDATE OTHERS.** Easy to forward to friends and family with the click of your mouse.

CHOOSE THE E-NEWSLETTER THAT INTERESTS YOU MOST:

- Christian news
- Daily devotionals
- Spiritual empowerment
- And much, much more

SIGN UP AT: **http://freenewsletters.charismamag.com**

8178